A Stone's Throw

A Stone's Throw

living the act of faith

*social transformation through faith
and spiritual practice*

Claudia Horwitz

stone circles
durham, north carolina

Published by stone circles. stone circles is a non profit organization which finds unique ways to integrate faith, spiritual practice, and social justice. Our work is based on beliefs supported by lessons from historical movements, political realities, and personal journeys.

To order additional copies of this book or request for-profit reprinting of *A Stone's Throw*, please contact: stone circles, 301 West Main Street, Suite 280, Durham, NC 27701.

Artwork by Andrew Boardman.
Cover design and layout by Claudia Fulshaw Design.

Printed in the United States of America by Harperprints.
This book is printed with soy ink on acid-free paper.

For my Great Uncle Manny,
who has always supported my work

and

for Fifer, my niece,
who was born at the same time as this book.
Welcome to the world.

contents

acknowledgements

Though my name is on the cover, there are people on whose shoulders I stand and whose arms have been wrapped around this book since its inception. Their spirits fill every page, and it is a privilege to know them. I am thankful for a family that has given me much love and strength over the years and for teachers who have added more to my life than they will ever fully know: Liz Cedillo, Arrington Chambliss, Ed Cohen, Katherine Fulton, George Lakey, Julia Scatliff O'Grady, David Sawyer, Nateshvar Ken Scott, Ralph Smith, Mitch Snyder, and Maura Wolf. I am grateful for those who were patient while we figured out what this work is about, especially those in the First, Second, and Third Circles. The greater the mistakes I made, the more I learned. And, I have the deepest admiration for those who agreed to be interviewed; their stories will be as rewarding to read as they were to record.

This book has been graced by colleagues from coast to coast who made it infinitely better. John Beilenson, Meredith Emmett, Alison Byrne Fields, Polly Guthrie, Margot Horwitz, Stuart Horwitz, Annice Kenan, Joan Kofodimos, Hez Norton, Jeanette Stokes, and Heather Zorn carefully read the work in progress and responded with constructive feedback. Elizabeth Warren offered to copyedit the text, which she did with enthusiasm and a keen eye. Because he believed in the work, Andrew Boardman created the extraordinary images that bring these words alive.

Thanks also goes to those who welcomed me into the spaces where this effort took shape: Iris Tilman Hill and Tom Kelley at the Center for Documentary Studies; the good people at the Weymouth Center for Arts and Humanities; and the staff at North Carolina Public Allies who gave me a warm, supportive place to work and put up with me when I know it was hard: Billie Burney, Daughtry Carstarphen, Meredith Emmett, Charles McKinney, and Amanda Sabin. And to Tony Deifell and the Institute for Public Media Arts who graciously served as stone circles' fiscal sponsor for four years.

And finally, praise larger than the planet goes to Thérèse Murdza — editor, and spiritual anchor of this project. Without her, this book would not have been this book.

welcome

In the midst of an ever-complex, ever-quickening universe, we crave time to pause and remember what matters.

In the face of devastating injustices and the inequity of our economic and political systems, we must find a way to respond.

    This book is inspired by these realities. It is an expression of my daily struggle to remember my own strength and the power of God and how both can be a force for justice. It is about living the act of faith, an ongoing and circular process. Turning inward toward truth and stillness gives us energy and the will to turn outward. Turning outward, we face the world around us with compassionate attention. Turning inward again, we reflect on our experience and grow in our understanding. It continues, this integration of spirit and action. Like a stone's throw, it creates ripples, the magnitude, direction, and duration of which cannot be predicted.

    And all along the path, we are offered the chance to choose love over fear. Love and fear. All the world's fire and breath is this. Action and intention born of fear and void of love wreak havoc on the mind, the body, and the soul. Fear holds us back and keeps our hearts closed. Between individuals, it breeds ignorance and isolation; between groups of people, fear paves the road for oppression and hatred. Fear is God's way saying, "There is another path. Another way to be with people. Another way to walk in the world." At any moment we can let go and make room for something else.

    Welcome to this book. It is here to give you new ways to remember what you already know—about yourself, the people around you, the place you find yourself, and the life force that runs through it all. I hope that the information and activities will be useful and inspiring to you, whether you are just beginning to think about the role of spirit in your life or feel rooted in a religious or spiritual tradition. You might use it only for your own journey, with a group or organization that matters in your life, or with a new circle of people that you gather together. I welcome your reactions, questions, and experiences. Please e-mail them to: astonesthr@aol.com Your comments and feedback will make the work stronger.

Enjoy.

Claudia Horwitz
Durham, North Carolina

a beginning . . . .

In the spring of 1995, I felt called to help bring a spiritual dimension into the work of social change. I wanted to find ways to nurture what is not easily nurtured in society—the still, small, silent space that invites a transcendent presence. I wanted to create places where people could rest a while and tend to their souls, surrounded by like-minded people who were doing the same. I wanted to pursue a path that I knew I didn't completely understand, and I didn't want to do it alone.

So, I started an organization called stone circles. I chose the name because circles of stones are found all over the world. They are mysterious and yet universally holy sites for worship and ritual, places where energy is renewed, and the life force dwells. To me, they represent strong individuals coming together to create strong communities with a lot of openings.

Over the past four years, my colleagues and I have experimented with many ways to integrate faith, spiritual practice, and social justice. We have provided training in spiritually-based organizational development to nonprofit organizations all over the country. We have convened Circles, collectives of activists who meet regularly for reflection and renewal. And, we have organized interfaith gatherings that foster celebration and discovery.

It has been a long walk through the wilderness, beautiful and terrifying at the same time. I have stumbled, gotten up, and been reborn. I have grown in my respect for others and for myself and been amazed at the wonders of the world around me. And I have come to honor three beliefs:

Spiritual practice helps us take care of ourselves. A daily practice brings us back to center, gives us a powerful way to *just be* in the world, and transforms the rhythm of our daily lives. The more depth we develop from within, the more we are able to maintain equanimity in the midst of chaos and distraction. Once uncovered, a calm heart is an alluring, vital, and renewable resource.

Life is about relationships—the relationship we have with ourselves, each other, and our own notion of God. We live in a world organized around short-term needs, but the process of change is long-term. It is not easy or safe work. Disrupting the status quo requires a propensity for challenge, ongoing support, and enough trust for real collaboration. Relationships hold a group of people together over the long haul, allowing us to move forward together with courage and boldness.

Faith plays a vital role in the ongoing struggle for true social change. "Faith is the substance of things hoped for and the evidence of things unseen." (Hebrews 13:21) Faith takes us outside of ourselves and encourages us to think of the broader reality that includes and yet transcends our own. Faith gives us a language of hope and stories of commitment, of love and responsibility, of reconciliation and redemption. It expands our notion of what is possible.

And with these beliefs, three questions emerge:

1. How do individuals turn inward to nourish their spirit?

Individuals and the quest for wholeness

Going out into the world every day to make some small change is no easy task; it takes energy, focus, and commitment. Every day, it seems, there are reasons to feel anger, anxiety, or insecurity. These emotions are energy—the raw material of our lives. Unexamined, this energy can manifest itself as self-criticism, judgment, despair, pain, or paralysis. Through spiritual practice, we can transform this energy into strength, joy, serenity, compassion, and love.

How can we give ourselves permission to be quiet for a little while each day in a world that prizes activity? How do we allow ourselves to rest and reconnect with what makes us brave? And what does it take for us to stay present to our deepest truth? Fortified with freedom, resources, time, and companions for the journey, we can ask these questions, explore our own concept of God, and take responsibility for our spiritual well-being.

2. How do organizations create relationships and a culture that mirrors their values and beliefs?

Organizations and the quest for excellence

Organizations and groups based on fear, chaos, and conformity attract those elements of fear, chaos, and conformity into their organizational culture. When organizations operate out of equanimity, creativity, and trust, they elicit equanimity, creativity, and trust from people who work there. Organizations which develop their own reflective practice and make space for a spiritual dimension reap numerous benefits:

- *Greater focus*: Opportunities to slow down and ground ourselves in purpose and meaning.
- *Stronger relationships*: Greater accountability and stronger communication. This includes clarifying needs and expectations, which enhances collaboration.
- *Effective teamwork*: Recognition and appreciation of individual strengths, more patience, and a better understanding of each other's challenges.
- *Better crisis management*: An ability to face obstacles with more creativity and calm.
- *Renewed commitment*: Reconnection with what is important about the work and a chance to become a part of each other's journey and development.

3. How do progressive people of faith strengthen their voice in communities, and in our social and political dialogue?

Communities and the quest for justice

In private, faith is a practice, an act of communion with what is holy. People gather to be with others who believe what they believe. Baptists pray with Baptists, Jews daven with Jews, Catholics kneel with Catholics, Zen Buddhists sit in meditation with Zen Buddhists, pagans worship the earth with pagans, those who follow their own individual spiritual path do so in the spaces they create for themselves.

In public, faith is a still a practice. Yet, in public, many of us are wary of revealing our religious or spiritual lives. Religious fanatics of all kinds have made us embarrassed and forced faith into a closet. We like to believe we are a nation organized and governed by secular principles. But that is not the case. For the past 50 years, over 95 percent of the American public have maintained that they believe in God. Faith, in all its incarnations and expressions, is embedded in our political system, our cultural connections, and our economic structure. Some people of faith have raised their voices, and they have been heard, but there is a broader spectrum of faithful people—from all paths and traditions—who believe in justice. If we are to create the radical change necessary for everyone to live lives of dignity and joy, we have to become more public about our convictions.

touchstones . . . .

As you delve into these questions, your spiritual life will evolve. It may involve other folks on a regular basis—a spiritual or faith community—or it may be more solo. You will have different teachers at different times; some you will choose, many will just appear. The road will be rocky; there will be forks, and you won't always know which direction to go. Chances are, you can build a meaningful life along whichever road you take if you can follow it with heart, integrity, and focus. Here are some things I remind myself:

Make space for quiet every day.

Always listen to your intuition; it will show you where your truth lies.

Whatever you draw energy to, will grow.

Tomorrow will be different from today.

In struggle, lie the seeds of strength.

how to use this book . . . .

what you will need

1. An open mind.

2. A blank notebook. Many of the activities invite you to do some writing. A journal or notebook will also help you to capture your reactions to what you are reading and notice any subtle changes that occur as a result. You can use it to record readings or prayers you find, as well as additional resources you want to explore such as teachers, books, articles, or workshops.

3. Quiet space and time. This book encourages reflection. I want to help you find some space in which to read, think, write, and be still as the ideas and questions settle in. If you don't live alone, carve out space and time when you can be alone without distractions. If that isn't feasible at home, be creative. Head for the library, a cafe, or a local park.

overview

Part I, *Turning Inward*, introduces three mainstays of spiritual practice: Silence, Meditation, and Prayer, and a fourth chapter on Spiritual Practice. Through ongoing, contemplative experiences, individuals cultivate their own personal expression of faith. These experiences give us a deeper sense of being from which to do.

Part II, *Sustaining Life*, looks at that which unleashes creativity, nurtures relationships, and therefore sustains the lives of individuals and organizations: Inspiration, Ritual, Words & Stories, Art, Earth, and Healing. These sources of strength and inspiration support us as we turn inward and turn outward, giving us a way to envision the path.

Part III, *Turning Outward*, explores four ways we can join with others to forge links between faith and social change: Relationships between people, Circles of individuals who gather with intention, Interfaith Celebrations that honor our differences and similarities, and Space that bring out our collective visions and harnesses our energy for justice.

the shape of each chapter

Each chapter follows a similar format. First, a context for the chapter is given. This includes a personal *turning point*, cultural context, and some thoughts about the topic's connection to *social change*. This is followed by a series of *activities to do alone* and *activities to do with groups*. Each activity section begins with low-risk activities and moves on to high-risk activities that build in intensity and require greater trust and more preparation. In the Appendix, you will find a list of all the activities, how long they take, and a risk-factor rating (low, medium, high). Materials needed for the activity are included. More details on both activities to do alone and activities to do with groups can be found below. Each activity is denoted by a 🄬 . Questions for Reflection have a 🄰 and writing activities are marked with ✏ .

After the activities, there is a list of resources for further exploration. The chapter ends with one or more stories of individuals who unite faith and action. In addition, worksheets have been designed for some of the activities to do with groups. They can be found in the Appendix; please copy as needed.

activities to do alone . . . .

Start with the chapters you are drawn to and look for activities which appeal to you the most. Many of the activities are introspective; they will ask you to reflect on ideas and feelings that you may not think about every day. Take it slow. One activity may keep you occupied for days. The activities can enhance a religious or spiritual practice you may already have. If you have a relationship with a clergy member, spiritual teacher, or guide, share this work with them. Ask them for support and guidance. Or, find a friend or colleague to partner with and share experiences.

activities to do with groups . . . .

It a tremendous privilege to do spiritual work with groups. When you facilitate a session on faith or spiritual practice for a group, you are creating a new learning community, and that community becomes your responsibility during the time you spend together. *You design space for groups to be at their best.*

You might use these activities with:

1. A community group you are already part of that is interested in exploring reflection, spirituality, and matters of faith;
2. An organization you work with that wants to deepen their connections to one another and to their work;
3. A social justice or community service committee of your religious congregation; or
4. A new group of peers or coworkers that you convene expressly for the purpose of pursuing the activities in this book. The "Circles" chapter can help you with ideas on how to do this.

As you read, focus on the sections that speak to you and those that you think might be of interest to others. You'll find that many of the activities consist of questions. When asked in an environment of community and trust, questions give people a chance to begin telling their story. If there is already a base of good communication and openness in your group, you can begin with an activity that involves a little bit more risk. If, on the other hand, this will be a brand-new experience, you'll want to start with some lower risk activities. As in the activities to do alone, the activities to do with groups start out low-risk and get progressively riskier.

before you begin

As you think about how to introduce an activity to your group or organization, it will be easier if you are cultivating:

- a commitment to your own spiritual path;
- enthusiasm and respect for your coworkers;
- a relationship with an ally, mentor, or a support system outside of the group with whom you can share your experience; and
- some background in group process or a willingness to learn by doing. Read over the next section on "Facilitating Spiritual Work with Groups." You might also seek local training opportunities in facilitation or group dynamics.

questions for reflection: activities to do with groups

1. *What is your primary goal? What do you think other people might be interested in?*
2. *What moves you? How might you share that with others? How might they share what moves them?*

3. *What is the mission of your group or organization? Where does spirituality or religion fit into that? Where might the connection seem problematic?*
4. *Who else can help you? What role(s) might they play?*
5. *How much time do you have? What can you realistically accomplish in that time? What physical space will you use?*
6. *Who makes decisions in your organization or group? How can you present your ideas to them?*

when and where to do it

1. *Regular group and/or staff meetings.*
2. *During the work day.* Short periods of reflection can be a way to stop and gain a fresh perspective during a hectic work day. This is useful when tense situations occur, when preparing for a big event or program, or when one person needs extra support. *Stopping to pause is a great alternative to moving blindly into chaos.*
3. *Staff/volunteer retreats and board meetings.* People come with an eye on the bigger picture of the organization, so it is a ripe time to bring in new ways of looking beyond the day-to-day work.
4. *Events out of the office.* This is especially useful if people are reluctant to take time out of the work day. And, people are less likely to be distracted.

It is beneficial to (1) integrate the work into your group or organization's workplace; (2) create new environments for reflection by going to someone's house or meeting in a central, public space; and (3) transform your office space.

three initial activities for groups . . . .

If you are working with a group that has never discussed these issues before, begin by giving people a chance to explore their own views and their relationship to faith and spirit. You can use the activities below, as well as the worksheet "Exploring Your Faith Background" found in the Appendix. These activities will help you (1) gauge your group's reaction to dealing with these issues, and (2) assess your own strengths as a facilitator and areas in which you want to grow.

faith stories

Have everybody pair up with someone. Give them the following list of questions and ask them to interview each other. Tell them that they have five minutes each, so that each person is encouraged to be thorough and thoughtful in their answers. Ring a bell or chime when the first five-minute period is up and ask people to switch.

1. *Did you practice a faith growing up? What was it?*
2. *What has your relationship to faith or spiritual practice been over the past year or two?*
3. *What is inspirational to you?*
4. *When do you remember experiencing the presence of spirit or God (or whatever else you call it) in your life?*

Come back together as a group and ask people to reflect on what they said and heard.

℮ words of power

This activity allows a group to become familiar with each other's thoughts about faith while sparking interesting discussion. It is particularly useful because it helps people clarify what they mean by certain terms.

The first part is done individually. Tell the group you are going to write a word on the board or a large piece of paper, and you want them to write, think, or draw stream of consciousness about what the word means to them. They will have a couple of minutes for each word. Write only one word at a time:

Faith   Spirituality   Religion   God   Justice

After you've gone through all five words, ask folks to gather in groups of four to discuss their definitions. Remind people that there is no right and wrong; they are here to learn from each other's definitions and notice similarities and differences. Come back together as a group and share your responses.

℮ faith map

You will need large pieces of paper (flip chart or newsprint size works best) and drawing materials such as crayons, markers, or pastels. The idea is to visually map out your journey with faith, starting with the first faith-related experience you can remember and moving to the present. Encourage people to be as visual as possible. You can ask folks the following questions to get them thinking:

What are the highlights of your faith journey? What are the hard times?
Who are key figures along the way?
What places or spaces figure prominently in this journey?
Where are you now? In what directions might you be going?

If the group is larger than eight people, divide everyone into groups of five or six. Ask each person to spend five minutes sharing his or her map, leaving a couple minutes after each person shares for reflections from the rest of the group. Remind people that these reflections should be personal statements, not generalized or judgmental comments.

after your first activity

Whew. You did it. Take a deep breath. Relax. When you feel ready, think about the following questions:

How do you feel about what you did?
How did the group respond? Which parts of the activity did people seem to enjoy?
What might be an appropriate next step?

facilitating spiritual work with groups . . . .

Doing spiritual work with groups has the potential to transform the way people see themselves and their work. It gets easier with time and practice, and you will learn as you go. Here are some things to keep in mind when doing the work laid out in this book.

1. prepare an outline

Know your goals and objectives. Have an outline for the session. In the beginning it's always better to overplan; as you gain more experience, you will have a better sense of how long things take. You should go over the outline at least twice and preferably three times. Visualize each component in your head, imagining how a group might move through the activity you have planned. When you have a good outline, you give others the opportunity to focus on the topic at hand; they don't have to worry about what comes next. This isn't to say you shouldn't leave open time for discussion; just build that into your agenda.

2. balance individual and group activities

Learning and spiritual exploration can take place in many ways. The more varied the formats you use, the more likely you are to appeal to a variety of learning styles. For example, some people will have a revelation during an individual reflection exercise, while others will gain new understanding through dialogue with one other person or a larger group. For this reason, try to combine individual reflection activities—meditation, silence, writing, art—with an activity for small groups of three to five individuals each and/or the entire group. You can start with the following framework and vary it as you gain more experience. This outline is designed to fit into an hour and a half:

1. opening ritual to bring the group together (5 minutes)
2. introductions (15 minutes)
3. individual reflection activity (20 minutes)

4. small group activity or dialogue (20 minutes)
5. large group reflections on the experience (20 minutes)
6. closing circle or ritual (10 minutes)

3. set up an intentional space in which to convene

Think about what kind of space the activity calls for. Will you be gathering in a circle? Make sure there is enough space to accommodate everyone. Is the space quiet and safe enough to encourage reflection and dialogue? Is it private? Do you want to do anything to alter the space? All spaces can be transformed with cloth draped in the center of the room, on the floor, or on a low table; plants, flowers, and other imports from the natural world; sacred objects that you bring and that you ask others to bring; candles or low lighting; and music.

4. think well about the whole group

You want to create and maintain an atmosphere that allows for deep listening, effective communication, the best use of the time available, and a healthy group process. And, you want to make sure that the group maximizes everyone's participation. Cultivating good facilitation skills—being able to read a group's energy and create space where people can access deeper and different parts of themselves—will serve you throughout your life. As you move through an activity, pay attention to how the experience is resonating with people. The challenge is to pay attention to two things at once: (1) how the overall content of the session is going and (2) how different individuals in the group are reacting to the session. This gets easier with time; you learn to pay attention to nonverbal cues of the whole group, while still listening to what is being said. Make notes. Notice who is speaking and who is not. Don't hesitate to check in with people one-one-one during a break if you sense discomfort or boredom; both can be a sign that deeper issues are surfacing and someone may welcome an opportunity to talk. If not, respect individual privacy while letting the person know that you are available if and when they want to talk.

5. set the tone

You want to create a safe environment for people to explore. Draw out opinions and help everyone to participate. Calling attention to diverse perspectives is particularly important with faith-based work. Be on the lookout for the "tyranny of the devout." Those who are most sure of and comfortable with their beliefs are often most likely to express them. Pay attention to those who don't seem as comfortable expressing their beliefs and help them find their voice in the group; they may need some extra support. You might also check in with them one-on-

one afterwards. If some folks seem to be generalizing and unwilling to speak personally, ask people to use "I" statements so that they speak for themselves.

Listen carefully to what people are saying; others will follow your lead. This is the best way to catch those "a-ha" moments, the times when connections get made for the first time or someone comes face to face with a new truth or idea. If the discussion gets heated, the circumstances may be ripe for a *teachable moment*. Intense situations, well-managed, have enormous potential to impact individuals and further group interaction. Your first instinct may be to "fix" something. Remember that the more you try to steer the conversation or bring it to a close, the more you risk limiting the group's learning process. Allow for chaos and do not attempt to control everything. People will be looking to you for cues; the more relaxed you are with conflict, the more you give the participants permission to relax into whatever is happening.

6. decide which questions are important

When asked in an environment of community and trust, questions give people a chance to begin telling their story. If there is already a base of good communication and openness in your group, you can begin with questions that involve a little bit more risk. If, on the other hand, this will be a brand-new experience, you'll want to start with some lower risk questions. Always try to ask strategic, open-ended questions to get people talking. These are the questions that go beyond "yes" or "no" answers, for example, "What do you remember about faith growing up?" Remember that even if the questions feel familiar to people, it will be a new experience to share their responses with a group of people.

7. what to do when no one speaks

Being comfortable with silence draws out meaningful voices. Don't be afraid to call on someone who hasn't spoken up and be aware of who monopolizes the conversation. (I have gotten to the point where I'm no longer afraid to say, "Thanks for your comment; I'd like to make sure we hear from other voices in the room.") In some cases, if folks aren't talking, it might be because the topic is too risky and/or people are reluctant to share in a large group. In that case, there are four possible actions to take:
— Reframe the question or activity;
— Break the group down into small groups of three or four;
— Use an individual reflection exercise that allows people to think about the topic first on their own; or
— Share an example from your own life.

8. give people the option to opt out

Keep in mind that not everybody will share the same level of comfort or enthusiasm for an activity. Sharing information about oneself and one's faith brings up lots of issues for people, many of which tend to be unresolved. And folks may not desire this arena (or any arena, for that matter) for exploration. As a result, people should be given the option not to participate without having to explain why. It's critical that you give the group some choices. Build this into the process of setting up an activity.

If it's a writing exercise, for example, encourage art as an alternative. If you're doing movement, encourage people to be still when they need to be still. We are used to following directions. Giving people permission to tune into and follow their intuition is a gift which opens up other doors. You are inviting people to become aware of and trust their own needs.

and remember. . .

As one of my mentors, George Lakey, says, "You'll never go wrong if you love your material, love your participants, and love yourself." Don't worry, however, if this love isn't always reciprocated. You challenge people when you ask them to think about hard topics or explore themselves. As a result you can become a target for whatever this stirs up for them.

Working with groups is a skill that can be learned, improved, and shared. You get better with practice, by reading about other people's experience, and by watching people. Many organizations and individuals run workshops on how to be a good facilitator or trainer. The best that I know of is George Lakey's "Training for Change" workshops. Based in Philadelphia, Lakey and his team of trainers run workshops all across the country and around the world. See "Resources" at the end of this chapter for contact information.

evaluation: how did it go?

As you convene groups, you will want to know how people received what you gave them. This will help you plan what might come next for this group, provide useful information for work with other groups in the future, and give you an indication of where you need to grow. If possible, create time for both written and oral evaluation. Written feedback is useful because often people will write things they'd never say out loud. Oral feedback is helpful because people may reach new conclusions during conversation. You might also consider two complementary types of evaluation: post-activity evaluation and long-term evaluation.

post-activity evaluation

Post-activity feedback occurs immediately following an activity or gathering.
This also allows people to begin synthesizing what they got out of the activity.
Because this may be a new, and therefore scary, topic for folks, they may feel
some discomfort with it. And they might be tempted to displace their uneasiness
onto you by jumping to evaluate your performance or the overall content and
structure of the session. Therefore, it is good to begin with questions that keep
people focused on their own experience of what happened.

What did you notice or learn about yourself today?
What did you notice or learn about others today?
What things did you like about this activity? What would you want to see repeated?
What would you change?
What questions do you still have?

long-term evaluation

Long-term evaluations measure impact over time. The strongest effect may be
felt long after the activity or group gathering time is over. It is difficult for
people to measure the full effect of an experience after it has just happened.
And, the impact of the work laid out in this book is difficult to measure. There
are so many factors that can lead to one's spiritual development and not all of
them are easy to gauge. People can report how many times they meditated in a
month, and for how long, but it is harder to discern what impact those
meditation periods have on the rest of their life.

The following questions were asked of members of the Circles (stone circles
sponsored groups which meet regularly for reflection and renewal) after we'd
been meeting for 6 to 12 months. They enabled each member to reflect on what
was different about their life since initiating their participation.

What have you gotten out of this Circle that you expected?
What have you gotten that you didn't expect?
What else did you expect to get out of your participation that you haven't yet?
What have you learned the most from?
Over the past year (six months, etc.) what stands out?
Which activities or gatherings were less meaningful to you?
How do you think this experience has changed your daily life?
What do you notice about your spiritual life?
How do you think this experience has changed your work life?

working with groups over time

Psychologist and author M. Scott Peck provides a powerful model for community-building; it is an incredibly useful framework for thinking about group process. A more detailed account can be found in his book, *The Different Drum: Community Making and Peace*. He outlines four stages:

1. *Pseudocommunity*. This is the stage where everyone is nice to each other. There is a lot of agreement, and conflict is avoided. Most individuals are looking for safe ways to interact within the group and deciding which pieces of themselves to reveal. During this stage, the group is very dependent on the leader for guidance. You will often find folks making lots of general statements (as opposed to "I" statements which indicate ownership), and there is little desire to challenge or be challenged. Once some of the generalizations are challenged, individual differences emerge, and you have . . .

2. *Chaos*. Don't be nervous. Chaos is a vital part of any group process, a must, if the group is going to deepen their connections to each other. This is the time when individual differences begin to come out, and chaos, according to Peck, "always centers around well-intentioned but misguided attempts to heal or convert." People don't want to be healed or converted so they resist. The first time a group goes into chaos the communication is sometimes loud and disrespectful. People are playing out old patterns of communication and defending their positions and their place. The leader's job is to (1) pay very close attention to the chaos, and (2) gently guide people out of it at the right time. This is like watching people arguing loudly in a building that they don't know is on fire. Once they're ready for direction, you can show them where the door is. The only good way out of chaos is through . . .

3. *Emptiness*. This will seem even harder than chaos for a while. Emptiness is almost like a death required for rebirth. It is a powerful time when people begin to get rid of that which is keeping them from communicating effectively and building real community. This is a time when folks will need to release their expectations, preconceptions, prejudices, assumptions, judgments, ideology, solutions, the need to heal/convert/fix someone, and the need to control the group. So it means folks are going to share some of their hardest stuff. And then you finally reach . . .

4. *True Community*, which will feel very different from the pseudocommunity you were in earlier. You can tell real community because people listen to each other better and longer, and folks are more comfortable revealing pieces of themselves. Chaos is a stage that groups may reach over and over again, but it will be different each time. As the group stays together, they will find ways to make the chaos more productive. Incorporating silence or reflection, for example, will make the chaos more graceful.

resources for group work

Bobo, Kim, Jackie Kendall, and Steve Max. *Organize! A Manual for Activists in the 1990s*. Washington: Seven Locks Press, 1991. A great manual for grassroots organizers with chapters on developing events with a message, fundraising, volunteers, meetings, public speaking, using the media, building coalitions, and more. Written by three organizers from the Midwest Academy, a group that has trained more than 20,000 activists since 1973. Full of useful charts, checklists, and worksheets.

Coover, Virginia, et al. *Resource Manual for a Living Revolution: A Handbook of Skills & Tools for Social Change Activists*. Philadelphia: New Society Publishers, 1985. A great reference for those working on social change efforts, includes sections on strategizing, group dynamics, facilitation, decision-making, conflict resolution, personal growth, and organizing. Lots of case histories, exercises, group building tools, and resources.

Fox, Matthew. *The Reinvention of Work: A New Livelihood for Our Time*. San Francisco: HarperSanFrancisco, 1994. Draws on a rich spiritual tradition to make greater connections between inner and outer work.

Marcic, Dorothy. *Managing with the Wisdom of Love: Uncovering Virtue in People and Organizations*. San Francisco: Jossey-Bass Publishers, 1998. Based on Marcic's theory of "new management virtues" that an organization's health is fundamentally based on the pivotal teaching of all religions: love your neighbor.

Peck, M. Scott. *The Different Drum: Community Making and Peace*. New York: Touchstone, 1987. A look at community as an experience of self-awareness and profound connection.

Senge, Peter, et al. *The Fifth Discipline Fieldbook*. New York: Doubleday, 1994. Resource for developing leadership and creating true organizational transformation; filled to the brim with exercises, examples, and advice, this is an indispensable resource for those committed to building a learning organization.

Shields, Katrina. *In The Tiger's Mouth: An Empowerment Guide for Social Action*. Philadelphia: New Society Publishers, 1994. Analysis and approaches for those working for change and in need of some support and healing. Ideas for activists on how to cope with bad news, develop survival tactics, nourish action, and build what Shields calls "fireproof" organizations (those that won't melt when it gets hot!).

Training Center Workshops/George Lakey, 4719 Springfield Avenue, Philadelphia, PA 19143; 215/729-7458. Web site: www.nonviolence.org/training

Part One:
Turning Inward

silence

*Let us be silent that we may hear
the whispers of the Gods.*

~ Ralph Waldo Emerson

*Our soul makes constant noise,
but it has a silent place we never hear.
When the silence of God enters us,
pierces our soul and joins its silent
secret place, then God is our treasure
and our heart. And space opens before
us like a fruit that breaks in two.
Then we see the universe from
a point beyond space.*

~ Simone Weil,
Random Thoughts on the Love of God,
translated by Robert Bly

questions for reflection

What kinds of silence are present in your life?

How are they different?

When are you most conscious of silence?

When are you most comfortable with it?

What aspects of your work might lend themselves to silence?

what is silence?

Silence is an opening that encourages a different voice to emerge. It is the voice of intuition and of soul, a truth that has depth and reality. This is the voice that we search for when we have to make difficult decisions, prepare for a life-changing event, or deal with great pain. Silence can enhance nonverbal communication with friends and loved ones as we explore ways to use our eyes, ears, hands, and facial expressions. It quiets our nerves and the endless chatter in our minds, brings us to greater states of rest, and provides space to regain perspective. Carving out space for silence is an act of paying more attention to one's self, to other people, and to the world. It is an act of resistance to abstain from unimportant conversation and thoughtless communication.

We live in an age of sound. At work, telephones ring, machines hum, people talk, faxes fax. We come home, and we turn on our radios, televisions, CD players, and VCRs. Some of us are so used to these sounds that it may take a city dweller days in the woods before he or she can actually hear all of the sounds there. It is hard to hear what the spirit has to tell you if you cannot get still enough to listen. The universe calls us to be silent, because spirit talks quietly. Silence ushers in greater awareness of God.

Fertile silence is like a placenta nourishing us from both emptiness and its connectedness with the greater organism of creation. Indeed, one aspect of silence is emptiness, and yes, it is often lonely. In the presence of silence, the conditioned self rattles and scratches. It begins to crumble like old leaves or worn rock. If we have courage, we take silence as medicine to cure us from our social ills, the suffering of self-centered alienation. In silence, sacred silence, we stand naked like trees in winter, all our secrets visible under our skin. And like winter's tree, we appear dead but are yet alive.

~ Joan Halifax, *The Fruitful Darkness*

turning point

In 1994, I make what will be the first of many visits to the Kripalu Center for Yoga and Health in western Massachusetts. My three-day stay is full of healing—yoga, meditation, workshops, healthy food, a beautiful outdoors to explore, and Danskinetics. A combination of dance, yoga, group interaction, and an aerobic workout, Danskinetics is accessible to people of all ages. The first Danskinetics class I ever take is taught by Ken Scott, who also goes by his Sanskrit name, Nateshvar. For an hour and a half, he leads us through a series of powerful dance movements and into free-form dance with an energy and excitement that I had never seen before or since. Through it all he radiates a sense of goodness and joy.

And he does not say a word.

Later that afternoon I look on as another guest approaches him in the hallway. He smiles at her, listens, smiles again, touches his finger to his lips, shakes his head, smiles a third time, and moves on. I watch and wonder. I find the woman at dinner that evening and tell her I couldn't help being intrigued by their exchange. She laughs and informs me that Nateshvar is on a silent retreat. He is only engaging in nonverbal communication, which allows him to continue teaching Danskinetics, yoga, and other movement classes.

The retreat is to last for one year.

Through this encounter, I become fascinated with the power of silence. I used to think I had to talk all the time. This was an unconscious response to the fear that I'd be perceived as boring, unintelligent, or clueless. If you send a very loud parade down the street, no one will notice the street itself or the house where you live. I begin to realize that the most intriguing and intelligent people I know did not seem to feel this similar compulsion. I start to think about what my talking attempted to hide but often exposed: nervousness, angst, ignorance, arrogance. I begin to wonder how I might rely less on verbal communication. And I start to incorporate intentional silence into my daily life, eliminating conversations for at least an hour after waking and an hour before going to bed.

In early 1998, I return to Kripalu for a month and spend four of those days in silence. The experience gives me a glimpse at how powerful prolonged silence can be, enriching both activity and rest. It opens up space for my own wisdom and enables me to live from my truest place. In my silence, I watch as idealized images of myself melt away, and I become more content with reality. Other people's faults and bad habits barely even register. I am exempt from mindless chatter, engaging less with people and more with myself, my spirit. And, it makes more space for other people as well. I pay greater and greater attention as friends there share parts of their own story, which had been previously unheard. Silence, it seems, is the path to a higher, deeper love. I have since found it to be a valuable tool when working with groups. If people can be silent together for more than just a minute or two, their bonds deepen in unpredictable ways. And, the impact is felt long after the silence has been broken.

silence and social change . . . .

Words, heard and unheard, spoken and held back,
are central to the prophetic mission. Since a prophet must understand
the place of words, so a prophet must appreciate silence.

~ David Wolpe, *In Speech and In Silence*

Silence can be a powerful tool for social justice work. Groups that have developed their ability to be silent with each other reap the rewards, both as individuals and as a unit. stone circles gatherings and workshops almost always commence with a couple of moments of silence. The quiet gives everyone a chance to become present to themselves, each other, and the task at hand.

Silence is also useful when a group is faced with a hard decision, serious disagreement, or a crisis. If the discussion is getting tense or going around in circles, suggest three minutes of silence. People can use this time for whatever they want to think about, but ask that they refrain from writing or reading. Silence with activity is different than silence with no activity at all. Sometimes people are resistant or skeptical at first because it is so different from what we are used to in the workplace. Experiment. One period of refreshing silence may be enough for people to see the benefits.

Frame the silence for people if necessary: "Why don't we take a couple minutes of silence to think about what our actual goal is?" This is particularly helpful if a group has fallen into the common pattern of "groupthink," circling around the same idea and therefore losing out on other wisdom. Eventually you can lengthen the period of silence, taking the first 10 minutes of any meeting together to sit in silence to clear your mind in preparation for the work that lies ahead.

silence in action . . . .

Silence can also be a powerful way to cope with tragedy, pay tribute to the fallen, or face unspeakable horrors. If you have ever attended a silent vigil or protest, you know how powerful it is:

- "Take Back the Night" marches give survivors of sexual violence a chance to walk, in silence, in the dark, with a supportive group around them.

- Memorials to the Holocaust and other genocides include moments of silence to remember the dead; there seems no more appropriate way to face these atrocities.

- People visiting the Vietnam Memorial maintain a solemn silence in its presence. There are few sounds other than tears and whispers to the dead.

- On May 4, 1995, three thousand people convened at Kent State University to mark the 25th anniversary of the clash between National Guardsmen and students that killed four students. Some stood in a silent vigil for over 12 hours to commemorate the shootings.

a powerful way to cope with tragedy...

- When hate crimes were on the rise in Germany in the early 1990s, thousands of citizens took to the streets for a silent candlelight vigil.

- People up and down the East Coast gathered for two minutes of silence a day during the summer of 1995 to offer a prayer for peace in Bosnia.

activities to do alone . . . .

silence in your daily life

How might you incorporate silence into your day? What if you were silent before 9:00 A.M. or after 8:00 P.M.? This is harder if you have children, but some parents make a habit of finding quiet time for themselves at one end of the day or the other.

Could you spend one whole day in silence? Pick a non-work day, if possible. Inform your family or living companion(s) of your intention ahead of time, even ask them to join you. Try not to stay at home all day, even if it's a weekend. Enjoy opportunities to interact with others nonverbally. At Kripalu, I wore a nametag inscribed with the words, "In Loving Silence." You can try that, or carry around a card that explains briefly what you are doing. In his article for the *New York Times Magazine*, "Silent Sundays," author James Otis explains that over the past three years of staying silent every Sunday, he has carried around printed cards that read "I don't speak on Sundays." These are given to anyone with whom he must interact.

Let the silence be all-encompassing: no radio, television, or stereo. Throughout the day, jot down your thoughts, reactions, the difficulties and joys, the reactions you receive from others. Or, just move through the day without stopping to process it. Later you can reflect on what was important about the experience. Remember that your commitment will inspire and intrigue others, even while it is confusing and strange to them. You may very well open the door for someone else, just as Nateshvar did for me.

silent retreats

Plan ahead to take two or three days for a silent retreat. A silent retreat can be an amazing time of integration, elimination, and stillness. You might seek out local retreat centers, monasteries, or convents, many of which have space for guests for a low fee or donation. Many meditation centers sponsor workshops in silence, with a nightly talk by one of the meditation teachers. These places are more common that you might expect. Many are included in two books on

sanctuaries throughout the United States. [See the Resource section for details.]
Bring a journal and maybe one inspirational book, but take care not to overload
yourself. Spend the time walking, thinking, meditating, praying, and resting.
Don't rush to fill up your days. Watch how your body slows down, how your
eating habits change, and what shifts in your experience through your senses. A
list of retreat centers is provided in the Appendix.

activities to do with groups

working in silence

- *Are there times in your work day now that are filled with silence?*
- *How might these be enhanced or lengthened?*
- *How could your group weave more silence into its days?*
- *What would it mean to have one afternoon, or even an hour, every week when
  phones (excluding crisis hot lines) went unanswered? How might the workplace,
  not to mention the work, be transformed?*
- *Where else could you add silence to your group's routine?*

> *Since the lengthy exercises we did on silence at one meeting,
> I have been much more aware of the noise in my life and have continued
> to make efforts to reduce it. Noise, it seems to me, is one obvious
> manifestation of the clutter, confusion, and overstimulation of
> modern life that interferes with spirituality.*
>
> ~ Elizabeth Warren, member of the First Circle

experiencing silence together

> *The experience of sitting silently together as a group tends to bring about
> a subtle shift in consciousness that strengthens the team bond.
> Sometimes we extend mindfulness to the court and conduct whole practices
> in silence. The deep level of concentration and nonverbal communication that arises when we do
> this never fails to astonish me.*
>
> ~ Phil Jackson, *Sacred Hoops*

If you can spend time together in silence outside of the office, try the following
activity, which I adapted from an exercise I learned from Zen teacher and
author, Cheri Huber. This works particularly well on a weekend or early evening
in the spring or summer when there is daylight left. Everyone will need to see
the instructions, so write them on a large piece of paper and post it in your
gathering space, or pass out copies to everyone. You will also need some kind of
bell or chime to signal different segments of the exercise; a piece of silverware
against a glass will also do.

WRITTEN INSTRUCTIONS FOR THE GROUP:

Welcome!

As you enter, please remain in silence.
You may, of course, find other ways to acknowledge and greet people.

Please do the following three things over the next 40 minutes.

(1) Find a comfortable place to sit in silence for 10 minutes; if weather permits you can do this outside, but don't go too far away. You can use this time for prayer, meditation, or thought. Please do not write or read. A bell will ring to signal the end of this 10 minute period.

(2) If you are inside, go outside at this time. Spend the next 10 minutes doing the following:

Take three slow steps in any direction and stop.

Check in with all of your senses.
- *What do you see?*
- *What do you hear?*
- *What do you feel?*
- *What do you smell?*
- *What do you touch?*

When you are ready, take three steps in another direction.
Repeat the questions above.
Continue this until the second bell rings.

(3) At this point, maintaining your silence, find a partner. Walk together in quiet for 20 minutes (perhaps 10 minutes in one direction and then back) before reconvening at our gathering place. It will be helpful if one partner is wearing a watch.

We will reconvene at _____ at _____ .
                     (time)   (place)

Once everyone has returned, the group can sit again in silence or do a more formal meditation. Invite folks to share their experience:

- *What did you notice?*
- *How did it feel to do the exercise?*
- *What was comfortable? Uncomfortable?*
- *What surprised you the most?*
- *What did you like about doing this?*

Sometimes, a group that has spent this much time in silence may not want to talk at all. The questions above can be answered in writing. These writings can be exchanged with another person or even passed around the circle. Or you may want to just sit together in silence for 10-15 minutes and then end the gathering.

℮ silence with others: communal retreats

If you live with family members, a partner, or in a group housing situation, you may want to try a communal silent retreat. A weekend is the perfect time for this. Begin with a meal or ritual together—a chance to set any intentions you each have for the period. Agree that you will not engage with each other for 48 hours. Reconnect at the end, giving everyone an opportunity to share their experiences and tell the stories of their silence. You may find that you have little or no desire to communicate upon breaking the silence; don't push it. Just enjoy the quiet of each other's company.

With all I have thought and read about silence, I found nothing more beautiful than the words of writer Pico Iyer in his essay for *Time Magazine*, "The Eloquent Sounds of Silence:"

> *We have to earn silence, then, to work for it; to make it not an absence but a presence; not emptiness but repletion. Silence is something more than just a pause; it is that enchanted place where space is cleared and time is stayed and the horizon itself expands. In silence, we often say we can hear ourselves think; but what is truer to say is that in silence we can hear ourselves not think, and so sink below our selves into a place far deeper than mere thought allows. In silence, we might better say, we can hear someone else think.*
>
> *Silence, then, could be said to be the ultimate province of trust: it is the place where we trust ourselves to be alone; where we trust others to understand the things we do not say; where we trust a high harmony to assert itself. . . In love, we are speechless; in awe, we say, words fail us.*

the sounds of nature

An article written in my local paper in May, 1998 reported the somewhat startling appearance of six species of cicadas. After living underground for 13 years, feeding off tree roots, the cicadas had crawled out of the ground. They were ready to attract a mate, lay eggs, and pass on to their next life in bug heaven.

Remarkable? Yes, nature is remarkable. I heard the cicadas that weekend and at first thought they were locusts. Their noise was intense, full of the celebration their liberation from the earth warranted. The article, however, reported, that "People have mistaken it [the buzz] for airplanes flying overhead, construction equipment, even burglar alarms. The sound is so loud, so annoying, and so puzzling that they're calling 911, wanting to know what's going on."

We no longer recognize the sounds of nature.

resources for silence . . . .

Davis, Bruce. *Monastery without Walls: Daily Life in Silence.* Berkeley: Celestial Arts, 1990.

Halifax, Joan. *The Fruitful Darkness: Reconnecting with the Body of the Earth.* San Francisco: HarperSanFrancisco, 1993. Stories from one woman's journey into the practice and ancient teachings of Buddhism and Shamanism.

Housden, Roger. *Retreat: Time Apart for Silence and Solitude.* San Francisco: Harper, 1995. A beautiful guide to retreats in many of the major religious and spiritual traditions. Includes information on retreats in meditation, yoga, art, music, nature, and silence.

Iyer, Pico. "The Eloquent Sounds of Silence." *Time Magazine*, January 25, 1993.

Oates, Wayne E. *Nurturing Silence in a Noisy Heart.* Garden City, NY: Doubleday & Company, 1979. Great guide for refocusing and making more room for silence.

Otis, James. "Silent Sundays." *New York Times Magazine*, January 18, 1998.

Sarton, May. *Journal of a Solitude.* New York: Norton & Company, 1973. The diary of one year in the life of this writer, poet, thinker, and gardener; a wonderful account of daily life spent largely alone and in silence.

Storr, Anthony. *Solitude: A Return to the Self.* New York: Free Press, 1988. The author explores his own solitude in the context of historical and religious figures who sought similar experiences.

Wolpe, David. *In Speech and In Silence.* New York: Henry Holt & Company, 1992. The importance of silence and words in Jewish tradition, practice, and text.

stories of silence . . . .

Evelyn Mattern

Evelyn Mattern, SFCC, is a member of the Sisters for Christian Community. Over the last two decades, Evelyn has worked with the Roman Catholic Diocese of Raleigh and the North Carolina Council of Churches as a lobbyist and advocate for the rights of farmworkers and other disenfranchised populations. Her most recent project is "Ears to Hear," which she created. Evelyn also taught English for 10 years at St. Augustine's College in Raleigh and in the North Carolina Community College system.

CH: Evelyn, tell me about your faith background

EM: Well, my family wasn't church-going people, but they were very ethical. My mother would talk freely about what she believed, and the presence of God was part of her life. My grandmother in particular wanted us to go to Catholic school, so from the age of six, life was integrated with religious meaning. I took it very seriously. I entered the convent, partly from not such good motives. I had this idea that I wouldn't be okay if I didn't give my life to God, so I did. I did a lot of reading about the lives of the saints, and I realized everyone was concerned with souls. Many years later I realized caring about souls was caring about people.

When I was in graduate school at Penn in the mid-sixties, Vatican II was happening—a [Catholic] Church Council that was telling us to look at the world. Students were burning draft cards, and I met the Berrigans. [Daniel and Philip Berrigan, brothers and Catholic priests who have been involved in the anti-war movement and other peace issues.] There was a local peace movement I'd gotten involved with, and my own brother was facing Vietnam. The Civil Rights Movement, Vatican II, and Vietnam came together, and I saw this was what God's work was in the world.

So you became an activist?

I did. And I paid a price for it. I wore a full-length habit with a black veil, but I also felt the need to be in anti-war demonstrations. The civil disobedience squad wouldn't arrest me, but they'd call up the Mother General. I remember the Sisters saying "You went to a demonstration with your habit on?!," and I asked "Well, did you want me to take it off?"

I think in religion there are these two elements. First, the stabilizing element—all dictators want a religious people, because they're going to be obedient. But then there's this other dimension—the prophetic or disruptive dimension. People like the Berrigans gave me confidence to examine that dimension and apply it to our world today.

> I remember the Sisters saying "You went to a demonstration with your habit on?!," and I asked "Well, did you want me to take it off?"

In 1975, I went to the first women's ordination conference in Detroit where hundreds of women felt they had a call to be priests in the Roman Catholic Church. It allowed me to take another path to this new community. They were feminists and didn't believe in hierarchy. I really liked the vision that they had.

In 1975 I also went to my first meeting of the Sisters for Christian Community We're non-canonical, meaning we are not governed by the Roman authorities. Usually non-canonical religious groups apply eventually to Rome for some legal approval, and we've decided never to do that. So nobody outside of us has authority over us.

And you got very involved in community work at the same time?

In 1972, I started going into women's prison. I had volunteered to work with the Defense Committee for the trial of the Harrisburg Seven, a 1972 political trial of the Berrigans and other peacemakers. I saw how similar their view of the world was to mine. They ended up in prison, and I thought, "Well, I'll probably end up in prison, so I better start getting comfortable with prison."

I started going to the women's prison one night a week, teaching creative writing. That was another world. I developed a notion of what the North Carolina criminal justice system was like. I heard our new bishop was open to peace and justice work. He asked if I would be willing to take on a general purpose peace and justice job.

What did you work on?

I started learning how to develop a response to migrant farmworkers. I basically rode around to all the Catholic parishes in the eastern part of the state to survey the population. Everyone said, "The issues are in the next county, look in the next county." I sensed a tremendous amount of denial, especially in light of the data I was getting from the state.

It was a denial of presence. Women can be looked through, prisoners can be looked through, black people can be looked through, migrant farmworkers can be looked through, even though they're all over the place. I was determined to get some kind of religious ministry to migrant farmworkers. When I left five years later, I had in place a full-time migrant minister who would spend 40% of his time in direct service and 60% on social change. That was my goal for all peace and justice efforts, to get people thinking in terms of policy change, not just Band-aid. It was the Dorothy Day idea: you have your soup kitchen, but you also try to make your changes in the "dirty rotten system." She said that, so it gives me permission to call it that.

I got increasingly radicalized as I looked at more and more of the system. I began to see how the system doesn't really work for most people. The North Carolina Council of Churches asked me to serve on the farmworker ministry committee, and then they asked me to be a staff person. So I spent nine years at the legislature lobbying and that radicalized me, too. I never quite believed in the system; I realized the legislators don't represent the people of North Carolina; they don't look like the people of North Carolina. Most are there to increase their wealth and power and connections.

> That was my goal for all peace and justice efforts, to get people thinking in terms of policy change, not just Band-aid.

You left the council and then came back to work on a new project, "Ears to Hear," right?

When I left the council the first time in 1990, the political process did not touch enough people to suit me. I wasn't sure change could come through the political process unless there were some deeper cultural changes. I wanted to work on cultural change for a while. I didn't know quite how to do that. I thought maybe through writing, which I wanted to do anyway. Then council called me back in 1996, and I was willing, because I wanted to continue work on this spiritual, cultural thing to get to the heart piece.

It seems to me that one of the best things I've gotten to do is hear people's stories. There are incredible people who have taken incredible risks, often in very quiet ways. They've managed to be very quiet leaders. Hearing those people's stories with the intention of inspiring other people to look and say if this person can do it, I can do it. It's trying to get at the heart as well as the head.

Evelyn, what's been the thread of inspiration running through your life, the spiritual sustenance that has helped you maintain your commitment?

I'm always interested in people's communions of saints—people dead and alive whom I look to with the question, "What would so and so do in this circumstance?" So I do have a lot of people. And I belong to a religious community. We're very scattered in a way, but I think if I were totally alone trying to live the way I'm living, I wouldn't be strong enough. There are times when you really need to know there are other people on the path with you. We share enough of a vision that I feel accompanied by my community.

Do you have a daily routine?

A regular morning for me is to get up early, to read first and do a little yoga, and meditate through centering prayer for a half hour. I sometimes skip that if I have to leave the house at 5:00 A.M. but I try not to, or I get it in later. At night I try to do some reading. Every now and then I take a day. It's a spiritual need, or maybe it's just temperamental: an introvert trying to operate in an extrovert world. And then the summers, I have three months off, and I go into monastic mode. Up early, more time for prayer, more time for physical work, more time for study. Not every day is the same, but I like to do prayer and writing in the morning, reading in the afternoon, work and a walk in the evening.

I feel I have to pray regularly, I have to have solitude regularly, I have to do spiritual reading regularly, and I get very nervous if any of those isn't happening regularly. That's why I call myself a hermit. It's not that I don't see people, but this society we live in is crazy, and it would eat every minute of your time and every iota of your attention. You can't let it. My claim on time for God, time for spirit, is to say I'm a hermit.

silence.

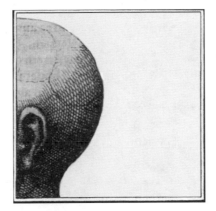

meditation

The spirituality of it [meditation] ambushed me. Unwittingly, I was engaging in a practice that has been at the heart of religious mysticism for millenniums. To separate 20 minutes from the day with silence and intention is to worship, whether you call it that or not. To be awakened to the miracle of existence—to experience Being not only in roses and sunsets but right now, as something not out there but in here—this is the road less traveled, the path of the pilgrim, the quest.

~ Marty Kaplan, "Ambushed by Spirituality,"
Time Magazine

questions for reflection

When do you notice yourself becoming distracted?

What, if anything, do you do to refocus your attention?

*Can you imagine what it would feel like if your mind was free of distractions,
if you were able to go through your day more mindful of each experience?*

Have you ever meditated before?

What was positive about your experience?

What was frustrating?

what is meditation? . . . .

Meditation is bringing your focus to one thing, in most cases your breath. It is observing with intentness. Reflection. The clearing of the mind. It can be practiced in the context of a religious tradition or completely independent of one. There are as many different definitions as there are practitioners, but the basis of most forms of meditation is the breath. Our breath is the one thing we always have with us. With each breath in, if we are conscious of it, we are breathing in energy. With each breath out, we breathe out something from ourselves, something we no longer need. All organisms breathe; it is one of the few things that all of nature has in common. The very definition of spirit, from the *Oxford English Dictionary, Second Edition*, is "the animating or vital principle in man and animals; that which gives life to the physical organism, in contrast to its purely material elements, *the breath of life.*" [Emphasis mine]

> *Breathing is the fundamental link between all things in nature.*
> *It is our conscious relationship to life. Breathing connects our awareness*
> *to every movement, every thought, every emotion we have.*
> *How we breathe is how we live. And the way we breathe can allow us to*
> *recover our wholeness, our balance of body and mind.*
>
> —Bija Bennett, *Breathing into Life*

turning point . . . .

It is the summer between my two years of graduate school. Shaken by an experience that I could only see as failure, I realize I need spiritual help, something beyond therapy. I make a pilgrimage to see two friends, David and Jennifer Sawyer, on their farm in Kentucky, and I try to describe my dilemma. They present me with three possible routes out of my despair: read, meditate, or pray. These are the three ways to God. I am already reading more than enough for school, and prayer is something I don't understand. I choose meditation.

In pursuing this course of action, I do what I always do—I buy a book—*Moon Over Water*, by Jessica Macbeth. Of all the books I've read on meditation since then, this one is still my favorite. Back in Durham, I set up a corner of my room with two plants, a photograph of the New Mexico mountains, rocks I like, and a clay pot that was given to me. I begin to practice. Every morning, I sit. Sometimes it is only five minutes, sometimes 10 or 15. Regardless, within just a few days a strange thing begins to happen. Every night I get home from school and think, "Today was a pretty good day." I don't overreact so much. I am nicer to people. I accomplish most of what I hope to accomplish for the day.

Within days, meditation is bringing me a sense of calm detachment that I've never experienced before. I worry less about what other people think and what I am missing in the world. My highs and lows aren't as gut-wrenching. In the six years since then, my meditation practice has had many variations. Some days I can't sit for 10 minutes without looking at my watch. Some days I can sit for a half hour without flinching. Some days I skip it altogether and then deal with the feeling of regret later. When I don't meditate, I simply feel "off." I'm not as focused or patient, with myself or with others. Little things cause a lot of frustration. I'm less hopeful, more easily overwhelmed.

Through it all, meditation remains a powerful tool for me. It is one of the building blocks of stone circles workshops, events, and training. In just 10 - 15 minutes, people can shift their energy, create a space of calm in their mind, and enter a silent, still place. In addition, sharing some of my meditation practice means at least one instance in every stone circles gathering when I take a risk.

meditation and social change . . . .

There may be no greater need for people of action than to learn to be still. When we meditate, we get a chance to be aware of what is going on, our breath, our sitting, a mantra, the candle in front of us—whatever we choose to focus on. And all we have to do is be aware. These things ask no response from us. What a switch from daily life, when we are constantly asked to respond. Pick up the phone when it rings, and you have to say something. Someone presents us with a problem, and we automatically begin to solve it. A crisis hits at work, and what have we been conditioned to do? More of the same—come up with something, and fast. In our urgency, it is easy to overlook vital information and the range of potential responses.

How might we give our best and achieve whatever form of justice we are seeking? What if we created another option for ourselves, not to react but to be in full, present, and loving awareness? And what if, in that space of being, we left lots of time for the voice of our true wisdom to emerge?

Meditation periods are often called a practice because we are setting aside this time to *practice awareness*. If we practice being aware in the morning, we are more likely to be aware the rest of the day. We can bike or walk or drive with a greater sense of attention. Cooking, eating, and cleaning can become acts of mindfulness. Every conversation and each interaction are opportunities to practice mindfulness in our speech, our actions, and the way we listen to other people. A meditation practice presents us with new ways of being, all of which have a positive impact on our work. For example:

Staying in the moment, staying present. We spend most of our time rehashing the past and anticipating the future. When we do this, we greatly limit our ability to think well about the present, thereby limiting the responses or options for action that are available to us. Staying present, we can listen more closely and without needing to respond as quickly. As we become more aware of our actions and our interactions, we also begin to notice and be mindful of our emotions—anger, joy, frustration, fear, excitement, despair—without becoming attached to them.

Thinking clearly and reconnecting with truth. The more aware we are, the more we can respond in a way that is truthful and wise. The closer our work is to issues of survival (meeting basic needs or addressing crisis situations), the greater the sense of urgency. As a result, we don't always feel as if we have time to think things through before making a decision. Meditation increases our ability to think clearly about our work and ourselves. It reveals insights which are often otherwise blocked in our day-to-day lives.

Concentration and focus. It's hard to learn when the mind is frantic. We're distracted, we drift, we're somewhere else, and suddenly we've missed the information, the question, the assistance we needed. Mindfulness is balanced awareness in every moment, the ability to ask "What is my truth? What else do I need to know? What is the wisest response? Do I have the energy to do it? Who else can help?"

Detachment. Through meditation, we learn to detach ourselves from hoped for results and from whatever seems to be consuming us in the moment. Meditation, and other forms of spiritual practice, allow us to relax our grip on life, our need to make everything work out, our desire to stay completely in control. The only thing we can count on is change. The trick is not to avoid the bad days, the frustrations, the stress, the pain. Rather we can watch it, as one might watch the weather, knowing it's bound to shift.

facing challenges . . . .

The challenges that arise during meditation are metaphors for what many activists face in their daily work:

Distraction. If there's one thing you can count on during meditation, it's distraction. Our minds are not used to this kind of quiet, and initially we do not know exactly how to handle it. Do not get discouraged; this happens to even the most experienced meditators. You start to sink deeply into a breath, and slowly a

The only thing we can count on is change. . .

few items for your grocery list float through your head. Or you remember something you wished you'd said in an earlier conversation. Or an idea for a new project appears. Suddenly you are not meditating; you are thinking. What do you do? First of all, relax. Just notice that you are thinking. You might even want to say calmly to yourself, "Oh, I'm thinking." Then refocus your attention on your breath. Let the distraction lead you back to the breath. And then watch how you begin to deal differently with distractions.

Discomfort. If your body feels tense or full of aches, it is a good idea to relax your body before meditating. Light stretching or yoga will help. You can also guide yourself through a body relaxation meditation like the one at the end of this chapter. You may also need to readjust your posture or lie down if sitting is too uncomfortable.

Fatigue. Falling asleep during meditation is also perfectly normal, especially at first. It may be a sign that your body needs a relaxation even deeper than meditation. You may not be getting enough sleep, or your mind may just be resisting this level of concentration. You may want to change your position or alter the time of day you're meditating. Many of us see fatigue as a weakness, but it is often the first sign of burnout. Let this be a clue.

Judgment. Nothing can kill a meditation practice (or any spiritual practice, for that matter) faster than judgment. Being disciplined about meditation is one thing. Being hard on yourself is quite another. Be kind to yourself, especially in the beginning, and don't worry if you think you're not meditating well, not doing it often enough, or not doing it for long enough. It may take a while before you feel like you are able to actually concentrate on your breath for more than a couple of seconds. This should be proof enough of how cluttered and busy our minds are and how badly we need to clear a space in there. Even when we're just beginning to explore the practice, we still feel the benefits. And, as we grow in compassion for ourselves, we become more compassionate with those around us.

No results. Some days you will feel many of the benefits meditation has to offer; other days you may not feel any. Just recognize that you will have a range of experiences with meditation as you will with other spiritual practices. All of these experiences are part of the practice. As with meditation, social change work can often mean dealing with the reality of "no results" without losing interest in the task or your focus on the goal.

Oh, I'm thinking . . .

activities to do alone . . . . 人

The practice of meditation can reduce tension and promote relaxation,
improve concentration and self-discipline, give a sense of improved well-being,
increase energy, aid the development of the psyche, enhance spiritual growth,
lower high blood pressure, decrease the frequency and severity of tension-related diseases,
aid the body in its recovery from physical fatigue, promote serenity,
and improve your ability to listen.
~Jessica Macbeth, *Moon Over Water*

℮ basic meditation

Thousands of books have been written on meditation; some are listed in "Resources" at the end of this chapter. Each book, teacher, and religious tradition offers different ways to meditate. Experiment until you find something that works for you. The basic building block of meditation is the focus on the breath. Below is one way to get started.

1. Before beginning a period of meditation, it may help to stretch. Light exercises or yoga can be a great way to get energy flowing more evenly through your body.

2. Find a comfortable, quiet spot. Sit in the same place everyday; over time, it will become a quietly enchanting corner in your house, apartment, or room. Your body temperature will drop as you relax into meditation, so dress to stay warm.

3. Sit either in a straight-backed chair or on the floor, cross-legged. If you choose the floor, put a pillow under your buttocks so your knees rest on the floor. Your back should be as straight as possible. You want a posture that will allow the maximum energy to flow through you. At some point, you may want to explore sitting on a prayer bench or Zafu cushion, used in Zen meditation. For now, a pillow will work fine. If sitting is uncomfortable for you, lie down. It is easier to fall asleep lying down, so meditate when you feel awake.

4. Rest your hands either in your lap or on your thighs in a position that is both comfortable and intentional. You may want to begin by reading an inspirational prayer or poem to enter a quiet space.

5. You can close your eyes or leave them just very slightly open, looking down and about six inches in front of you. In Zen meditation, the eyes are left

open. The belief is that if you practice awareness in meditation with the eyes open, it will be easier to maintain that awareness during the rest of the day, when your eyes are open. In the beginning, closing your eyes will eliminate distractions.

6. Begin to notice your breath. Let it deepen and lengthen as your body starts to relax. Get settled in your body, your breath, and the space around you. Many people begin their meditation practice with a ritual, which can be something as simple as lighting a candle or saying a short invocation.

7. Begin to meditate, or focus on the breath. One very simple way to do this is just to count to 10 breaths. On the in-breath, silently count "one" in your head; on the out-breath just listen to the sound of the exhale. On the next in-breath, hear "two," and so on. If you lose count (which you surely will—our minds need practice to stay focused!), start over at one. When you do get to 10, start over. Try consciously to notice your breath as it moves up and down through your body. Another variation is to pick one word like "peace" or "love" to say to yourself on the in-breath.

8. End your meditation as consciously as you began it. If your eyes were closed, open them very slowly. Give yourself a couple of minutes just to rest in the quiet of the moment. Those moments following meditation are some of the most blissful. Before moving your whole body, wiggle your fingers and your toes. This is a more gentle way to come out of a relaxed state. You may want to end with a closing ritual or prayer.

Do this practice in the morning and the evening. Five to 10 minutes twice a day can make a revolutionary difference; eventually you can work your way up to 15-20 minutes. I like to meditate first thing in the morning, immediately after I wake up, and sometime in the late afternoon/early evening. If you have an alarm that is not too loud, set it for the desired length of the meditation period. That way you can meditate without having to worry about how much time you have left.

℮ full-body meditation for relaxation

Lie down on a comfortable floor or sit comfortably (but straight) in a chair. If you want to lie down and you have a bad back, put a pillow under your knees. Make sure you're dressed warmly enough, as your body temperature will drop as you sink deeper into the meditation. What follows is a "script" for full-body relaxation. You can:

1. Read it over a few times to get the general flow, memorize a few key phrases, and then repeat it to yourself. Keep this next to you and refer to it periodically. You may find this less relaxing the first few times you do it, but you'll find in time that you've committed much of it to memory and no longer need the script.
2. Record it on a tape player and play it back.
3. Pair up with a friend and lead each other through it.

This is also a great thing to do with a group. See "guided meditations" below under activities for groups.

NOTE: Each time you see "..." it indicates that it's time to pause for a couple of seconds. The main thing here is to take it very slowly, but not so slowly that you fall asleep in the middle of the meditation.

Begin by settling into the space underneath you... feel your body sink into the floor or the chair... feel it getting heavier... let your body relax... turn your attention to your breath... just watch your breath... notice it getting deeper... focus your attention only on the breath... as you breathe, become aware that each breath in is a chance to breathe healing energy from the ground below you... each breath out is a chance to rid the body of tension... use whatever distractions may arise as reminders to return to your breath... this is time just for your body and your mind to relax... loosen any clothing that may feel tight... readjust your body if you need to to feel more comfortable....

Now bring your awareness to your feet... they've been carrying you around all day... let them relax... breathe into your feet, noticing any points of tension or stress... just let your feet relax... clench the muscles in your feet and toes for a moment... feel the relaxation deepen as you release... let your feet and your ankles just sink into the floor beneath you... now move your awareness to your calves and your knees... notice any tightness or tension here... tighten these muscles and let them relax... keep breathing deeply as you begin to focus on your thighs, your pelvis, your buttocks... tense up the muscles in your thighs and your pelvis... then enjoy the release as you let this part of your body relax... continue to breathe deeply and evenly, as you notice the calm in your lower body....

Next, begin breathing into your back... you may notice many different points of tension in your upper and lower back... this is a common place to hold stress... tense up the muscles of your back and let them go into a state of calm relaxation... just breath into your back and breathe out, letting yourself sink deeper into the ground or the chair... bring your awareness next to your chest and your stomach... tighten the muscles in this area and then let them relax... notice your breath as it moves through

washing the dishes: mindfulness as daily practice

If you cannot wash the dishes in mindfulness, neither can you meditate while sitting in silence.
~ Thich Naht Hanh,
The Miracle of Mindfulness

Thich Naht Hanh, a Vietnamese Buddhist monk, talks about washing the dishes just to wash the dishes, not to finish them and get on to the next thing. When engaged in work, we will be more likely to focus on one task or activity at a time if we practice aware-ness. Tibetan monks use chimes throughout the day to bring them to awareness of the moment and to remind them to do whatever they're doing more mindfully. We may find that specific things can remind us to be mindful. I went through a period of being annoyed whenever the phone rang at work. I realized I was being rude sometimes as a result. One day, I decided that each time the phone rang, I'd smile to myself and breathe deeply and then pick it up. What a difference this made! I found myself less bothered by the phone, and I treated the person on the other end of the line better, listening more thoroughly, and opening my heart wider. Even now, when the phone rings, I am reminded to be mindful. I have a friend who remembers his commitment to God and his faith every time he puts on his seat belt.

you. . . the chest and stomach moving in and out in an easy rhythm. . . let this part of your body relax. . . .

Imagine drawing a breath in through your fingers and letting it drift slowly up your arms. . . let your fingers and hands, elbows and arms relax. . . tighten the muscles in your arms and let them relax. . . bring the breath and your awareness to your shoulders and your neck. . . notice how you feel. . . you may have stress or aches in this part of your body. . . you may want to let your neck roll slowly from side to side, being careful not to strain any muscles. . . breathe slowly into this part of your upper body. . . let the gentle breath bring healing to your shoulders and your neck. . . let them release. . . let every breath out carry tension away from the body. . . .

With the breath, begin to notice your head and your face, your mouth, nose, eyes . . . become aware of any tension. . . let the breath flow through your face and let it relax. . . give your face and head permission to just let go and release. . . drop your jaw. . . let your eyelids droop. . . notice your face and head getting heavier as they become more relaxed. . . .

Breathe relaxation into your whole body. . . let the breath wash up and down. . . let it flow over every muscle, every bone, every cell. . . with your breath, notice how relaxed your body has become. . . know this is a state you can always return to. . . that it is the breath, your breath, which brought you here. . . your body and mind and soul are relaxed. . . this relaxation will stay with you. . . .

Slowly, return your awareness to the floor beneath you and the room around you. . . leave your eyes closed. . . when you're ready, begin to wiggle your fingers and your toes. . . stay focused on your breath. . . slowly roll over to one side. . . very slowly, when you're ready, sit up. . . notice that you are relaxed and refreshed. . . notice how different your body feels. . . when you are ready, open your eyes. . . .

℗ walking meditation

Walking meditation is a chance to pay attention to both your breath and your footsteps. The basic instruction is to be mindful of every step you take. Be mindful as you pick your foot up, as it is in the air, as your body shifts its weight, as that foot comes down and the other one comes up. You might be amazed at how slowly you can walk. You can do this anywhere. Beautiful, scenic locations offer wonderful opportunities for walking meditation. It would be interesting to try this on the streets of a big city. Small spaces like your living room are great and even better for concentration, because you won't be as distracted by the scenery. Thich Naht Hanh's *A Guide to Walking Meditation* is a good resource for more information.

℮ guided meditations

Find guided meditations to listen to. Many use imagery as a way into relaxation. There are plenty of great tapes around, and many public libraries have them. Many books contain guided meditations that can be recorded and played back. A couple of good ones to check out are *Working from the Inside Out*, by Margo Adair, and *Healing Unto Life and Death*, by Stephen Levine.

activities for groups: getting started . . . .

℮ leading meditation for groups

The first time I led a meditation for a group, I was nervous. When you actually begin, it feels wonderful to know that just the sound of your voice is bringing people to new states of relaxation.

Preparation. Have the whole meditation written out in front of you. You can start with written guided meditations such as the full-body relaxation above or one from another book. It's important to practice a few times by yourself and on one other person, before doing this with a group. You need to get a feel for the words, the pauses, the flow of the meditation. I've found that many people love guided meditations, so it shouldn't be hard to round up a volunteer or two. Ask them to give you some feedback afterwards on the timing, the pace, the sound and volume of your voice, what worked for them, and what didn't.

Think about your goals. If you are doing a guided meditation for a group of hardworking, stressed-out colleagues, you might choose one that asks them to imagine a peaceful location, a place they can return to in their mind when they need a sanctuary. As you do more and more guided meditations and you get a feel for how they work, you can start writing your own.

Guided meditations can range from the very simple, such as a body relaxation, to the very complex. I attended a workshop called "Women and Power" at the Omega Institute a few years ago. Jean Shineda Bolen, a Jungian psychologist steeped in Greek mythology, led us through what must have been a 40-minute guided meditation. She took us through rooms in a house, had us discover objects we needed for our journey, and brought us face to face with someone who'd be a great guide. It was the most involved guided meditation I'd ever experienced.

<u>Timing</u>. Be sure you have enough time. You need at least 20 minutes—a few minutes to get settled, 10-15 minutes for the meditation itself (many are longer), and a few minutes at the end for folks to return to the present.

<u>Beginning</u>. Ask everyone to assume a comfortable position. Dim the lights or turn them off if it's during the day. It's better to have a little light than complete darkness so folks don't fall asleep. Don't be surprised if there is some moving around during the first few minutes as people get comfortable, change positions, and loosen clothing.

<u>Pace</u>. With guided meditations, you want to take your time but not go so slowly that you give people's minds a chance to drift away. As you gain experience, you'll learn the right pace and how much time to leave between phrases.

<u>Closing</u>. Most guided meditations will end with a way to come back to the present. You want to make sure that people don't get up too quickly, or they will get dizzy. Suggest that they wiggle their hands and toes, roll slowly over to one side, and then very slowly come to a seated position. A few minutes of silence at the end of a guided meditation is important for this transition.

<u>Debrief</u>. If you use a guided meditation that is focused on something beyond relaxation, give people a few minutes to debrief with one other person.

℮ meditating on challenge

1. Ask everyone to pair up and spend three to four minutes each discussing a challenge they are currently facing in their life. Partners are not to give advice but merely to listen to each other. Tell them that you will call "switch" when three minutes are up and it is the other person's turn to share.

2. Lead folks through a 10-minute guided meditation. Start with a full-body relaxation. Before you have folks start to come out of the meditation, add the following:

   Feel the sense of peaceful relaxation in your body. . . realize how much energy is available to you. . . the challenge you have identified is not as big as it might appear. . . you have everything you need to face and resolve this issue. . . know that there are people in your life who want to help you. . . the intuition within you already knows a creative response. . . you approach the challenge with courage and joy. . .

3. Finish the end of the full-body relaxation.

4. After a few minutes of quiet, have everyone reconnect with their partner and revisit the challenge they discussed earlier. Ask them to talk about how they are feeling about it now.

    What if anything has shifted?
    What else might they do in this situation?
    What else is available to them?

℮ meditation in pairs

This activity is adapted from the work of therapist Virginia Satir. Satir helped develop many personal growth centers and created experiential techniques now widely used by therapists. Have people pair up with someone they don't feel they know well and have them sit facing each other, either in chairs or on the floor. Ask one partner to close his/her eyes while the other remains meditating, eyes open, on the other person's face. This meditation is for the person with their eyes open, so direct your instructions to them. Leave time after each phrase (each time you see ". . .") for the participants to consider what you're saying or asking them. This exercise may provoke laughter or tension, anxiety or joy; ask people to notice these as they arise and let them go.

TO READ TO THE GROUP:
Begin by taking a couple of deep breaths. . . settle into the chair and get comfortable so you can feel grounded. . . look at the person in front of you. . . first notice surface things about the person in front of you. . . what does he or she look like? . . . does this person remind you of anyone you've seen before?. . . how are they similar or different to you in age?. . . gender? . . . ethnic background?. . . what else do you notice about them on the surface?

Now, go a bit deeper. . . what have you already noticed about their life?. . . their personality?. . . continue to look at them. . . realize how they are similar to you. . . what dreams might they have?. . . which ones may have come true?. . . which ones may have been dashed or deferred? . . .

Buddhism, enlightenment, and the four noble truths

Meditation comes from the Eastern tradition of Buddhism. Buddha is the Sanskrit word for "awakened one." The story of the Buddha begins in 560 B.C.E., when a young man named Siddhartha was born a prince in northern India. His father the king hid all unpleasantness from him. It wasn't until Siddhartha got outside the palace walls at age 29 that he caught a glimpse of suffering: sickness, aging, and death.

This experience transformed him forever and sent him on a pilgrimage. For years he wandered throughout India, studying Hindu teachings, fasting, and practicing Yogic exercises, all in search for a solution to the suffering he had witnessed. Eventually he abandoned religious teachings but continued to meditate. He sat and struggled until finally one day he experienced what Buddhists now call *enlightenment*: a feeling of complete oneness, no separation. Soon afterward he began to teach his message of hope, that there is a way beyond suffering.

His message is conveyed through the Four Noble Truths:
1. *Dukka*, or suffering, is a necessary condition of life.
2. The cause of suffering is *tanha*, or the desire for private fulfillment. We must accept this suffering and take full responsibility for it if we are to find a way out of it.
3. Everyone is capable of relieving suffering by overcoming this desire.
4. Suffering can be relieved through the Noble Eightfold Path: Right Knowledge, Right Understanding, Right Speech, Right Behavior, Right Livelihood, Right Effort, Right Mindfulness, and Right Concentration.

Realize they've been hurt in their life and have probably hurt others as well. . . notice that they have regrets and shame just as you do. . . they are full of fears, hopes, and dreams. motivated by a need to receive love and a desire to give love, probably like you. . . breathe deeply as you take in this connection. . . these similarities. . . recognize the oneness that exists between you right now. . . when you are ready, put your hands on the shoulders of your partner. . . this will be a sign to them that they can open their eyes. . . sit together in the quiet for a moment and just acknowledge each other. . . .

Repeat the exercise with the other partner closing his or her eyes.

resources for meditation . . . .

Adair, Margo. *Working Inside Out: Tools for Change.* Oakland: Wingbow Press, 1984. Full of guided meditations to use with groups engaged in social and political action. Focuses on energy, planning, healing, relationships, and visioning.

Bennett, Bija. *Breathing into Life: Recovering Wholeness Through Body, Mind and Breath.* New York: HarperCollins Publishers, Inc., 1993. A compact collection of short meditative exercises on the breath.

Chödrön, Pema. *When Things Fall Apart.* Boston: Shambhala, 1997. Radical and compassionate advice for what to do when things go wrong from one of the first Western women to take full monastic Buddhist vows.

_____. *The Wisdom of No Escape and the Path of Loving Kindness.* Boston: Shambhala, 1991. A wonderful collection of talks given by Chödrön at a month-long meditation retreat at Gampo Abbey.

Hesse, Herman. *Siddhartha.* Translated by Hilda Rosner. New York: Bantam, 1951. One classic version of the story of the Buddha.

Kabat-Zinn, John. *Wherever You Go, There You Are.* New York: Hyperion, 1994. A simple and clear guide to bringing mindfulness meditation into everyday life. Short chapters, each with a meditation exercise to try.

Kaplan, Marty. "Ambushed by Spirituality." *Time Magazine*, June 24, 1996.

Levine, Stephen. *Healing Unto Life and Death.* New York: Anchor Books, 1987. Like many of Levine's books, this one has great guided meditations.

Low, Albert. *An Invitation to Practice Zen.* Rutland, Vermont: Charles E. Tuttle Company, 1989. The Zen Buddhist approach to meditation, complete with background on Buddhist philosophy and detailed instructions for developing a Zen practice.

Macbeth, Jessica. *Moon Over Water: Meditation Made Clear with Techniques for Beginners and Initiates.* Bath, United Kingdom: Gateway Books, 1990. A great guide for anyone wanting to know the basics; includes many practical exercises.

Mitchell, Stephen. *Tao Te Ching: A New English Version.* New York: HarperPerennial, 1988. A beautiful translation of the ancient Chinese text.

Nhat Hanh, Thich. *A Guide to Walking Meditation.* Translated by Jenny Hoang and Nguyen Anh Huong. Nyack, NY: Fellowship Publications, 1985. Describes the approach of this engaged Vietnamese Buddhist monk.

_____. *The Miracle of Mindfulness.* Translated by Mobi Warren. Boston: Beacon Press, 1976. Thich Nhat Hanh sees every act as a meditative one and provides simple, beautiful commentary on how to lead a mindful life.

_____. *Peace is Every Step.* New York: Bantam, 1991. How to walk the path of mindfulness in everyday life; includes commentaries, meditations, and stories.

Rahula, Walpola. *What the Buddha Taught.* New York: Grove Press, 1974. An account of the Buddha's Four Noble Truths, written by a Buddhist monk and scholar. It includes texts as remembered and recorded by a group of disciples shortly after the Buddha's death.

Thondup, Tulku Rinpoche. *The Healing Power of the Mind: Simple Meditation Exercises for Health, Well-Being and Enlightenment.* Boston: Shambhala, 1996. Meditations and visualizations from the basic teachings of ancient Tibetan medicine.

Wilhelm, Richard. *The I Ching, or Book of Changes.* Translated by Cary F. Baynes. Princeton, NJ: Princeton University Press, 1950, 1977. First published in 1924, this is one of the oldest of the modern translations of the *I Ching*; includes a forward by Carl Jung.

Arrington Chambliss

Arrington Chambliss recently earned a Masters of Divinity at Harvard Divinity School and a teaching certificate at the Graduate School of Education. Prior to entering Divinity School, she spent 10 years working with young people and doing organizational development with two community service organizations, ACCESS and COOL (Campus Outreach Opportunity League), and Project LEEO, which provides leadership, education, and employment opportunities to young men at risk. Discerning for ordination as an Episcopal priest, she also maintains a strong meditation practice.

CH: Arrington, tell me how you got into meditation.

AC: Tension and intensity in my work, and my own experience of illness catalyzed a conversation with two friends, David and Jennifer Sawyer. We talked about the need for spiritual grounding. David introduced me to the *Tao Te Ching* and the *I Ching** and that's when I started studying Taoist philosophy. I connected with the philosophy the first time I learned it. There was a lot of talk about change in communities and systems, but there was rarely talk about change in the individual and how one could channel energy in a positive way towards change.

I was fascinated by how the *I Ching* told me that it might not be time to move forward, that non-action might be the best strategy, that I didn't always have to be assertive with my opinion. The best thing was to sit still. I immediately noticed an impact on my relationships in the office. I began to wonder how systemic changes would shift anything unless there was a shift in consciousness around power and love. My practice gave me a new framework: (1) sometimes I didn't need to do, and (2) systemic change became connected to spiritual change.

> It was clear I needed to learn to sit still. The tension inside me was a mirror for the world outside in many ways. I needed to understand that was a passing phenomenon.

And so I learned to sit. That's when I learned to meditate. It was clear I needed to learn to sit still. The tension inside me was a mirror for the world outside in many ways. I needed to understand that was a passing phenomenon.

*The *Tao Te Ching*, written by Lao-tzu in fifth century China, can be translated as *The Book of the Way*. It is a treatise on the art of living in harmony with the way things are. One surrenders to the Tao and finds their own truths about life. The *I Ching*, or *Book of Changes*, is a book of wisdom and an oracle. The last three thousand years of Chinese culture and history have been profoundly affected and inspired by this text. It is the source of Confucianist and Taoist philosophy. There are hundreds of translations and interpretations of the *I Ching*.

You have made a serious commitment to meditation. Tell me about your practice.

Three to four years into it I didn't have a name for it, but I came to learn it was mindfulness practice, focusing on the breath. As I've learned more, I've decided that the lineage and practice I want to settle in is Tibetan Buddhist meditation practice, primarily because it uses the material of life—the everyday material of our anger, our life circumstance—and teaches us to transform and rechannel that energy. I practice twice a day, for about 30 minutes in the morning and 20 minutes at night. I have one meditation that is one to two hours, once a week; I belong to a small group of meditators who meet once a month; and I go to classes every Wednesday night.

You have a teacher?

Yes. Three or four years into my practice, I'd reached a plateau about what I was able to teach myself through reading and practice. I felt like I needed a guide, someone who knew more than I knew. I also needed someone to help me structure my practice so I could go deeper with it.

What impact has meditation had on your life?

I feel like I'm a different person. The people I look to for guidance are different people—people who can embrace both the inner and outer world, who embrace justice and peace both inside themselves and outside in the world. My inner and outer work are connected. The messy, inner work that I sometimes try to avoid by pouring myself into justice work needed to be dealt with.

And what impact has it had on your work?

I was working at the East Boston Ecumenical Community Council with 12 youth organizers in East Boston, one of the most multiethnic communities in Boston. We'd spent nine weeks planning and training them how to organize other young people. It was to culminate in a youth-led, community development planning day, paralleling a process being driven by condo developers in the area. There was a fear that young people, working-class people, and people of color wouldn't have a voice in that planning process.

On the actual day, the youth had a list of 50 other young people who said they were coming. The event was to start at 11:30, and we got there at 8:00 A.M. to set up. By 11:40 only four young people were there. The youth organizers became more disappointed. Before, I might have immediately jumped into some kind of action or felt pressured to do something immediately. The other adult organizer and I gathered them in a group and told everyone to take a deep breath and focus on why we were all there, why we felt like this was important, and how powerful all the work we'd done was.

After silence we went around and talked about one thing we needed to do or didn't need to do. There was space to reconnect, to not wallow in their hopelessness and feeling of failure but instead place their attention in a different place—what they'd already done and what could still be done. They ended up walking up the street to recruit young people to come to the event. They brought back 25 young people and the day was a great success. They got press coverage and came up with youth priorities for the neighborhood. It wasn't a success in terms of the original goals, but they'd seen they didn't have to give in to that feeling of hopelessness. Organizing wasn't always about bringing in great numbers, but it was creating a sense of momentum to see how they, as organizers, could do something. I don't know if I would have reacted that way in the past. There was a detachment; it wasn't about me, and it also wasn't about them. Creating the space to take that leap is what I think meditation teaches you, to take the pause.

What would you say to activists who were thinking about meditation or developing a spiritual practice?

Figure out the practice which grounds you within yourself, whether it be meditation or movement or dance or prayer. Spend time with yourself in that way regularly whether it's three minutes or an hour or whatever you can figure out. And spend that kind of time with a group of people that you work with, time where you're not expected to do anything but recognize your connection to one another and the common purpose. Don't look outside of yourself for the answer. It's the hardest lesson that I still struggle to remember.

> Figure out the practice which grounds you within yourself, whether it be meditation or movement or dance or prayer.

stories of meditation and vocation . . . .

Cheryl and Jim Keen

Cheryl and Jim Keen are professors at Antioch College in Yellow Springs, Ohio. Cheryl is a professor of Self, Society, and Culture, and Jim is a professor of Social and Global Studies. Together they founded and ran the Governor's School of Public Issues and the Future of New Jersey for 13 years. They have also taught at Harvard University, Lesley College, and Goddard College. In 1996 they and two others co-authored Common Fire: Leading Lives of Commitment in a Complex World. They have been married for 23 years.

CH: *Tell me about your faith background.*

CK: I grew up Lutheran. My father was the head of the Sunday School, and he would ask for small dollars to support the work with the kids, and they would always spend money buying property instead. It outraged him. He quit right when I went to college, so I went on a spiritual quest for a better spiritual home. When I went to graduate school and met Jim, he took me to Quaker meeting, and it was exactly what I had been looking for, and I hadn't even known about Quakers before. The first meeting I went to I said, "This is my spiritual place to grow."

What was it about it?

CK: The sense that everybody's equal and that you all wait for the spirit to move, the very strong women who were there, the feeling in the room, the lack of hierarchy, the social commitments of people. It embraced everything that I cared about: feminism, social action, spirituality, mysticism, and intellect.

And you had opened the door for that, Jim?

JK: I grew up being a Quaker. I studied Quakerism in college, particularly the mystical side of Quaker tradition. Later, I journeyed to the East and spent time in an Hindu-oriented ashram and learned to teach meditation. That whole journey to the East brought me back to my Quaker roots. It was more comfortable to stay within a tradition that I'd been nurtured in, particularly because it was a very good tradition from which to practice a spiritual or religious orientation that was not centered on one religion but was open to a variety of religious traditions. I've been meditating regularly for 27 years; Cheryl's been meditating regularly for almost 25. So that's something that we've been doing together.

Do you meditate together?

JK: At times, and at times separately. More separately.

CK: Largely because of the demands of family life. I'll meditate, and you get the dinner started.

JK: But we meditate in the same space, and there's something about meditating where other people meditate that has value to it.

Can you talk about how you see your mission in the world?

CK: I'm open to a different vision of my work in the future, but I don't think it will be that radically different. I feel called to reform the face of secondary and higher education. I would like to help it get to a place where it's not what it is now and hardly recognizable because it's returned so powerfully to best practice.

And what role does your spiritual life play in acting on that calling?

CK: Trying to be loving in all of my dealings and the Quaker piece is very strong for me—to look to that of God in every person. I really try to practice that. I get razzed for always giving the other person the benefit of the doubt, which is the popular culture way of interpreting that.

> Trying to be loving in all of my dealings and the Quaker piece is very strong for me—to look to that of God in every person.

JK: Cheryl creates authentic contexts in which people can practice a greater obedience to the truth. It's a very spiritual approach to education and reform. There's always this sense of concern, not only for people but also for how people come together and support each other and become transformative agents in the world. Wherever we go, eventually she develops a flock. There's something ministerial about her, much more than I am.

My orientation is toward trying to develop and understand settings in which transformative education takes place. And trying to understand the patterns through which people become world servants in a significant way. The spiritual dimension is certainly a very important dimension of that. We did this 15 year research project on how people develop and sustain lives of commitment to working on behalf of the whole human family. The most important thing we found was that people had had important encounters that had taken them across thresholds of difference in ways that helped them develop a larger sense of inclusion in their self-construction.

I'm interested in how people preserve themselves in the context of living lives of commitment. How does spirituality make the difference in each of you being able to sustain yourselves over many years of work?

CK: Meditating daily, twice a day, keeps me healthy and stable and energized, because I work into the evening. I don't know if it's personality or meditation, but I don't worry. I hold people in the light. If I'm worried about an individual, I hold them in my mind and wait for an intuitive moment about how to be of service to that person on their path. It might be me who sees what the next step is in someone's life, and I need stay open to that, spend more time with them and listen.

Meditation helps with that. Going to Quaker meeting in a small town like Yellow Springs where other people have powerful commitments keeps me inspired and humbled. There are other people who need support. So meeting replenishes me; it doesn't always, but I'm willing to spend an hour a week to go to meeting on the chance that someone will address my condition or the experience will renew me in a powerful way.

If I'm feeling spiritually awake, I'll read Rumi's poems and feel even more alive. If I'm struggling, if I play two particular hymns, I cry and feel humble in the face of God and rally myself. And I read the *I Ching*. That kind of expectant waiting fits with me, the thinking, "Well, this is interesting, what's happening now. I'll wait and see. It must be something I can't figure out, so if it's painful, I'll just wait." The *I Ching* helps me if I have to make a choice that is off the linear path.

> And I don't have much interest in working alone. One way in which that obviously manifests itself is Cheryl's and my relationship as collaborators over the years.

JK: It's important for me to feel good about the work I'm doing, that it isn't something necessarily that anyone who came along might do. I have to find some ways of taking what I've learned, my background, my particular gifts and try to be of service with them at this point in my life. Spiritually I feel good about that, much better than trying to walk into somebody's preexisting job description. I'm better off spiritually when I'm myself instead of trying to play some role that isn't me.

And I don't have much interest in working alone. One way in which that obviously manifests itself is Cheryl's and my relationship as collaborators over the years. I've always been kind of a communal type, and while I like solitude, the solitude is in counterpoint to community, rather than being highly individuated. That's the balance for me: the solitude, coming at things in ways that have a lot of self-authorship in them and yet doing that in a way that is highly collaborative with other people. Being able to get that into balance is almost a spiritual discipline. I'm constantly reframing and seeking balance, and I've been doing that for years.

You've both spent a lot of time with young people who are beginning to discern a spiritual direction. What do you feel is important for them?

CK: Having spaces in which they can share fragile expressions of things they care about or avenues of exploration that seem fruitful. Having people keep them company in the exploration, whether it is in dialogue, or music, or poetry. To create a moment in which something just a little different is happening because someone has opened up and said something much more honest than they ever expected to hear—and to honor that. There they can see the potential of the quickening of the spirit.

JK: I think it's important that people develop reflective habits. I try to build it into every learning environment opportunity. For people who do it, it's a welcome thing. And for people who have not yet learned how to do it, nothing will serve them better than becoming self-reflective—assessing what they're learning, what they know, what they're feeling, looking for connections, becoming explicit about what's surprising them. I'm always interested in seeing young people become authentic, qualitative researchers of everyday life, including their own.

I'm very interested in people having experiences like internships and travel abroad, opportunities to experience the world in different ways. That's one of the reasons I think community service programs are so important; it's so bizarrely missing from the lives of many 18-22 year-olds. The other thing is a mentoring environment in which the mantle is passed, and people step up and start to take on the world's challenges in significant ways. Part of the opportunity of being a young adult is to find yourself in situations where you learn important stuff from older folks who have been around. All of that is really important.

I'm not really interested in environments that do not challenge people to move across the threshold of significant difference, so that the self evolves at a wider gyration and wider increments of evolution take place. That will, from my point of view, lead to a greater chance that the person will make a larger contribution over time and that it will be on behalf of the whole human family.

meditation.

prayer

Prayer is an invitation to God
to intervene in our lives.

~ Abraham Joshua Heschel,
Man's Quest for God

Pray according to who you are.
If you are an extrovert, pray in an extroverted
way. If you are quiet, pray quietly. Pray to God,
pray to Allah, pray to The One, pray to
The Only, pray to your Ancestors. It's all received.
It's all acted on. Pray with acceptance and
gratitude. Pray for connection, pray for your love
to be felt, pray for the ability to show it.
Pray for people you know to feel better.
Pray on your bike. Pray in the bathtub.
Pray in silence. Pray in song.

~ Dr. Larry Dossey

questions for reflection

What do you remember about prayer?

Do you have any favorite prayers?

What do you love about them?

What about prayer has enabled you to connect with spirit or God?

What about prayer has kept you from this connection?

what is prayer? . . . .

Prayer allows us to bring forth something from within and give it a consciousness of spirit. It's a way of articulating an intention, expressing gratitude, and releasing our own wisdom. Prayer enables us to reach beyond ourselves to something else. It is an opportunity to engage in a direct conversation with a higher being, to bridge the gap between our very finite, human ourselves and an infinite spirit. Like meditation, prayer invites us to be still and to focus. But while meditation is a practice of paying attention, prayer is a practice of voicing our intention.

> *Prayer is an act which enables you to become an instrument, surrender your own will and be led by God's will. Prayer restores whole(r) consciousness.*
>
> ~ Stu Horwitz

turning point . . . .

It is January 1991, and I am at a retreat for young people doing community service. The United States is getting ready to bomb Iraq. War is imminent but somehow far from my mind. I have just begun to create an organization called "Empty the Shelters" with a group of people in Philadelphia. We hope to draw young activists to the city to support the organizing that poor people were already doing. I am lost in program development, relationship-building, and fundraising. Only later will I start to see the incredibly entrenched connections between our work on economic justice issues and a war thousands of miles away.

On the second day of the retreat, a participant named Katrina Browne reminds all of us of this and says, "I don't know if you pray, or how you pray, but you might want to pray for Butros-Butros Gali [then Secretary-General of the United Nations] who is on his way to try to bring peace to the Iraqi crisis." Suddenly everyone is silent for a few minutes. I don't know who is praying, who is hand-wringing, who is thinking, but we are all lost momentarily in our own personal response to the situation. I sit there, wondering exactly how to "do it." Up until then, I was used to praying in synagogue: reading words in unison in Hebrew and in English with the rest of congregation. How would that possibly translate to this situation? I know I am against the war, that I am irate that so many people of all nationalities are going to have to risk their lives over oil supply. I'm not sure how to use prayer to face my frustration, but I stumble around with some words in my mind.

During the rest of that month, and in the months that follow, there are protests, marches, and vigils. In Philadelphia, we carry signs and candles down Broad Street and pack the pews of local churches for town meetings that feel like revivals. Some of my colleagues get arrested at the largest rally in Washington, D.C. Through it all, I come back to prayer, and I am grateful that someone gave me a way to rise above the despair and helplessness of war.

prayer and social change . . . .

The Reverend Ann Jeffries calls prayer the silent partner of action. Through prayer, we find ways to give up control of the outcome, allowing us to focus on the task at hand. Through prayer, we can strengthen our faith when we are scared. Through prayer, we can ask for guidance when faced with difficult situations or decisions.

Communal prayer is powerful. In the past few years, prayer vigils have been used by Protestant and Catholic coalitions interested in providing an alternative to the religious right, by protesters unhappy with Supreme Court Justice Clarence Thomas' anti-civil rights voting, and by anti-death penalty advocates in support of death row inmates. Vigils have helped communities resist hopelessness and cope with violence and grief. Many urban neighborhoods have organized prayer vigils as part of their efforts to fight gangs and drug activity. In most cases, religious and lay people gather together to bring a sense of peace and hope to their community, if even for one evening. In many cities, interfaith groups now hold vigils at murder sites. These have proved healing for the families of victims and for the broader community.

sabbath of domestic peace . . . .

The Annual Interfaith Worship and Healing Service of the Sabbath of Domestic Peace is co-chaired by a minister from the Philadelphia Baptist Association and the executive director of the Board of Rabbis of Greater Philadelphia. Sponsored by a different faith tradition every year, the Sabbath of Domestic Peace is an interdisciplinary, interfaith coalition that encourages and supports the involvement of religious congregations in the effort to prevent and reduce domestic violence. The Sabbath of Domestic Peace was started in 1995 by SaraKay Smullens, a family therapist, and Mimi Rose, the head of the Sexual Assault and Domestic Violence Unit in the District Attorney's office. They provide accurate, integrated resources for worship and education. This effort draws on many fields, including law enforcement, social work, advocacy, community service, medicine, psychology, academia, and theology.

prayers for change . . . .

To pray is to take notice of the wonder, to regain a sense of mystery
that animates all beings, the Divine margin in all attainments.
Prayer is our humble answer to the inconceivable surprise of living.

~Abraham Joshua Heschel

prayers of praise or thanksgiving

What are you thankful for?
What, if anything, is new in your life or your work?
When might you or your organization say a prayer of thanksgiving?
Whom do you have to appreciate?

The She-he-ki-hi yanu, a simple Jewish blessing, is said every time something
new and joyful happens:
Blessed are you, force that rules the universe
Who has kept us alive, brought us together,
and made it possible for us to reach this sacred moment.

The Twenty-Third Psalm is another example of simple praise. This feminine
version was written by Bobby McFerrin:

The Lord is my shepherd, I have all I need;
She makes me lie down in green meadows.
Beside the still waters, she will lead.

She restores my soul, she rights my wrongs,
She leads me on a path of good things,
And fills my heart with songs.

Even though I walk through a dark and dreary land,
There is nothing that can shake me,
She has said, she won't forsake me,
I'm in her hand.

She sets a table before me, in the presence of my foes
She anoints my head with oil,
And my cup overflows.

a powerful way to cope with tragedy. . . .

Surely, surely goodness and kindness will follow me,
All the days of my life,
And I will live in her house
Forever and ever.

Glory be to our Mother and Daughter
And to the Holy of Holies,
As it was in the beginning is now and ever shall be,
World, without end, amen.

prayers of surrender

What forces surround your work that are out of your control?
What fight are you willing to give up for now?

12-Step Programs use the "Serenity Prayer" in this way:
God, grant me the serenity to accept the things
I cannot change,
The courage to change the things I can,
And the wisdom to know the difference.

prayers of petition/supplication

What do you need? How would you ask for it?
What does your work need? How would you ask for it?

When he lived in New York City, my brother would occasionally hand guests pieces of paper when they entered his apartment. People were offered the chance to write their prayers and throw them into the non-working fireplace filled with candles. The pieces of paper accumulated. Eventually he buried them, letting them decompose and return to the earth.

Juliet's soliloquy from act 3, scene 2, of *Romeo and Juliet*, is a poetic form of prayerful petition.
Come, night; come Romeo; come, thou day in night;
For thou wilt lie upon the wings of night
Whiter than new snow on a raven's back.
Come, gentle night, come, loving, black-brow'd night,
Give me my Romeo; and, when he shall die,
Take him and cut him out in little stars,
And he will make the face of heaven so fine

That all the world will be in love with night
And pay no worship to the garish sun.

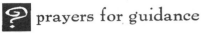

prayers for guidance

Where do you feel stuck?
What additional wisdom do you need to resolve this situation?

From the First Congregational Church of Berkeley, United Church of Christ, author unknown:
Eternal God, day by day your love is bourne into the world and into our lives. You work imperceptibly—we cannot see your love working any more than we can watch a seed grow. But you also work steadily and we have faith that in our lives you are moving and working. Grant us renewed trust in your gentle will, which is working for love in the world. Strengthen us to work for the harvest, in fields that are the people and the events of our daily living. Amen.

activities to do alone . . . .

beginning to pray

> *There are a hundred ways to kneel and kiss the ground.*
> ~ Rumi

> *How you pray, when you pray, and why you pray is a direct reflection of your understanding of the Divine and the role that it plays in your life.*
> ~ Iyanla Vanzant, *One Day My Soul Just Opened Up*

There are a hundred ways to talk to God. Some religious traditions stress certain forms; others mandate the words. Take stock in the role prayer has historically played for you and how, if at all, you remember praying. You may need to unlearn or adapt old styles of praying in order to fulfill your current needs. If you have not drawn strength from organized religion or the religion you practiced as a child, then prayer may have negative connotations for you, reminding you of an experience that was less than fulfilling. You may be more comfortable exploring the prayers of other traditions, reading sacred poetry, or writing your own prayers. In time, you may or may not find that your own tradition has some new territory for you to explore.

Check the library or bookstore for collected prayers or sacred prose from one or many different religions. Take a prayer you've known for a long time and recite it. You may find a deeper meaning as you say them aloud, alone and quiet.

There are many books of daily prayers, reflections and meditations now available. Or, begin a simple conversation with the spirit, the life force, God, or Christ.

℮ prayer as a daily practice

Begin to develop a practice of prayer for yourself. Perhaps you'll pray in the morning, maybe when the sun is rising and you are greeting the day. Maybe you will pray before going to bed in the evening, remembering what has been holy about the day, the times the spirit was present, what you are thankful for, and even your hopes for the day to come. You might find that prayer becomes something you do anytime you take time to stop and collect your thoughts.

Where would you feel comfortable praying?
What time of day?
In what position?

℮ centering prayer

Centering prayer was developed by the Reverend Thomas Keating, a Trappist monk, in the 1970s in order to make contemplative practice more widely available outside of monastic living. During this time, many people in America were turning to Eastern practices such as yoga and meditation. Keating wanted to make similar experiences available to people within their own tradition.

In centering prayer, you sit in silence for 20 minutes twice a day, and repeat one word that invokes a sense of peace and draws you into an inner silence. Repeating the word is also a reminder to return to silence in the mind. The word is really a symbol of your intent to open yourself up to God, to possibility, and to your inner knowing. The word might be "God," "love," or "peace." It is used as a way to refocus in a prayer state when one gets distracted. Two books on centering prayer are listed in "Resources" at the end of this chapter.

✑ write it down: keep a prayer journal

Some people keep a regular record of their prayer life: which prayers they are saying, why, and what other thoughts or feelings these prayers invoke. Writing down what comes to mind during or after prayer can enrich the experience. It will help you to capture the essence of your prayer.

℮ writing your own prayer

Crafted over time, your own prayer can be a simple statement of what you want to remember each day. Think about the following questions to get started:

What do you hope for?
What do you honor?
What do you want to pledge to yourself?
What do you welcome into your life?

I wrote my first prayer on a lazy summer day, on a friend's porch swing. I used it every day for many months:

> Today
> Let me live fully and love completely.
> Let me honor and celebrate others and myself
> So that the best of what lies within might come forth
> And let me be present enough in the world around me
> To choose love over fear.

About a year later, I needed some more specific daily guidance, so I wrote the following:

> I give thanks for this new day of possibility that stretches out
> before me.
> Every day I make choices.
> Today, in grace, I choose to pray often, love as well as I can,
> remember everyone is a child of God, breathe deeply, work hard
> and work smart.

activities to do with groups

prayer bundles

You will need the following materials: pretty cloth cut into small (4"x 4") pieces, cord or string, herbs like lavender or tobacco, small pieces of paper, and writing implements. Prayer bundles are a wonderful way to introduce prayer to a group. First give everyone a slip of paper and ask them to write a prayer for themselves. Next, have each person choose a piece of cloth. Place the prayer, folded or rolled up, in the center of the cloth. Sprinkle some herbs over it and say a blessing if you wish. Wrap the cloth up and bind it with the cord or string. When everyone is finished, ask them to stand in a circle with their prayer bundles cupped in their hands in front of them. Ask if anyone has a prayer they'd like to offer for all of the bundles.

prayer and healing

The subject of prayer and healing has been getting more attention recently. A poll conducted for *Time Magazine* in 1996 found that 82% of adults believe in the healing power of prayer. Dr. Jeffrey Levin at Eastern Virginia Medical School and Dr. David Larson of the National Institute for Healthcare Research have found 200 studies that look at the role of religion and prayer in healing. They have found strong evidence that religion and prayer both make a difference—in heart disease, cancer, strokes and other life-threatening illnesses.

One of the most famous studies was done in 1988 by Dr. Randolph Byrd at San Francisco General Medical Center Hospital. A cardiologist, Byrd spent 10 months studying 393 patients admitted to the coronary care unit. Some patients were prayed for (by three to seven people they did not know and who did not know them,) and some were not. In this double-blind study, neither the doctors nor the patients knew who was being prayed for and who was not. Those who were prayed for were three times less likely to develop complications like congestive heart failure, cardiopulmonary arrests, and pneumonia. They were five times less likely to need antibiotics.

@ communal prayer

Communal prayer is often called worship. Worship can be prescribed using a predetermined collection of prayers, but it doesn't have to be. A group might come together informally, as in a prayer circle. Prayer circles can include people of many different faith backgrounds. Ask folks to bring a prayer to share if they choose. Find a place to meet where everyone will feel comfortable and where you won't be disturbed.

SAMPLE OUTLINE FOR PRAYER CIRCLE:

1. Begin with a few minutes of silence so everyone can center themselves.

2. Have everyone introduce themselves. Ask folks to talk about prayer and its significance for them.

3. Share the prayers that people brought. These may be read aloud by one person or the whole group, or they may be read silently.

4. Open up a space for people to share their joys and concerns, so that others may add their prayers and energy. Many Unitarian Universalist Fellowships share in this way, and it always seems to be the time when members of the congregation feel most connected to one another. You may choose to go around in a circle and let each person share his/her joys and concerns. Leave a few moments of silence for everyone to pray about them before going on to the next person, or you may just have one period of silent prayer at the end.

5. Close with a song or a reading.

---

resources for prayer . . . .

Bly, Robert. *The Soul is Here for Its Own Joy*. Hopewell, NJ: The Ecco Press, 1995. Sacred poems from various cultures; includes Emily Dickinson, Kabir, Mirabai, Rumi, Rilke, Sappho, Simone Weil, and more.

Carse, James P. *The Silence of God*. San Francisco: HarperSanFrancisco, 1991. How to determine, in the "silence" of response, your own intentions for praying and thus find a way to begin to answer those prayers.

Castelli, Jim, ed. *How I Pray*. New York: Ballantine Books, 1994. People of various religious traditions share information about their own prayer life. Includes Baptist, Buddhist, Catholic, Episcopal, Hindu, Jewish, Lakota Sioux, Lutheran, Mormon, Muslim, Quaker, and Presbyterian perspectives.

Dunn, Philip. *Prayer: Language of the Soul*. New York: Daybreak Books, 1997. Three thousand prayers from around the word on themes from abundance to peace. Includes locations for prayer in the United States and abroad.

Fellowship in Prayer. *The Gift of Prayer*. New York: Continuum, 1995. A collection of personal prayers from many spiritual traditions, East to West, ancient to modern. Includes prayers for relationships, gratitude, protection, peace, telling God's greatness, and more. Fellowship in Prayer is an interfaith journal with readership in 80 countries. Contact: Fellowship in Prayer, 291 Witherspoon Street, Princeton, NJ 08542-3227.

Gibran, Kalil. *The Prophet*. New York: Alfred A. Knopf, 1951. Gibran was a Lebanese poet, philosopher, and artist. This is his timeless collection of prayerful essays on family, work, love, children, marriage, and more.

Keay, Kathy. *Laughter, Silence, and Shouting: An Anthology of Women's Prayers*. London: HarperCollins Publishers, 1994. Great collection of poems about God, creation, daily life, self, relationships, work, aging, peace, justice, hope, and suffering.

Matthews, Caitlin. *Celtic Devotional Daily Prayers and Blessings*. New York: Harmony Books, 1996. A combination of traditional blessings and prayers written by the author. There are practices and prayers for morning and evening of each day of the week and they change with the seasons.

Ming-Dao, Deng. *365 Tao Daily Meditations*. San Francisco: HarperSanFrancisco, 1992. Beautifully written meditations on Taoist principles.

Mitchell, Stephen, ed. *The Enlightened Mind: An Anthology of Sacred Prose*. New York: HarperPerennial, 1991. Passages from an array of sacred texts and the writings of mystics, rabbis, priests, ministers, teachers, nuns, and philosophers from the 6th Century B.C.E. though the modern day.

a word about public prayer

In 1994, the Georgia General Assembly adopted the Moment of Silence in Schools Act, legalizing a daily 60-second period of quiet reflection in the classroom, not as a religious exercise but as an opportunity for silent reflection. This is in contrast to the Alabama law that allows a moment of silence for meditation or "voluntary prayer" in a state where the legislature has a history of making attempts to return to organized prayer in the classroom. Supreme Court Justice Sandra Day O'Connor agreed with recognizing a distinction between a moment of silence and a state endorsed religious practice. Her argument? "A moment of silence is not inherently religious. . . a pupil who participates in a moment of silence need not compromise his or her beliefs. During a moment of silence, a student who objects to prayer is left to his or her own thoughts and is not compelled to listen to the prayers or thoughts of others."

Reininger, Gustave, ed. *Centering Prayer in Daily Life and Ministry*. New York: Continuum Publishing Company, 1998. This book is a collection of pieces on centering prayer, written from individuals from numerous Christian denominations. Includes contributions from Thomas Keating and M. Basil Pennington, two leading voices on the subject.

Rilke, Rainer Maria. *Rilke's Book of Hours: Love Poems to God*. Translated by Anita Barrow and Joanna Macy. New York: Riverhead Books, 1996. The simple prayers of German philosopher and poet Rainer Maria Rilke define a reciprocal relationship between the divine and the ordinary.

Roberts, Elizabeth and Elias Amidon. *Life Prayers from Around the World: 365 Prayers, Blessings and Affirmations to Celebrate the Human Journey*. San Francisco: HarperCollins, 1996.

Sabbath of Domestic Peace, Web site: www.angelfire.com/sd/sabbathdomesticpeace

Sewell, Marilyn, ed. *Cries of the Spirit*. Boston: Beacon Press, 1991. Poetry and prose celebrating women's spirituality, including self, intimacy, mothering, generations, death, sacredness, and spirit.

Williamson, Marianne. *Illuminata: A Return to Prayer*. New York: Riverhead Books, 1994. An inspiring and useful collection of prayers on everything from the body to work to relationships. Sections on prayers for the world and rites of passage ceremonies.

stories of prayer . . . .

Rabbi Sid Schwarz

Rabbi Sid Schwarz is the Founding Director of The Washington Institute for Jewish Leadership and Values, an educational foundation dedicated to the renewal of American Jewish life through the integration of Torah, Judaic study, and Tikkun Olam, (repair of the world.) He is also the founding Rabbi of Adat Shalom Reconstructionist Congregation in Rockville, Maryland.

CH: Sid, tell me first about your faith background.

SS: I grew up in a very traditional Jewish home and went to an Orthodox *yeshiva*[1] as a child. I went to synagogue every Saturday with my Dad. I got more involved because the rabbi invited me to lead the junior congregation. In leading the youth services on Saturday morning, I learned how to make it interesting for the kids. It became really gratifying.

Then, I made a trip to the Soviet Union between my junior and senior year of high school which opened up a whole different avenue of what being Jewish was about: the oppression, the religious discrimination, the Jewish experience. I spent my senior year doing work on Soviet Jewry. My school principal, who was the youth chairman of a synagogue on Long Island, asked if I wanted to run their youth program. I got a job directing a youth group of a synagogue, even though I was only in high school. That started me on a career of doing Jewish youth work. I felt that I was a lot more effective getting Jewish kids to be excited about their Judaism than rabbis or teachers I had encountered. It was my youthful brashness. My Judaism had this political dimension because of my Soviet Jewry work. I wasn't interested in being a rabbi until my last year in college. It was between being a rabbi and a lawyer. I figured good lawyers were a dime a dozen, but there were so few people working in the Jewish community who struck me as able to effectively communicate the message.

Did your Judaism always link back to a social commitment?

For me, as for most Jews, those two things were very compartmentalized. I finished rabbinical school when I was 26 or 27. I had the opportunity to come to Washington to head up the Jewish Community Council, a very political job. Getting that job put me right in the center of the action, in terms of the Jewish political activist community.

My launching of the Institute was in part an outgrowth of my frustration there. I was seeing that, on the one hand, synagogue Jews were very parochial, with little interest in engaging with politics. In the political world, there was very little interest in the spiritual world, or in Judaism as a religion. I felt that those two things had to be brought together; they were meant to be intertwined. That was the vision that launched the Institute, to build a bridge between the world of politics and social justice, and the world of Jewish knowledge and Jewish religion.

---

[1] an Orthodox Jewish school

What would you say about the role of prayer in your own life?

In the way that you or I might think about it now, it was pretty nonexistent, even after I became a rabbi. I knew the liturgy backwards and forwards—the body of Jewish prayer was part of the air I breathed—but it was all rote. There was never a deep spiritual component to it. As I matured as a rabbi and as a Jew, I found ways to pull people's spiritual journeys out of them. I found myself automatically connecting their stories to pieces of Jewish texts and Jewish liturgy. The whole prayer thing began to make sense to me. It was like a code had been broken.

> The whole prayer thing began to make sense to me. It was like a code had been broken.

I remember the first time it happened. I was entering my senior year in high school. I made a trip to Russia, and we went into a synagogue in Moscow. There were 25 of us in the group. We had brought a lot of religious artifacts to give away to Russian Jews, which were contraband. We were told they were eager to meet us, and that there were KGB[2] operatives in the synagogue. The usher brought us to the dignitary box, alongside the *bimah*[3]. It dawned on me; we were being put in quarantine. He didn't want us to mix with the Russian Jews.

But I was desperate to make a connection. When they brought the Torah out for the service, they brought out a dozen. There were 12 tables and 12 torah readings going on at once. We got out of our box, dispersed through the synagogue, and we did begin to make connections. I kept introducing myself, saying I was a Jew from New York, etcetera, and people kept moving away from me. It turns out, the KGB had trained people to entrap the Jews; they would pose as Jewish tourists to get someone to say something inflammatory. So, I was doing all the wrong things, although I didn't know it at the time.

In frustration, I started to pray. When I finished the *Amidah*,[4] I suddenly had a throng of people around me. Because the one thing they couldn't teach KGB agents how to do was *daven*[5]. We had found a way to connect in a nonverbal way. They knew that I could be trusted. It spoke to me about how vital it was to know the code. There's a part in the Amidah which literally says "to the informers, the tattletales, let them have no success." That prayer starts to scream out of my head, because what we had experienced was just that. Suddenly I was living the prayer, and it began a process for me of recapturing every prayer I knew by heart and saying, "What in my life experience makes this prayer come alive?" I started doing that for myself, and now I do it for other Jews. I never considered myself to be a deeply religious person. I'm observant, but the meditative mode has never worked for me; it's not who I am. But prayer becomes a deeply spiritual experience for me when I am able to penetrate the code of our sacred texts, understanding meanings that may or may not have been intended by the authors. I connect the texts to part of my life experience.

[2] the Soviet secret police
[3] the pulpit in a synagogue where Torah scrolls are kept
[4] one of the central prayers of Judaism, said standing three times a day; the Hebrew word *amidah* means "standing"
[5] Hebrew word for prayer which usually denotes a complete immersion in worship

I started this tradition at synagogue of having members give talks where they would take a prayer or piece of biblical text and connect it to their experience. One woman who lost an infant this past year gave a talk during Rosh Hashanah and connected that trauma with the story of Hannah in the Bible when she gives up her son Samuel to priestly service. The fact that she put it into a Jewish framework and a Jewish context made the talk extremely powerful.

Where does your social justice work fit into all of this?

A lot of the work at the Institute is finding people who are really plugged into doing justice work and giving them sustenance to keep going. The burnout rate in people who do justice work is incredible, because the odds are against you. You're working against the system, against prejudice, against class bias. The ones who stay in it for the long haul are usually those who find some spiritual sustenance. Why is it that some of the most important people in the history of justice work were people of faith? Jesus, Mother Theresa, Dr. King—that's not a coincidence.

But if you don't have a spiritual base, where do you start?

I've got this group that meets once a month of 20-25 people who are in major political positions, and we do Torah study. Most are not connected to Judaism, but they have these continual "a-ha" experiences where they find a text that speaks to what they are wrestling with. First, they connect it to a personal struggle about how they keep to their mission. And embedded in the heritage of which they are a part is something that can give them a certain amount of comfort and support.

Second, when they share with each other their own struggle, in the context of *Pirke Avot*, the Ethics of Our Ancestors, they feel very connected. I don't know another way to have that conversation without putting it in the context of Jewish texts. I think the reason is that I believe that there is some wisdom embedded in the text, that is equal to more than all the wisdom of the people in the room. Thousands of minds have poured over these texts for centuries. There's an answer there, if we can ferret it out.

What advice would you give younger activists who are starting a spiritual path, Jewish or not?

The biggest problem is that we're looking for God in all the wrong places. I worry about it a lot. There are places in our society that are called houses of worship, and most people think that that is where you go to find religious wisdom, insight, solace. It's not. Certainly not when you first walk in. You get a lot of straight, habitual religion which, if you're not familiar with it, is hard to access. It's hard to crack the code. As a result, I am not confident that suggesting a synagogue as a starting point is the right path. It can be, as likely, a dead end.

There's not one book I can say, this is it. What we call spirituality is a matter of taste. What's spiritual for you might leave me cold. I can't read someone's mind and know what's going to work.

I'd say, do your best to find a small circle of people with whom you can create a community, with whom you can travel a road together. And structure it in a way so that you're learning about yourself, about the world, about fortitude and character, matters of faith. Share that with a minimum of two other people, and as many as eight or nine other people. That will be your spiritual circle for a time, until you can move to the next level.

---

stories of God . . . .

Thérèse Murdza

Thérèse Murdza is an organizational development consultant with Lambda Rising, a chain of independent bookstores committed to serving lesbian, gay, transgendered, and bisexual people and their allies. She is also a painter. She lives in Washington, D.C.

CH: Tell me about your faith background.

TM: I was raised Roman Catholic, and both my folks had gone to Catholic schools, Catholic colleges. My sister and I went to CCD [education for Catholic youth] every Saturday, and we went to church every Sunday or Saturday night. It wasn't a question, it was just what you did. I really loved it. The sacraments were very important. Communion—I loved that. The body and blood of Christ. The pagan mystery, the magic. It's not the representation of the blood and body of Christ, it *is* the blood and body of Christ! It was so dramatic and full of passion. I remember wanting to be a priest as a child.

The messages came subtly and not so subtly that it wasn't possible. It wasn't even possible at that time for girls to be altar attendants at my parish; only boys could do that. Even women lay readers were new, so I felt really disheartened. I remember being told I could be a nun, and I remember thinking, "Well, that would be cool, but how come I can't be 'up there' on the altar with God?" There was a certain disillusioning that began pretty early. What was it about me that wasn't good enough to be that close to God? How could there be something not good enough for God? Those were big questions for a little girl to be carrying around.

And eventually you lost interest?

I felt a lot of hypocrisy. In school, I was reading about the Inquisition and the Crusades. Something just didn't add up. Once I left for college, I never went to church. I started becoming friends with Jews. It was an adult realization: that Catholicism grew from Judaism; that Jesus was a Jew. I started realizing the value of understanding where something comes from.

And I learned the difference between cultural Judaism and religious Judaism. I thought, "Oh, these people are Jewish, and yet they don't go to temple, but they have some familial connection to Judaism." I felt like I had that too, though I didn't call it that. My whole ancestry is Catholic. I got interested in genealogy and how Catholicism was integrated into the very cells of our family. I got the message that Catholics were somehow better, that Catholicism is the only true religion and that we had to pray for everyone else. I never felt proud, per se, but it was something I bore as part of my cultural heritage.

What has changed?

Well, I attended some 12-step meetings, and I found that God was being spoken about right there out loud. People talked about God all the time. It was the first time outside the Catholic church that I had heard people talking about God, about their faith—their faith that things were going to pass or their faith that things were going to get better. Story after story. I went into an intense period of suffering and was also learning to connect with people. My nose was right up against the abyss, and at that time, there was this feeling that I had two choices: death or insanity. So, there was a small group of us who talked about God.

> I mean, how do we tremble through what it is to be alive? It is a frightening, awesome, awe-filled, and awful thing. How can one person stand it alone?

For all the hype, 12-step meetings take place in a public space where people go to talk about God, something higher, bigger than this great and small life. It feels like experiencing grace, like the mystery of how we survive our suffering and our joy. I mean, how do we tremble through what it is to be alive? It is a frightening, awesome, awe-filled, and awful thing. How can one person stand it alone? In those rooms you hear people who talk about being able to face a deep level of suffering, because right there is also God. So I guess I started counting on something being there. Then, even when I was walking around in my daily life, it was there. And then it just felt like it was there all the time.

What is "it"? Can you describe it?

A presence of something, a hum. It's the only "count-on-able" thing. It *is* the change. It is witness to the change. It is everything. It is in everything. And I notice things that hum in a way that they always are humming. I always say that if you stick your toe in the river, wow! When you listen for it, there you are. Then there are moments when you're actually *in* the river, however briefly.

What moments?

I think they come unexpectedly. They're windows of grace. They almost feel like God is checking in: "Just wanted to let you know, it's still here." Just when I think, "Oh, it's just a big old random mess," I realize, "Oh, it's a big old divine random mess."

Do you call it God because that's a recognizable word?

I used to say "The Universe". God: it's just three letters, and there's a need I have as I get older to not always be the lone wolf so much but to be in common language with people. It gives me a serenity that I didn't have or particularly need before.

Is there something you do to remember it, to feel it?

I'm not sure that I do something separate. Allowing every action to turn towards God or away from God. I've tried to embody that and have that inform everything I do. I read it in this book about Trappist monks. Though since then, it shows up in books about other religious lives.

How do you remember that?

When I get into a quandary or I want to be mean, or someone hurts me or I feel hurt, or I read or witness or hear about something really horrible—it reminds me not to act in the same way. It helps to guide me. It's a really simple thing, not a whole bunch of rules, things I have to remember. It's weird to articulate these things; it feels uncomfortable to even talk about it.

But vital?

If I don't find a way to recognize the mercy, I might as well crawl under a rock. There's so much suffering. So many people are in so much pain, and every day I participate in something that hurts somebody else. If I let all that stuff in, I couldn't hold it. It reminds me that it's bigger than I can remotely think about. There's no way I can undo it all, fix it all, alleviate it all, and that doesn't mean that I am allowed to go crawl under a rock. I feel like I'm responsible for whatever I can do. My piece of turning the tide.

> It says, "You don't have to climb the whole mountain today. Just take one more step. Go a little bit further and then you can rest."

I guess it all just helps me go a little further. It says, "You don't have to climb the whole mountain today. Just take one more step. Go a little bit further and then you can rest." When I can't possibly hold it all, I know that the river is way longer and bigger. There are other people along the banks. I can lay the burden down, even if it's just for a moment. And then I can pick it up and go on again.

prayer.

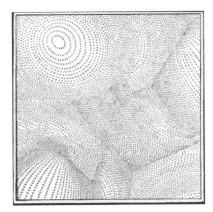

spiritual practice

As one matures in spiritual life,
one becomes more comfortable
with paradox, more appreciative of life's
ambiguities, its many levels and inherent
conflicts. One develops a sense
of life's irony, metaphor, and humor
and a capacity to embrace the whole,
with its beauty and outrageousness, in
the graciousness of the heart.

~ Jack Kornfield, *A Path with Heart*

The man or woman truly on the path
[to inner peace] seeks every moment
as the one in which to activate
life's highest blessing.

~ Paul Fleischman, *Cultivating Inner Peace*

questions for reflection

What do you do on a regular basis that connects you to your faith or spirituality?

How do these current activities enhance your life?

What makes them important?

What types of spiritual or faith-based activities are you curious about?

what is a spiritual practice?. . . . .

A spiritual practice forms a habit that brings our focus back to the presence of spirit. It can be anything that reconnects us with our center, gives us fresh energy, grounds us in the here and now, and reminds us of what's most important. There is so much competition for our attention. The television blares, a child tugs at our leg, colleagues make their demands known. All the while, the spirit sits quietly off to one side, watching and waiting its turn.

A spiritual practice reawakens our faith and strengthens our ties to other people. Jews observe the Sabbath from sundown on Friday through sundown on Saturday. During this period, no work is to be done. It is a time for prayer and rest. Catholics attend confession and pray the rosary as part of practicing their faith. Muslims pray to Mecca five times a day, a practice that engenders a constant awareness of their duty to and love for Allah.

Each of the three preceding chapters—Silence, Meditation, and Prayer— describe contemplative disciplines which ask us to slow down and pay attention. A regular connection with spirit, however we define it, enhances our ability to deal with daily life in a way that we might even rejoice in from time to time. It may happen in a house of worship, out in the woods, near a body of water, or in a corner of a room that has become sacred.

turning point . . . .

My spiritual practice is an act of remembering who I am and who God is in my life. Though it is undefinable to a certain extent, I can begin to explain my practice in two ways. First, it is an ongoing awareness of the energy that pervades every living thing and every interaction between all living things. My practice is an attempt to be continually aware of this energy, the life force, that which I often call God. Second, and more specifically, my practice is the time I take every morning to be quiet and sink below the surface of my daily routine and my mind's chatter. Sometimes I read; sometimes I write. Many days I pray. Most days I meditate.

I have realized that I need this time of solitude in the morning to live deeply in the world during the rest of the day. When I take time to honor myself and my relationship to God, I notice the extraordinarily ordinary and beautiful things that happen in my life. I slow down, listen more, feel more present to others, and ask better questions. My relationship with myself and with others deepens. I am more likely to embrace change and even surrender control. I find I have more energy, and my overall health improves. My patience grows. I look for ways to honor myself and others. I am more joyful. When I neglect my practice, I feel its absence. I am more hurried, less focused, and somewhat scattered. In my interactions with others, I feel preoccupied, more competitive, less open. I talk more, but the words seems to mean less. It is almost as if my ego expands into the space that usually fills up with the energy of spirit.

I try to remain faithful to my practice for the same reason that a marathon runner develops a training program. Discipline does not happen by accident. If someone wants to run 26.1 miles, they have to make a serious commitment to running. That means they run when it's raining or snowing. They run when they don't want to run. They run when it seems like everyone else is just hanging out, reading the paper. But as they keep running, they realize they can go farther than they could the day before. Their body becomes more flexible; they see what they are capable of.

Although it continues to elude me, I believe that an individual spiritual practice and a more organized, communal faith experience can be very complementary. I was raised Jewish, and I believe this will always be a fundamental part of my cultural identity. I find, however, that my spiritual practice, my experience of prayer, and my relation-ship to God do not feel inherently Jewish to me. I have not yet found a way to practice Judaism that feeds me spiritually, on a daily basis, the way I need to be fed. The synagogue is a big place, with many windows and doors. I may find a way in some day. For now, there are days when I get scared, fearing I will languish in a state of spiritual isolation for the rest of my life, flying solo without other passengers. On good days, I remember that we all see a different piece of the sky, but there is only one sky. There are many routes to God.

spiritual practice and social change . . . .

Through my work as an organizer and now with stone circles, I believe there is no greater challenge than the integration of spirit and action, faith and justice. Every day I become more keenly aware of the nuances of this challenge. The challenge of speaking with the voice of justice, raised on protest politics, and the voice of the soul, eager to bring light. The challenge of trying to treat people with honor when I am angered by their actions or words. The challenge of shedding violent language from my vocabulary. The challenge of distinguishing between right and wrong without passing judgment.

Activist, educator, and writer Parker Palmer talks about the move from the false self (the ego) to the true self—the self joined with God. This journey, he contends, transpires through contemplation. At a speech in October of 1998, I heard Palmer say that contemplation is "any way you have of penetrating illusion and touching reality." As we become more and more inundated with information, the need for this contemplative time increases exponentially.

Palmer goes on to explain that social engagement is at the heart of this fundamentally spiritual practice. The move toward authenticity, towards the true self, is what Palmer calls "the decision to live divided no more." As we become more clear about what we know is true inside of us, we are more eager to see it manifest on the outside. Anyone striving for justice does this. We recognize that something is fundamentally wrong; we know it because we can feel it within. And then we know we can no longer act the same on the outside.

activities to do alone. . . . .

developing a spiritual practice

Use Grid One below to notice what you already do that you might consider spiritual. This can be anything from a walk in the woods to reading the Bible in the morning to attending synagogue to meditation. Be as specific as you can. You may not remember everything right away so fill the grid out over the course of a couple of days. Don't worry how many boxes are left blank.

GRID ONE:

	Alone	With others	At work
Daily			
Weekly			
Monthly			
Yearly			

Once you feel your grid is complete, reflect on it:

Do you nurture your spiritual life mostly alone, mostly with others, or both?
How often do you do each activity or practice?
Do these activities cost money?
Are they convenient or do any require a special trip away from home?

Here are some possible activities; note your reactions to them:

reading	art	keeping a Sabbath
meditation	music	silence
prayer	dance	planting/gardening
yoga	exercise	sports
writing	fasting	other?

Now revisit the same grid, only with a different intention. Brainstorm. Grid Two is an opportunity to write down everything that comes to mind as a possibility—whatever interests you. Maybe there was one thing you remember doing two years ago or something you heard about from a friend or something you read about that sounded interesting. Write it down.

What do you want more of in your life?
What helps you in difficult times?

GRID TWO:

	Alone	With others	At work
Daily			
Weekly			
Monthly			
Yearly			

Reflect on the questions below. Again, these questions do not have to be answered in one day. It's better to reflect on your responses over the course of a week or even two. Different times and different moods will yield new responses and ideas.

What is the best time for you to incorporate a practice?
What is/are the best place(s)?

What do you need to make it happen? What might stand in your way?

In beginning or developing a spiritual journey, it is vital to consider who in your life might support you as you develop your practice and who might want your support as well. The process will have its highs and lows. You may feel as though there is never enough time or the right time. It may feel strange at times, and it's easy to lose sight of why you are doing this at all. A partner can help you through this.

Do you have a support system now?
If yes, is it adequate? How might you shift or strengthen it?
If not, how could you develop one?
Who are some possible candidates?

retreats

Retreats can be an effective way to jump-start a new spiritual practice or rejuvenate one that is waning. Don't be fooled by the word "retreat." You are not escaping anything. It is a period of rest and renewal that everyone needs, regardless of whether or not our culture easily allows for and accepts it. We tend to put off this type of activity until the time is right. Of course there are better and worse times. The best way to work up to a longer period of time away is by starting with shorter ones. A day spent in a quiet location with no distractions may inspire you to attend a weekend workshop. That, in turn, may lead you to begin planning an even longer visit, such as a month long work-study program at a spiritual center you are drawn to. A list of retreat centers appears in the Appendix.

write it down: keeping track

As you begin developing a spiritual practice, you may want to write in a journal or notebook to keep track of what you're doing and what is working for you. You can use it to record experiences and your reactions to them. Writing about them will only increase your understanding of what is happening and what changes are taking place internally. You will find yourself becoming aware of new information about yourself and the world around you and more conscious of certain emotions that are surfacing. You might also write down prayers, meditations, and other exercises that have been useful to you. Lastly, the journal is a great place to organize resources your hear about: books, articles, workshops, teachers, and groups.

labyrinth

The labyrinth, a circular pattern found in many religious traditions, has become a metaphor for spiritual journeying. It is one meandering path that goes from the edge of a circle (usually 40 feet in diameter) and then back out. It can take well over an hour to complete the journey. The labyrinth is a mysterious design whose origin is not known for sure. The oldest form is Cretan and is carved on a rock in Sardinia. It dates circa 2,500-2,000 B.C.E. The most well-known labyrinth is on the floor of the Chartres Cathedral in France; it was created in 1220.

Walking the labyrinth has become a tool to awaken the soul and allow it to surrender. On the way in, the walker releases what is no longer useful to her and her spiritual journey. Once in the center, she might receive a new insight through med-itation or contemplation. The trip back out of the labyrinth is an opportunity to integrate this new knowledge. Dr. Lauren Artess, a canon at Grace Cathedral in San Francisco, has been using the labyrinth in this way since 1990. As a result, thousands of people in this country have now walked the labyrinth, and many are creating their own out of elements as diverse as paper, canvass, stone, and grass. See "Resources for Spiritual Practice" for contact information on the Veriditas: Grace Cathedral Labyrinth Project.

activities to do with groups ....

℮ helping individuals think about spiritual practice

The worksheet "Developing a Spiritual Practice" in the Appendix can be used to help a group of people think about how to develop or deepen their spiritual practice. Once you've used this tool for yourself, you may want to share it. This works well in combination with freewriting. (See the "Words and Stories" chapter for more on freewriting.)

℮ organizational spiritual practice

You can help your organization develop a spiritual practice by carving out time during meetings that are already set up, such as staff meetings. Begin with 10-15 minutes. This short exercise is a good way for folks to get their feet wet and see what this is all about. Pick one of the following words or choose one of your own:

gratitude	humility	simplicity	cooperation
forgiveness	discipline	patience	wisdom

1. Think ahead of time about what the word means to you and use your thoughts to initiate a discussion.

2. Ask everyone to write/think about three ways this concept is currently manifesting itself in their lives *outside* of work. For example: "How do you know when you have forgiven someone? How do you know when you're being patient?" Then, have everybody choose one of their responses and share it with the group. If you are doing this with a group larger than eight, have people share in pairs or groups of three.

3. Next, ask everyone to write/think about three ways this concept is currently manifesting itself in their lives *at work* and again share with the group, in pairs or small groups.

4. Invite people to share positive things they've noticed about others in the room. You can model this by saying, for example, "I've noticed that you often wait before answering a tough question, and this has been a great lesson in patience for me."
   NOTE: The idea is to highlight the positive, what is working, and thereby enforce that.

℗ stations of reflection

This is a simple and meditative way for people to engage in individual, silent reflection in the presence of others. The "stations of reflection" are based around thought-provoking questions. These questions can pertain to anything that is relevant for the group. There are two examples below, for two different purposes.

Set up clusters of chairs in five different areas; each one will correspond to one of five reflection questions. There should be a few more chairs than people so that folks don't have to wait for someone to get up before moving to that part of the room. You can set each question up in such a way that makes it sacred. You might use pieces of material, lit candles, plants or flowers, or other items available to you.

Have the group gather *outside* of the space you intend to use if at all possible. Ask people to center themselves, perhaps by taking some slow breaths, or merely closing their eyes for a few minutes. Invite them to bring their journals with them.

TO READ TO THE GROUP:
Please do this exercise in complete silence. When you enter the room, take a seat in a chair, reflect on the question in front of you, and then write something about it. If you don't want to write, you can use the time for reflection. Once you feel like you've finished with a question, move on to a question in another part of the room. The order in which you answer the questions does not matter. You will have 30 minutes to finish all of the questions. I will make an announcement when we are halfway through this time period. If a question touches you in a particularly powerful way, you might choose to spend a few extra minutes with it.

example one: reflections on a work experience

These questions are for a group of people who have been working together and will continue to work together.

1. *Remember a time over the past _____ (fill in time period) when you felt particularly good about your work. What was good about it?*

2. *Recall a time when you felt very frustrated with this group. What prompted your frustration? How did you respond to it?*

3. *Recall a time when you took leadership in this group.*

There is a Zen story of a professor who goes to see a monk. The monk welcomes him, and the professor explains that he has come seeking wisdom from the monk. With that, the professor begins to talk endlessly about his knowledge and what he has done in the world. Finally, the monk asks the professor if he would like some tea. The professor nods yes, continuing to speak about his accomplishments.

The monk sets a cup in front of the professor and begins to pour. He continues pouring the tea until the cup is overflowing, and the tea is spilling all over the floor. The astonished professor jumps up.

"What are you doing?" he asks.

"This cup," the monk replies, "is very much like your mind. It doesn't have room for anything else because it is already full."

4. *What else would you like to see this group achieve in the future?*

5. *For whom in the room are you especially grateful? What is it about them that you appreciate?*

example two: reflections on faith and social change

These questions on issues of faith and social change can be used with any group, regardless of how well they know each other.

1. *How would you describe your belief system? Can you recall an event or turning point in your life which helped shape these beliefs?*

2. *What was your experience with faith, religion, or spirituality while growing up? What role, if any, do these play in your life now?*

3. *When, if ever, have you felt the presence of God or spirit in your life? Do you have a different name for it?*

4. *What role, if any, do faith and/or spiritual practice play in the work you do? How has it been an asset? How has it been a barrier?*

5. *How would you begin to define the role of faith in our society and culture? Where, if anywhere, does your own experience of faith or spirituality fit into this picture?*

Be sure to announce the halfway point; you may want to make a second announcement when there are about five minutes left in the half hour.

After people have had a chance to answer all the questions, have them return to the question that was the hardest for them to answer. When they get to that question, they should take a few minutes to talk and share experiences with others who had trouble with the same question. Next, ask folks to return to the question that was the most inspiring or powerful for them. And similarly, have them dialogue with the other people who show up at the same question. Complete this exercise with some reflections in one large group. Ask people what it was like to do the activity and what they learned.

resources for spiritual practice . . . .

Arrien, Angeles. *The Four-Fold Way: Walking the Paths of the Warrior, Teacher, Healer and Visionary.* San Francisco: HarperSanFrancisco, 1993. A look at each of these four archetypes, their principles, and tools for cultivating them.

Bass, Dorothy C., ed. *Practicing Our Faith.* San Francisco: Jossey-Bass Publishers, 1997. A resource for Christians looking to deepen their faith. This book touches on economics, hospitality, the body, Sabbath, community, healing, and song.

Bell, Richard H. *Sensing the Spirit: Spirituality and the Christian Life.* Philadelphia: The Westminster Press, 1984. How we forget, and can remember, God.

Borysenko, Joan. *Fire in the Soul: A New Psychology of Spiritual Optimism.* New York: Warner Books, 1993. Stories of the spiritual growth that arises from the darkness of fear, illness, and tragedy. Practical exercises and resources for meditation, prayer, and healing.

Brussat, Frederic A. "27 Ways to Live a Spiritual Life Every Day." *Utne Reader*, July/ August 1994. Quotations that provide examples of concrete, day-to-day spirituality on topics such as "Washing your hands," "Doing chores," "Sharing gossip," and "Throwing out the garbage."

Chittister, Joan, OSB. *Wisdom Distilled from the Daily.* San Francisco: Harper & Row, 1990. Written by the former prioress of the Benedictine Sisters of Erie, PA. This book looks at the Rule of St. Benedict as a foundation for listening, prayer, community, monasticism, work, leisure, and obedience.

Dass, Ram and Mirabai Bush. *Compassion in Action: Setting Out on the Path of Service.* New York: Bell Tower, 1992. A personal and practical guide to recognizing and living the interdependence of compassion and action, of social and spiritual development.

de Mello, Anthony. *Wellsprings: A Book of Spiritual Exercises.* New York: Image Books, 1986. Beautiful meditative passages from a Christian perspective that blend Eastern and Western teachings.

Elgin, Duane. *Voluntary Simplicity: Toward a Way of Life that is Outwardly Simple, Inwardly Rich.* New York: Quill/William Morrow, 1993. A classic on how to live in balance and make daily adjustments in response to the complex dilemmas of our time.

Fields, Rick with Peggy Taylor, Rex Weyler, Rick Ingrasci. *Chop Wood, Carry Water: A Guide to Finding Spiritual Fulfillment in Daily Life.* Los Angeles: Jeremy P. Tarcher/ Putnam Books, 1984. A guide for using daily activities as a way to live and apply spiritual insights. Includes chapters on relationships, sex, family, work, money, play, body, and social action.

spiritual quick hits

These simple actions can bring you to a different place, shift your energy, or give you a new perspective.

- Memorize a poem or prayer that you like and share it with one or many.
- Take one day to help people you know. Work at their organizations or at their homes. You might concentrate some energy on new/young parents with small children who need relief.
- Spend a whole day in silence.
- Spend a full day with children. Let them plan part of it and then take time to do what you loved most as a kid or feel like you didn't get to do often enough.
- Attend someone else's house of worship.
- Lie on the floor and spend 30 minutes listening to your favorite music in the dark.
- Go to a museum and spend at least 15 minutes with one painting that moves you or that you don't understand.
- Get on your knees and ask for forgiveness.
- Write a letter to an ancestor.
- Meditate on a photo of yourself as a child.

Fleischman, Paul R. *Cultivating Inner Peace*. New York: Tarcher/Putnam, 1997. Eight principles for making peace a way of life. Also includes stories of individuals who inspire the path.

Gatlin, June Juliet. *Spirit Speaks to Sisters*. Chicago: The Noble Press, 1996. Written for Black women, "to inspire, praise, enlighten, elevate, and liberate." Minister, activist, singer, and writer, Gatlin's voice calls readers to spiritual fitness and a more intimate relationship with God.

Kaufer, Nelly and Carol Osmer-Newhouse. *A Woman's Guide to Spiritual Renewal*. San Francisco: HarperSanFrancisco, 1994. A step-by-step workbook for women seeking to renew, create, or heal their spiritual selves. Written in two parts, the first on "Healing your Spiritual Alienation;" the second, "Seeking Spiritual Connection." Includes chapters on nature, beauty, creativity, rituals, intuition, and relationships.

Lerner, Michael. *Jewish Renewal: A Path to Healing and Transformation*. New York: Grosset/Putnam, 1994. Lerner sheds modern light on Jewish texts, God, prayer, and the practice of the faith.

Palmer, Parker J. *The Active Life: A Spirituality of Work, Creativity, and Caring*. San Francisco: Harper & Row, 1990.

_____. *To Know as We Are Known: A Spirituality of Education*. San Francisco: Harper & Row, 1983.

Petsonk, Judy. *Taking Judaism Personally: Creating a Meaningful Spiritual Life*. New York: The Free Press, 1991. The author weaves her own story with those of colleagues, friends, and mentors.

Richardson, Peter Tufts. *Four Spiritualities: Expressions of Self, Expressions of Spirit*. Palo Alto, CA: Davies-Black, 1996. A psychology of four spiritual paths corresponding to Jungian dimensions of personality: Journey of Unity, Journey of Devotion, Journey of Works, and Journey of Harmony. Each Journey includes underlying tenants, practices, mentors, and texts to read.

Spretnak, Charlene, ed. *The Politics of Women's Spirituality: Essays by Founding Mothers of the Movement*. New York: Anchor Books, 1994. A chorus of feminist voices explore spirituality and its role in transforming politics.

Underhill, Evelyn. *Concerning the Inner Life*. London: Methuen & Company, 1926. An exploration of how we can strengthen our inner resources, Underhill's essays were intially addresses delivered to clergy in the 1920s.

Vanek, Elizabeth-Anne. *From Center to Circumference: God's Place in the Circle of Self.* Mahwah, NJ: Paulist Press, 1996. Short essays about a woman's quest to deepen her relationship with God.

Vanzant, Iyanla. *One Day My Soul Just Opened Up.* New York: Fireside, 1998. Inspirational readings and exercises for 40 days and 40 nights.

Veriditas: Grace Cathedral Labyrinth Project, 1100 California Street, San Francisco CA 94108; 415/749-6356. E-mail: veriditas@gracecathedral.org Web site: www.gracecathedral.org

stories of spiritual practice . . . .

David Sawyer

Educator, writer, speaker, and consultant, David Sawyer spent 10 years at Berea College as the Director of Students for Appalachia (SFA). SFA, a campus service organization, teaches adults to read, tutors and mentors kids, and develops student servant-leaders. He also led the team that designed the national training for Summer of Service, the pilot for President Clinton's Americorps program. David is a native Kentuckian. He lives on a farm in the Cumberland Mountains in a log home he built with friends. He believes in hard work and living close to the land.

CH: David, your spiritual base is a powerful part of who you are. Tell me how it all developed.

DS: My spiritual base is a formal practice, under vow to a spiritual teacher, but it hasn't always been so. I rejected Christianity at age 13. I experience a dark night of disbelief and unhappiness about "God." As a senior in college, after a year of depression, I encountered Eastern religion and philosophy. I saw that the spiritual process did not have to be about believing in God but that it is better understood as a journey. The idea was very liberating to me. One spring day, I had what I guess could be called an "enlightenment" experience. For three days my depression and confusion were lifted, and I experienced a state of grace. Trying to regain this state of being got me serious about the spiritual path. I thought it might take me a couple of years! Twenty-five years later it is still a tremendous effort.

I began to explore Hinduism, met a Hindu teacher, and received my first "initiation." Later, I was given my first spiritual name, Karmananda, which I didn't like, because it means "he who attains realization or liberation through selfless service to humanity." At the time I wanted to go to a cave and get the hell away from humanity. Halfway through my 10 years with SFA I realized, "Holy shit, that teacher knew exactly what he was doing." I grew disenchanted with that particular school of Hinduism, because it was very much about leaving the world, putting your energy into your spine, and rising through the chakras to an ascended state of being. I called this the "up, up and away school."

> For three days my depression and confusion were lifted, and I experienced a state of grace. Trying to regain this state of being got me serious about the spiritual path.

Around this time, I had another turning point. I was meditating with a friend one morning, trying to concentrate on my mantra [a sacred word or phrase repeated during meditation]. Her cat was rubbing against me, irritating the hell out of me, looking for attention. A tremendous tension had been building in me, and it surfaced in that moment. I looked down at this little being seeking to be loved. I picked up the cat and petted her for the rest of the meditation practice—something quite unusual for me. I made a fierce decision that I have not forgotten: any spiritual practice that denies the needs of others is not for me.

After that I struck out on my own for awhile. I had read the spiritual teachings of Adi Da, but the demands in his community were more than I was ready for at the time. But I felt a strong connection with him and his teachings. Then, in 1995 the chance to see Adi Da for the first time presented itself. There was an outreach to those of us who had been on the fringe for a long time, people who were paying a nominal yearly fee to get the literature and stay in touch. On Easter day of 1996, he and I had our first personal exchange. It was very intimate; we kissed. I was able to speak words of love and respect in his ear, and he did the same. It was a very tender and special moment in my life.

Later, he created a new form of association based on his experience with me and other people, because he could see that we had work to do in the world, and yet, we were sincere about our spiritual work with him. He said humorously to me, "You won't do the practice like I've given it to you, and you won't leave, so I had to figure out some way to include you!"

And you took a vow; what did this mean for you?

Taking a formal vow is a real commitment, like a marriage vow. It has the same seriousness. I sit every morning, which I was doing anyway, but the difference is that when you have a true teacher, you are met halfway. You still struggle to be clear, to reach out, but there's an actual reaching back toward you as well. Somehow, the spiritual presence is activated in your particular case. Then it's not such a lonely, private endeavor. Practice becomes a matter of actually turning to the spiritual presence and being with that rather than trying to "get somewhere." Your side of the equation is that you have to do the turning, which is, of course, very difficult. A true teacher, in all traditions, helps quicken that process and somehow enables you to experience the spirit.

> The principle of my outer life is maximum positive impact. The principle of the inner is maximum spiritual realization. I was scared when I took the vow that it would weaken the outer side, but the converse has been true. It's made me more effective personally, because I'm clearer. I listen better.

How has your spiritual practice impacted your work?

A couple ways at least. There's been more strength, power, and clarity and less internal noise and confusion. I experience more synchronicity with the outer world. The principle of my outer life is maximum positive impact. The principle of the inner is maximum spiritual realization. I was scared when I took the vow that it would weaken the outer side, but the converse has been true. It's made me more effective personally, because I'm clearer. I listen better. My bullshit detectors are keener; my compassion and love are greater. People sense that I'm earnest even in my desire to make a contribution, so there's a receptivity in others. Spiritual work has cleared away a lot of my inner garbage and helped me be more effective in the world.

And, the students with SFA must really feel the effects of all this?

Without talking about my own spiritual journey, I've tried to create a work environment that honors both the inner and the outer. Last year I started talking in terms of excellence and love. Excellence means uncompromising quality. But there is also love. When I say love, I don't mean lovey-dovey. I mean respect, integrity, and if possible, affection. I started using this word to describe the texture of the interactions among ourselves and with those we serve. There's a lot of challenge in this environment, because we have this expectation of excellence. If you're not cutting it, you'll hear about it. There are tears, too, because people are always coming up against the thing they need to improve and transform in themselves. It surfaces your stuff. This kind of work environment seems to maximize others' ability to bring their inner convictions into their outer work.

What changes as a result?

The way you feel about work, other people, about yourself. There's a dynamism and a vitality, a frankness, laughter, creativity, and depth. It's a good place to be. People hang around there even if they're not working. Real relationships are established and maintained. It's a true community. Individual issues are surfacing all the time, and a lot of personal healing occurs.

People at age 21 and 22 are developing incredible sophistication about group dynamics and subtle leadership abilities. Most people don't even know exactly what it is they're getting, but I've heard from so many students five, 10 years out that they've seen the effect of that learning as they've gone on with the rest of their lives. The environment puts everyone on a steep learning curve—not least of which me.

If folks were going to try to bring some of what you're describing into their lives, where would you tell them to start?

Start doing some daily inner work. You don't have to have a spiritual teacher to do real spiritual work. And you don't have to meditate either. Inner work includes anything that helps you work through your issues: therapy, great friendship, read great books. Do something every day—even if it's just taking a book that touches your heart and spending five minutes reading.

If you have the capacity to influence your work environment, and let's hope you do because otherwise you're powerless, then just try to understand how important it is to deal with the side of the work environment that is rarely dealt with—the love side. Understanding that is what helps you and others grow.

Tell me about the high touch framework.

There are four possible ways a work environment can be structured. The first is high task/high touch. That's what we're always striving for. You get the job done, and you have great working relationships. That's excellence and love. People in this type of environment will be more creative, have more impact, and take more true risks. We're all going to have to take some risks if we're going to create a just world.

My humorous description of the other three ways goes like this: With high task/low touch you get a lot done, but you hate each other. With low task/high touch, everybody loves each other, but you don't get a damn thing done. Low task/low touch is true hell: you hate each other, and you don't get anything done

It's shocking and sad how common these three situations are. The stories of people committed to social justice with horrible work environment are legendary. We purport to create a better world for others, and we live in hell ourselves. And that's absurd. Gandhi said, "We ourselves must be the change we want to see in the world." Amen.

Over my door at Students for Appalachia is a quote from Dag Hammarsjköld, the Secretary-General of the United Nations during the dark years of the cold war. He said, "In our era, the road to holiness must pass through the world of action." That pretty much sums up my sense of who I am and what I must be. I've always been very much a person "of the world," and I keep believing that it's possible to live an American contemplative life—a life that is intensely involved in the reshaping of the world but also profoundly committed to realization. This is my challenge and my commitment.

stories of a faith journey . . . .

Darryl Lester

Darryl Lester has worked in adult and youth development since 1990 with organizations like North Carolina Public Allies, the Counseling Center at Shaw University, African-American Student Affairs at North Carolina State University, and most recently the 4-H Youth Development School-age Care Project. He is now the Program Officer at the Triangle Community Foundation.

> I still go to my church, but now it's more about principles and values and things that need to happen outside of that building.

CH: *Darryl, start by telling me about your faith.*

DL: I grew up in a small town in South Carolina, and I guess I would describe it as somewhat rural, large family. Going to church was a tradition. The church was the center, and you went more out of habit. You got involved, went to Bible school in the summer, participated in the choir, you were an usher; it became a ritual. I came from a family whose values came out of that foundation of the church.

I grew up African Methodist Episcopal, which was very laid back, driven by older people but now I'm in a Baptist church that has a more upbeat tempo. The pastor's younger; there are more things going on. It is a little less rigid than the church I grew up in, but it's still tradition-based. As I've grown older, I've widened my lens on Southern religion to more of a spiritual path. I still go to my church, but now it's more about principles and values and things that need to happen outside of that building. And I realize that as I grow, I can connect with other folks whose foundation may not be the same as mine.

It's about the spiritual foundation, what your center is, and what you're required to do based on that faith. I'm trying to keep the peace in my own life, and my faith allows me to keep that peace, but it also helps me make sense of some of the things going on in the world and about how some folks can get some peace in *their* life. And it doesn't always mean, "Come into this building."

What's hard about being on a slightly new path for you?

It's going to put you in conflict with a lot of the things you may have been taught. I'm questioning things more; in going to that building on Sunday, I interpret what the pastor is saying with a different lens. That path of trying to make sense of it put me in conflict with myself, my family. Sometimes it's like being out there by yourself. You pull away from the tradition, but you come back to it, and you come back to it with a totally different mind set.

Tell me about your spiritual practice outside of the church.

Integral to that is a time of prayer and acknowledging that there is this force that you can't see, but you do know has some control over things that are happening. I think through prayer you're able to communicate with that force. There are also guiding principles that go along with that. Being humble is one for me and that the more I walk this path, the more humble I want to become. And the value of being genuine. You don't say one thing and do another. You try to be consistent in how you live your life. It's not a rigid walk; I'm always trying to connect with people where they are. When we did the Annual Black Church Week of Prayer for the Healing of AIDS we had a litany [call and response], but there were comments made around the table—

> I think through prayer you're able to communicate with that force. There are also guiding principles that go along with that. Being humble is one for me and that the more I walk this path, the more humble I want to become.

Comments about people who have AIDS?

Yes, and I had to educate people without backing them into a corner. I wanted to snap their heads off, but I couldn't; I had to educate them, and next year they'll be in a different place. There's this unconditional love. Even though you might be on a different side of the coin, you can still have some appreciation for where they stand.

Is prayer an important aspect of being able to do that?

Yes, and I try to connect with people that help me reinforce those same thing. I see that in other people and that helps me a whole lot. I love basketball. In the mornings for the last year and a half, 15 guys have met to play, and we start off with some quiet time. Some guys bring a prayer or something inspirational. Then we play ball, and we play hard, intense. But guys aren't arguing with each other, aren't cursing. When we have disagreements, we don't get slowed up by arguing about a call or something like that. We all play hard, but it's about guys trying to get their bodies in shape, because part of their spiritual walk is trying to take care of themselves. Now we're looking at how this same group of individuals can come together and address some things that are happening in our community.

In addition to exercise, I know you also fast often.

Yes, it's the whole thing: taking care of myself, watching what I put into myself. As you're able to clear your system, it puts you more in alignment with that spiritual force. Now I try to do it anytime before I do something in public. I'm really asking for the supreme being to clear my mind. It's not about folks looking at me, but about trying to get them to hear what I'm saying that has meaning for me. And so far I can get up there, and my thoughts really connect well. It's like getting in the zone.

Do you ever feel a conflict between your faith and other things you believe in?

Dealing with AIDS issue. Here I am, I say I'm a part of this church, and it's a small Southern church, but when I hear folks make comments, it almost makes me not want to be a part of this. But I realize everywhere I go it is like this. So I get what I need from there, and I back away from it. My wife and I work with the young folks in the church, and we find they're not being prepared for the world; they're coming out of a box, and the world may deal them something they're not going to be able to handle. So that's my way of dealing with it—bringing issues to them that they need to know.

What about at work? What role does faith play there?

In the work environment, folks try to separate out their faith if they have one. Folks that are at peace with themselves, you can tell by how they operate at work. If we've got a deadline to meet, I don't have to snap at you. My faith is going to determine how I'm going to treat people at work.

I pick and choose my battles. I can't afford to spend energy dealing with trivial stuff at work; when I leave work I'm trying to deal with other stuff. Being a person of color, when I walk out of work I'm going to encounter different things than my coworkers will.

> Folks that are at peace with themselves, you can tell by how they operate at work. If we've got a deadline to meet, I don't have to snap at you. My faith is going to determine how I'm going to treat people at work.

History has shown that my chances of sometimes being taken the wrong way are increased. I've been in Wellspring grocery, and I can watch folks' demeanor with their pocket books. I try to laugh it off, but it's still frustrating. When you don't have faith and you encounter that kind of tension on your life, you don't always know where to go with it. My faith has given me a high threshold; my faith gives me peace.

What advice would you give to activists about building spiritual strength?

I think first of all they need to be at a place where they can accept who they are, even the things they don't like. Folks have to say that I'm okay, there's some things I have to work on. And they have to go through a time where they turn down the noise. They need to have some quiet time. In growing up, I realized I never dealt with the death of my brother and my sister, and the only way I could deal with it was to take some quiet time to sort through it all. Once you get in that quiet space, you have to face those things that always make you want to turn and go the other way. The other part that weaves through all is spending some time in prayer, fasting, and connecting all the pieces.

D, last question. What is your favorite scripture?

In Romans, it says "Be not conformed to this world, but be transformed by the renewing of your mind." What that means is something has to take place in here [the head], and when it talks, you get out of that whole conformist thing, that fear of being a trail blazer. When I engage with folks in church, actions always come out of their thinking. So when they can get their thinking right, then their actions will change.

spiritual practice.

Part Two:
Sustaining Ourselves

inspiration

*I believe in beauty. I believe in stones
and water, air and soil, people and their
future and their fate.*

~ Ansel Adams

questions for reflection

What or whom has inspired you recently?

What are the things, places, experiences, and people in your life
that have helped you to see new possibilities?

What do you do when you are in need of fresh ideas or a new direction?

what is inspiration?. . . . .

I turn to Webster's dictionary, and the definition resonates: "the infusion or arousal within the mind of some idea, feeling or impulse, especially one that leads to creative action." Inspiration is what gives us a vision of what else is possible. It allows us to climb out of a box that has confined our thinking; once we are out of the box, we look around for new directions. Inspiration comes through an infinite number of sources: people, experiences, words, music, art, movement, prayer. It may come in an instant, a sudden flash of light we experience while something powerful unfolds before us, or within us. Or, it may hide in the corners of what might otherwise seem like an "ordinary" conversation.

turning points . . . .

I am in the fourth grade; we have to pick a country and learn everything we can about it. I am in the "Italy" group, and I know almost immediately that this place touches me unlike any other. It goes beyond pasta and the red and white checkered tablecloth that we draw on our country poster. It sparks an affinity for all things Italian that continues for me to this day. The same year we also study the different bioregions of the world: desert, rain forest, tundra, jungle. Our classroom contains a purple bathtub. Every day one person is chosen, by virtue of good behavior and academic effort, to spend reading period in the tub. *This classroom seemed to break all the conventional rules; there wasn't a year in elementary school when I learned more.*

In September, 1997, the *New York Times Magazine* does a cover story on the new Guggenheim Museum in Bilbao, an industrial city in the Basque region of Spain which was once a center of steel making. The museum is like no other. Step back from a photo of it, and the physical structure looks like crumpled pieces of aluminum foil thrown together. Step closer and the beauty of the space is unparalleled, the originality undeniable. Made of limestone and titanium, the museum presents a drastically different and striking view from every angle. The windows slant in crazy directions, forms thrust at you almost from nowhere, the curves are as graceful as architecture can be. Built on an old river site, architect Frank Gehry paid homage to the museum's location, interfacing directly with a set of railroad tracks and a suspension bridge that are both still in use. *Every time I look at it I am reminded of what it means to think outside of the box with no limitation on beauty.*

In 1996 I have the privilege of hearing Bill T. Jones speak. I have not been more amazed by a single human being. A choreographer, dancer, writer, and lecturer, Bill T. Jones uses his body, words, and spirit to captivate us, to make us think, wonder, and question. He is one of the first people I hear speak fearlessly of God in a secular setting: "God is change, and life is a spiritual activity."

Jones asks us what we are offering the world. He tells us that he cultivates the perception *daily* that it is worth it to make something because, as I write in my notes, "creation is NOW." He assumes the posture of the Hindu God Shiva to illustrate the dance we do daily, the effort we must make to balance different parts of ourselves and of society. He explains to this group of activists that we must constantly test the potential of our ideas and our vision. That such tests often mean going into a foreign place with our ideas, getting kicked, and coming back to our community to recover before going back out again. Jones believes that society needs philosophers, artists, and scientists; he seems to be all three. *He is genius and poetry in motion, growing, changing, and taking us into the process.*

My favorite road in Durham is Alston Avenue and what lies near its end. It starts out as a busy four-lane road in the neighborhood surrounding North Carolina Central University, Durham's historically Black university. It quickly becomes a two-lane back road, winding its way past storefront churches, groves of pine trees, boarded up gas stations and thriving communities proclaimed with signs like "Welcome to Alston Heights" and "Bryan Heights Community." After a few more miles, signs of the New South appear. There is land available for sale, as well as buildings connected to the Research Triangle Park with names like Tricenter South and West Park Corporate Center. These complexes sit squarely across the street from old homes and uncultivated fields, interspersed with signs for barbecue and flower shops.

Then, you come to the old Lowes Grove Elementary School, now boarded up, waiting, pleading for someone to come along with energy for a revival. The school is a series of five red brick buildings stretched across a few acres of land. Before I have a chance to fully contemplate the cause of the building's demise and the whereabouts of its children, I am at the intersection of Alston Avenue and Highway 54. Fast food restaurants try to reassure me that everything is okay, as time and progress march on. I have fantasized about that school many times and wondered how much financial and political capital it would take to turn it into a community center for spirit and education. *So, I make the trip down Alston Avenue. It reminds me that my town has a past, present, and future and that they're not all so far removed from one another. It helps me remember the tenuous links between what has been, what is, and what will be someday.*

We open up new doors for each other.

inspiration and social change . . . .

Working to rebuild communities takes hard work, planning, commitment, and resources. It also takes inspiration. It would be nearly impossible to build a movement for change without this. Inspiration can serve as a reminder of what happens when one has a real thirst for going into unchartered territory. Sharing what influences and inspires us with others allows us to learn things about each other that would otherwise go unnoticed. We open up new doors for each other.

In the fall of 1990, I helped organize a conference on poverty issues at the University of Pennsylvania. Hundreds of students attended, as well as a group of activists and advocates from Philadelphia. The students were energized and ready to act, so we began thinking about next steps. We knew we wanted a more concentrated, intense opportunity to join the energy of young people with the experience of older activists and those whose lives had been directly affected by homelessness.

One night we gathered to discuss the possibilities. We knew Philadelphia was a city with thirty to forty thousand units of abandoned units of housing. One of the activists present claimed it was time to "rip the boards off the doors of those units and empty the damn shelters." Empty the shelters, we thought. It seemed like a good goal. But how? We began talking about the 60s, the student movement for Civil Rights, and Freedom Summer in particular, when hundreds of college students came South to help register Blacks to vote. (Only later would we begin to wrestle with the implications of outsiders coming in to help local people with their own struggle.)

We decided to try and create our own Freedom Summer, to invite college students to come to Philadelphia that next summer and work side by side with low-income people. Six months later, 40 students from across the country arrived in Philadelphia. We spent eight weeks working with poor people's organizations, getting trained in group dynamics and dealing with oppression, educating ourselves further about poverty issues, and living in community. Like so many activists before us, the Civil Rights Movement provided inspiration for how to build student-community partnerships, how to live together, and how to educate ourselves.

In my work, I love asking people to return to their sources of inspiration: to bring a reading to share, sing a song, retell a favorite story from history, or reminisce about a mentor's role in one's life. All are simple and powerful ways of calling on inspiration and sparking new possibilities.

activities to do alone . . . .

℗ seeking inspiration

If you've never thought much about this in any systematic way, try some initial brainstorming. Gather different colored pens, magic markers, paints, or colored pencils and one sheet of 8" x 11" paper.

1. Draw your favorite shape so that it fills the entire space.

2. Figure out a way to divide it into six parts, any way that you want. Be creative.

3. In each of the parts put one of the following words:
   Written sources (books, poetry, magazines, etc.)
   Music
   Visual sources (art, movies, video, etc.)
   Colors
   Places
   People

4. Slowly fill in each section with the relevant sources of inspiration. Brainstorm possibilities. Create other categories and add to the shape to make room for them.

5. Notice any patterns or themes. What images came to mind while you were making your lists?

Use the worksheet "Seeking Inspiration" in the Appendix to do this activity with groups.

℗ models of faith: inspiration for the journey

We can be moved by other people's stories, their approach, the spirit they radiate, the actions they are not afraid to take. When I am discouraged or hopeless, when I need advice, or when I need to be reminded of the bigger picture, I return to a mental list of people from whom I draw strength. Some of them I know; some of them I've only read about or heard speak. They are all part of what Evelyn Mattern calls my "community of saints."

Who are the people you turn to in your mind for inspiration? Make a list; it may be short. These may be folks you envision when something gets difficult in your work or in your life. Some Christians now wear a bracelet with the initials "W.W.J.D.", which stands for, "What Would Jesus Do?" You can ask this question of anyone whose life and outlook you admire. If you can, keep something she's created or given to you on hand. If it's someone you know, make lunch for him and interview him about his life journey, his beliefs, and his code for living. Write down or tape-record his responses.

sources of inspiration

How might you begin to "collect" or record your sources of inspiration?
Is it a notebook for poetry, quotes, ideas?
A folder full of images that call certain things to life for you?
A box or crate in the corner of your room?
Is there a wall in your house or apartment or office that could be covered with canvas or large brown paper and serve as an ongoing scrapbook of your life?

outings

In every community, city, or town, there are places which feed the spirit and provide inspiration. Imagine you are making a map of your community for God of those places which most inspire you.
Where might you go? What would you say about each place?
What would you take with you? When would you go? How long would you stay?
With whom would you share the map ?

activities to do with groups . . . .

sharing inspiration

Ask everyone to bring in something that inspires them in their daily life or something from their spiritual or religious tradition to share with others. It might be something written, an object in their home, or something else. It might be a ritual, a practice, a poem or prayer, a song—anything. Give each person three to four minutes to share their inspiration with the group.

personal models of faith

In pairs or groups of three, ask people to talk about their models of faith or community of saints.
Who taught you about faith growing up?
To whom do you turn to for advice or inspiration when things get rough?
Why are these people so important to you?
Are they people you know, don't know, or both?
If you were going to introduce them to a friend, what would you say about them?

nonviolence

Pioneered by Mohandas Gandhi in India and used during the Civil Rights Movement, nonviolence is both a personal practice and a methodology of resisting oppression. Gandhi believed that evil and injustice only exist when we support them. He developed a new instrument of social action, a form of civil disobedience he called *satyagraha*. Satyagraha is a Sanskrit word which means "holding on to truth" or "soul-force." This spiritual force had the power to bring an end to injustice, because Gandhi believed it could awaken the heart of oppressors.

Because it is a spiritual practice, nonviolence does not rely on attacking or belittling people in power. Rather, it seeks to reveal the truth in such a way that those in power can understand and accept it. The goal of nonviolent action is to reveal the truth of a situation and solve conflicts through non-injury. Many of the activists who have embraced nonviolent strategies were people of faith, relying on their religious and spiritual convictions. As King said about nonviolence, "We have a power, a power as old as the insights of Jesus of Nazareth and as new as the techniques of Mahatma Gandhi."

(continued top of next page)

℮ spiritual biographies

This exercise takes some research, so agree to spend some time preparing ahead of time. The idea is to pick someone and get to know more about how faith and action collide in her world. It might be someone who lives her faith daily. It might be someone famous on a national or international level, someone in your own community, or a member of your own family. It's just as important to validate your own history as it is to learn more about the history of faithful people. You might start with someone in your own faith tradition and then move on to other traditions.

Possible people might include:
– your Hebrew school or Sunday school teacher
– a minister, rabbi, priest, nun, or other religious figure
  you know
– elders in your family or your community

There are thousands of examples of famous people to choose from. Here are a few of my favorites:

Dorothy Day (1897-1980) founded the Catholic Worker Movement with Peter Maurin in 1933 on principles of nonviolence, communal sharing of possessions, solidarity with the poor, and resistance of coercive state power. There are now 150 Catholic Worker "houses of hospitality" in communities of need across the United States and Canada and around the world. The movement also includes community forums and newspapers. Day has often been called the "soul of the American left" and the "saint of the common ground."

Fannie Lou Hamer (1917-1977) grew up a plantation worker in the Mississippi Delta. She lost her livelihood after attempting to register to vote. After working with SNCC (Student Nonviolent Coordinating Committee) and serving as a state representative for the progressive Mississippi Freedom Democratic Party, she organized the Freedom Farm Cooperative. She became a national spokesperson on issues of hunger and poverty in the South and helped leverage federal funding to improve housing in rural Mississippi.

Rabbi Dr. Abraham Joshua Heschel (1907-1972) was born in Poland and raised in a Hasidic community. Escaping Poland just six weeks before the Nazi invasion, he eventually moved to the United States where he became a preeminent scholar, author, activist, and theologian. His teachings have influenced many to develop a more personal relationship with God. Heschel marched with Dr. Martin Luther King, Jr. in Selma, Alabama in 1965 and later formed an organization to opposed the war in Vietnam.

His Holiness, the 14th Dalai Lama, (1935-) is both the religious and political leader of the Tibetan people. When the country was invaded by the Chinese in 1950, many Tibetans fled to India. The Dalai Lama now leads an exiled community there. He has seen his religion labeled a "disease" by the Chinese, one million monks and citizens killed, and six thousand monasteries destroyed. But still the Dalai Lama preaches a message of nonviolence and compassion towards the Chinese. He has spent many years raising awareness worldwide about the plight of Tibet.

Thomas Merton (1915-1968) was a Trappist monk, peace activist, and prolific writer. A committed Christian, Merton also felt a deep connection to the monks of Hindu and Buddhist traditions. One of the most important spiritual writers of the 20th Century, Merton spent the second half of his life at Our Lady of Gethsemani, a Trappist monastery in Kentucky. A committed pacifist, Merton was a keen witness of social change on a global scale and maintained relationships with many of the most powerful, faith-based activists of his time.

Peace Pilgrim (unknown-1981) walked 25,000 miles for peace over three decades. With only a comb, toothbrush, pen, and copies of her message, she crossed America, speaking to groups and individuals along the way about peace. She believed that when enough individuals found inner peace, war would no longer be necessary. She began living a life of voluntary simplicity and started her pilgrimage on January 1, 1953, giving up "home, possessions, age, and name." She spoke about peace on television and radio, in university classrooms, from the pulpit of churches, and to people she met along the way.

Bishop Desmond Tutu (1931-) is the Anglican archbishop of Cape Town in South Africa. The son of a teacher who entered the ministry because he couldn't afford to go to medical school, Tutu was a critical force in the dismantling of apartheid. Motivated by his deep faith, he called for economic sanctions and the boycotting of elections in the 1980s. He won the Nobel Peace Prize in 1984.

nonviolence, cont'd

Nonviolence had tremendous psychological importance to the Negro. He had to win and to vindicate his dignity in order to merit and enjoy his self-esteem. He had to let white men know that the picture of him as a clown— irresponsible, resigned and believing in his own inferiority—was a stereotype with no validity. This method was grasped by the Negro masses because it embodied the dignity of struggle, of moral conviction, and self-sacrifice. The Negro was able to face his adversary, to concede to him a physical advantage, and to defeat him because the superior force of the oppressor had become powerless.

- Martin Luther King, Jr., *Why We Can't Wait*

mysticism: inspiration for the journey

Mysticism is the way in which one truly understands what it means to be one with the Divine. Through a personal mystical experience one reunites with the divine in themselves and gets closer to the unknowable: God. Over the past two thousand years, many saints, teachers, rabbis, nuns, and monks have described the content and impact of mystical experiences. Their writings are an inspiration.

Baal Shem Tov (1700-1760), whose name means "Master of the Good Name," spent years contemplating and studying the Kabbalah, the Jewish mystical tradition. The Baal Shem Tov preached to and inspired thousands in Poland and founded Hasidism, a Jewish tradition that emphasizes mysticism and religious zeal. The Baal Shem Tov believed that ritual is not enough for faith, that faith requires a vibrant relationship with God which can be achieved through joyful prayer.

The Desert Fathers is a term for generations of monastics who left Jerusalem and other cities for more remote locations in order to live their faith. St. Antony, born in 250 B.C.E., inspired the movement. He lived as a hermit for many years before emerging in public life as a healer and preacher. Others were moved to take up a similarly monastic life in caves and cliffs throughout the Mediterranean region.

Meister Eckhart (1260-1328), a German Dominican, belived mystical experiences were possible if one emptied one's mind of all activity. Throughout his life, he was preoccupied by the relationship between divinity and humanity. He believed there was a "little spark" of God, the divine kernel, in each being's inmost self: "Where the creature stops, there God begins to be. Now God wants no more from you than that you should in creaturely fashion go out of yourself, and let God be God in you." For these and other inflammatory writings, Eckhart was condemned as a heretic

Hildegard of Bingen (1098-1179) entered a Benedictine monastery at the age of eight. As a child, Hildegard had prophetic visions which continued throughout her life; they inspired her to write and illustrate three books. A cloistered nun, Hildegard founded two monasteries. She was also an herbalist and a scientist who catalogued medicines of her medieval era. Her liturgical chants have been rediscovered in recent years. Hildegard wrote, "For the shape of the word exists everlastingly in the knowledge of the true Love which is God: constantly circling, wonderful for human nature, and such that it is not consumed by age and cannot be increased by anything new."

Mirabai (circa 1498-1546) was an Indian noblewoman who rejected her station after her husband's death and devoted her life to the Hindu God, Krishna. She wrote religious poetry and music to express her love: "Like a bee trapped for life in the closing of the sweet flower, Mira has offered herself to her Lord. She says: the single Lotus will swallow you whole."

Jelaluddin Rumi (1207-1273) was born in Persia. A scholar and teacher under royal patronage, Rumi's life was transformed when he met Shams of Tabriz, a wandering dervish. "What I had thought of before as God, I met today in person," Rumi wrote. Their relationship and shared mystical experiences sparked Rumi to write ecstatic poetry, describing his longing to be with, for, and of God. For Rumi, it is through the suffering and sacrifice of love that one finds God. His writing addresses longing and satisfaction, separation and union, the worldly and the spiritual, love and pain.

St. Teresa of Avila (1515-1582) was a Spanish Carmelite nun who detailed her visions and revelations of God. In numerous writings, she describes the various stages of a mystical life from her first meditative experiences to an almost ongoing connection with the divine through which the soul loses itself to its love for God. With a few companions, she founded an enclosed convent at Avila in Spain. It became one of the foundations for the reformation of the Carmelite order.

resources for inspiration . . . .

Besserman, Pearl. *The Shambhala Guide to Kabbalah and Jewish Mysticism.* Boston: Shambhala, 1997. An introduction to philosophy and practice written by a descendant of the Baal Shem Tov. Includes meditation techniques.

Carmody, Denise Lardner and John Tully Carmody. *Mysticism: Holiness East and West.* New York: Oxford University Press, 1996. An academic survey of mysticism in Hinduism, Buddhism, Judaism, Christianity, Islam, and the religious practices of native people in North America, Latin America, Africa, and Australia.

Coles, Robert. *The Call of Service: A Witness to Idealism.* Boston: Houghton Mifflin Company, 1993. Stories from the author's experiences while working on civil rights and living a life committed to service.

Crawford, Vicki L., Jacqueline Anne Rouse, and Barbara Woods, eds. *Women in the Civil Rights Movement: Trailblazers and Torchbearers, 1941-1965.* Bloomington: Indiana University Press, 1993. Includes the story of Fannie Lou Hamer.

Dalai Lama XIV. *Freedom in Exile: The Autobiography of the Dalai Lama.* New York: HarperCollins, 1990.

Day, Dorothy. *The Long Loneliness: The Autobiography of Dorothy Day.* New York: Harper, 1952.

Eckhart, Meister. *Meister Eckhart: A Modern Translation.* Translated by Raymond Bernard Blakney. New York: Harper Torch Books, 1941.

Gandhi, Mohandas K. *Gandhi, An Autobiography: The Story of My Experiments with Truth.* Boston: Beacon Press, 1957.

Ghiselin, Brewster, ed. *The Creative Process.* Berkeley: University of California Press, 1985. Originally published in 1952, this book contains original commentary from 38 writers, artists, and scientists on creativity. Contributors include Einstein, Mozart, van Gogh, and Nietzsche.

Heschel, Abraham Joshua. *Moral Grandeur and Spiritual Audacity.* Edited by Susannah Heschel. New York: Farrar, Straus & Giroux, 1996. A collection of Heschel's greatest essays, edited by his daughter.

_____. *The Circle of the Baal Shem Tov.* Edited by Samuel H. Dresner. Chicago: University of Chicago Press, 1985.

Jones, Bill T. *Last Night on Earth.* With Peggy Gillespie. New York: Pantheon Books, 1995. Jones' fascinating life history, told autobiographically with beautiful photographs.

Kamenetz, Rodger. *Stalking Elijah: Adventures with Today's Jewish Mystical Masters.* San Francisco: HarperSanFrancisco, 1997. Story of the author's journey to seek counsel from Jewish spiritual teachers across the country.

Lakey, George. *Powerful Peacemaking: A Strategy for a Living Revolution.* Philadelphia: New Society Publishers, 1987. A five-stage strategy to create social empowerment and global transformation: cultural preparation, organization-building, propaganda of the deed, mass noncooperation, and parallel institutions.

Mayers, Gregory. *Listen to the Desert.* Liguori, MO: Triumph Books, 1996. Writings and stories of the Desert Fathers.

McGreal, Ian P., ed. *Great Thinkers of the Eastern World.* New York: HarperCollins Publishers, 1995. Short biographies and analysis of one hundred thinkers from China, India, Japan, Korea, and the world of Islam.

Mills, Kay. *This Little Light of Mine: The Life of Fannie Lou Hamer.* New York: Penguin, 1993.

Muschamp, Herbert. "A Masterpiece for Now." *New York Times Magazine,* 7 September 1997. Article about the Guggenheim Museum in Bilbao, Spain and its architect, Frank Gehry.

Peace Pilgrim. *Peace Pilgrim: Her Life and Work in Her Own Words.* Compiled by some of her friends. Santa Fe: Ocean Tree, 1991.

Rumi. *The Essential Rumi.* Translated by Coleman Barks with John Moyne. Edison, NJ: Castle Books, 1997. A new and definitive collection of Jelaluddin Rumi's ecstatic poetry.

Saint Hildegard. *Hildegard of Bingen's Book of Divine Works: With Letters and Songs.* Edited by Matthew Fox. Sante Fe: Bear & Company, 1987.

Saint Teresa of Avila. *The Interior Castle.* Translated by John Venard OCD. Sydney: E.J. Dwyer, 1988. This is considered the essence of St. Teresa's doctrine of prayer.

Tutu, Bishop Desmond. *The Words of Desmond Tutu.* Selected by Naomi Tutu. New York: Newmarket Press, 1989. Some of Tutu's greatest speeches, chosen and introduced by his daughter.

Wallis, Jim and Joyce Hollyday. *Clouds of Witnesses.* Maryknoll, NY: Orbis Books/ Sojourners, 1994. Short biographies and personal testimony of Christian peacemakers, martyrs, and saints.

stories of spirit in action . . . .

Arun and Sunanda Gandhi

Sunanda and Arun Gandhi run the M. K. Gandhi Institute for Nonviolence in Memphis, Tennessee. The grandson of Mohandas K. "Mahatma" Gandhi, Arun was born in South Africa. He was working as a journalist in India when he met Sunanda, the nurse who cared for him after surgery. The Institute, which they co-founded in 1991, provides training and education on the theory and practice of nonviolence.

CH: How would you describe the core of your spiritual life?

AG: Well, I think I came from a really strange spiritual background. Grandfather believed very early in his life that the only way we can bring peace to the people is by bringing unity in religions, bringing all the religions closer together. Which did not mean that he wanted them all to become one, but that there should be respect and an understanding for each other's religions. There's a wonderful saying from his writings, "A friendly study of all the religions is the sacred duty of every individual." And he emphasized the word "friendly." He made that friendly study of all the major religions of the world and incorporated from each one of them what he thought was useful in his daily prayer service.

> Grandfather believed very early in his life that the only way we can bring peace to the people is by bringing unity in religions, bringing all the religions closer together.

SG: Not only prayer service, but in his life.

AG: His beliefs, he made it a part of his mission. I grew up with prayer services every morning and evening, including hymns from every major religion of the world: Christianity, Islam, Judaism, Buddhism, Hinduism, all of them. We had the prayers in a room or under a tree where hundreds of people gathered to participate. That's what we have followed, respect for all the different religions.

SG: I actually grew up in a very traditional Indian spiritual upbringing. It was more ritualistic and bound by certain traditions. But somewhere deep down in me, there was a reckoning consciousness for service. Although in the traditional India taking a profession like nursing was looked down upon—girls from good standing did not go into a service profession like that—I chose to go into it, and it was one step against the tradition of a very well-blessed family. From there on, I started realizing the leaning of my heart, of serving people and being with them. I met Arun and we married. Then I saw people in his family, and all the people who came into our lives, their dedication to service, total dedication. It made me realize that was my path, my spirituality, my way of understanding religion.

Do you think spirituality is key to living a life of nonviolence?

AG: Yes, I think so. First of all, we need to understand what we mean by spirituality. We have a very limited notion of this, and we mix it up with religion. My own perspective of religion and spirituality is that religion is more ritualistic. Spirituality to me is something that goes above religion, where all the different belief systems meet, and they respect and understand each other. When we reach that level of spirituality, where we can appreciate and accept each other, then we are on the right way of serving.

But as long as we get bogged down in religious rituals and insist that my way of life is the only way and no other can be accommodated, then we are not really practicing religion. All the scriptures talk about love, compassion, understanding. That's the foundation of every scripture in the world. And yet we don't incorporate that in our lives. We have misinterpreted many of the religions. The most important thing is to translate that religion or scripture into our lives, into our daily actions. Not just go and mouth it two or three times a day in church or temple or mosque or wherever and then forget about it.

> Spirituality to me is something that goes above religion, where all the different belief systems meet, and they respect and understand each other. When we reach that level of spirituality, where we can appreciate and accept each other, then we are on the right way of serving.

SG: We do all these things, the rituals and the practices, like robots. We follow them because we're so used to it. We don't try to shake ourselves out of it. If we look around, we'll find much more to life, if we seek that love and that understanding. But we have already made up our minds. Just because someone looks different than you or has a different way of walking, we have preconceived notions without even trying to start a dialogue and find out, "If you are different, why you are different?" Once we start to do that, it becomes so apparent that what seems to be different, is really not different.

When does the daily commitment to living the compassion, seeing God in everybody, get difficult for both of you?

SG: When we are put into a corner. Like, we are told that the flight is cancelled or delayed. You get into the line, people rush from behind and get in front of you. That's the time when you start wondering, "What is happening, now?" And your beliefs, for that split second, start getting a little doubtful in your mind. Then you try to think, as much as you are stressed, the other people are stressed, and they have their own ways. And sometimes you try to smile your way out of it, or laugh. Or sometimes you let the stress get hold of you. But these are normal human reactions.

AG: I think it's an ongoing process. It's not something you can learn within a week, or even 10 years. It's a process that has to go on throughout your life. And every day is a new learning day. Every night is a new learning night. A lot depends on how open you keep your mind and how willing you are to learn from other people. If you close your mind and don't have any willingness to accept other influences, you stagnate. There was this very powerful lesson that Grandfather taught me. He said, "As you grow up, your mind should be like a room with many open windows. Let the breeze flow in from all of them, but refuse to be blown away by any one of them." We need to absorb things from all different sources, use whatever we find useful, and grow from it.

What else would you tell someone who was trying to create some small change in the world?

AG: The first thing I would like to tell them is what I learned from my parents and grandparents. You must look at yourself like a farmer. A farmer goes out and plants the seeds in his fields, and then he waits and prays for those seeds to germinate, and he gets a good crop. What we are doing today is planting those seeds, and we hope those seeds will germinate, and we'll get a good crop.

SG: You can help the natural environment and the natural surroundings, like a farmer, to allow that seed to germinate. And not just leave it to its own fate. That little seedling needs a helping hand. Be a support system.

AG: The important thing to remember is that we can't change the whole world, but we can change ourselves, and we can change people around us, so we should concentrate on that. When we try to change the world, or take up big issues, that's when we get burned out. Set yourself goals that can be achieved and achieve those goals, and then move to another goal. Take it one step at a time. The tendency I find in most young people is they want to change the whole world. I've noticed that most young people are always looking at political conflicts all over the world, but not many people seem to focus on economic conflicts or social conflicts that are going on, even in our neighborhoods.

SG: I'll cite an example. In earlier days, we found that there were many neighborhood watches. The crime situation in Memphis is really very, very grave. Unfortunately, it ranks sixth in the nation in crime, and everybody is worried about it. We were going to troubled neighborhoods and talking with people, just having dialogue with them. We said, "You have neighborhood watches, and you have neighborhood meetings where you talk about all the problems that you have. We have attended those neighborhood meetings, and people are getting frustrated and tired of them. Slowly the meetings are becoming smaller and smaller."

We suggested, why not let us have a street party? Now, once or twice in a month we have a potluck party. Everybody comes out, brings something, has fun, and plays games. Children are there and the next door neighbors. We get a chance to know who they are, what they are doing, what their family situation is. In the beginning people were a little doubtful about it, but recently we have found that they're really having wonderful results. People have started knowing each other; people have started taking interest in each other instead of just gossiping about each other.

AG: When we get too bogged down in problems and negativity, we become very oppressed and depressed, and we don't know what answers to find. We need to have a more positive attitude towards things.

The two things we have to learn in applying nonviolence in our personal lives is to use our anger constructively, rather than destructively. We have to find ways of channeling that energy properly. And the other is how to build relationships with people that are based on respect and understanding, not on selfishness. That's not a relationship; it only adds to the conflict and violence. We have to learn how to have a relationship with each other because we are human beings; we are part of one whole. People in the West tend to believe that we are independent individuals, that we can do whatever we like, and that's our business. But we are not independent; we are interdependent, and we have to look at ourselves as part of a whole big picture. We are all part of this whole creation, interlinked with each other.

SG: Many of the people who are on this quest for nonviolence help me understand that it is the truth all of us are after. Truth has many facets. And yet there is only one truth that we are all seeking.

stories of faith and justice. . . . .
Rebecca Reyes and Sue Gilbertson

Rebecca Reyes is an ordained Presbyterian minister who grew up in Corpus Christi, Texas. A clinical social worker, she is currently working with high risk mothers in the OBGYN clinic at Duke University Hospital. She counsels women around issues of economics, health, domestic violence, substance abuse, and HIV. Sue Gilbertson, MSW, CCSW is the regional director of Catholic Social Ministries for the Piedmont region, which covers nine counties. Raised in the Presbyterian church, she has been fed by both the Presbyterian and Catholic traditions. Rebecca and Sue have been comrades for eleven years.

CH: I know both of you make a strong connection between faith and vocation. How did that start?

SG: I was raised in Kent, Ohio. I was very influenced by the anti-war movement, and the shootings at Kent State were a formative memory for me. It was at the height of the Vietnam War, and there was a possibility my brother was going to be drafted. The shootings and the turmoil around the burning of the ROTC building was really visible in our town, in our church, and even in our family. Our church provided a forum for the town to talk about the situation. People came and talked about things like: "In light of the gospel, what do we do with the situation that's happening in our town? How do we look at the Vietnam War? What we do with that?" That was really powerful for me. There were two or three ministers from the South that had been involved in the Civil Rights Movement They talked in terms of "gospel values," taking a stand about what you believe even if it's not popular.

At an early age, I felt at a deep level what was important in life—being associated with trying to make things better, bring about justice, bring about the reign of God.

> At an early age, I felt at a deep level what was important in life—being associated with trying to make things better, bring about justice, bring about the reign of God.

RR: Mine is more environmental. I grew up in a very Hispanic home. It was religious, but it was also very spiritual. I think it was ingrained in me, especially by my grandmothers who were living close to the earth, using herbs, and recognizing the mystery of the earth. In the summer, I'd be watering the grass, and if I was playing with the water, my grandmother would say, "Be sure and get some water and put it on top of your head." Water was a force, and it wasn't just meant for playing. It was protection. That spoke to me, that my family believed in mystery.

My parents have been married for 52 years now, and they raised a family that was together all the time. We went to church all day on Sundays and Wednesday evenings. It was an understanding that that was what the family was going to do. And the Presbyterian church is the most demystified. The missionaries did a great job of making sure you don't have any of that in church—incense, candles, statues.

You two had very different church experiences.

SG: I remember being impressed that the church took a stand to open the doors and to invite people in to talk. It was a brave move on their part. People in town whose windows were smashed and cars turned over were really angry with the students, and it was a volatile time. The church was willing to open the door to the chaos.

RR: We were products of missionaries. The white people came and told the brown people to let go of Catholicism, because to believe in saints and icons was bad. We became Protestants. The missionaries were more conservative than people living in Kent. Their mission was to save souls. But the Presbyterians gave me education, one thing my parents would never have had without the Presbyterians. Few families could afford to send their child to a school. When you're poor and your parents are illiterate, education is great. My mom went to a Presbyterian school, which was a rare thing. My uncles and my mother learned trades. My parents graduated from high school, and all of their children graduated from high school, got graduate degrees.

And each of you pursued somewhat different paths as a result of your experience.

SG: One of my ministers talked about what an amazing impact the church could have on the world if we really lived the gospel, if we took our faith seriously. I always took that as a challenge. I've always worked through religious institutions. I worked at Lutheran Family Services in Wisconsin, and I volunteered at a church organization in Mexico. Now I'm working with Catholic Social Ministries. I like to be in an atmosphere where questions of faith and issues of faith are part of the dialogue. Personally, I get a lot out of that. It's kind of an accepted part of the culture of my workplace; our work comes out of a faith vision.

Rebecca, you've followed a different path. What made you decide to pursue ordination, given your ambivalence about the Presbyterians?

RR: I was a grad student working in environmental issues back in the 70s when oil companies and the ecological movement were just starting to blossom. I was struggling with what the church had to say about taking care of the earth. I was also taking leadership in the church. Someone asked me if would consider going to seminary. I applied and that's what I did.

Because I happened to be one of two Hispanic women in seminary, I had access to a lot of conversations with prominent theologians that broadened my theology. I never went to be ordained. I didn't see going to seminary as a spiritual decision; I saw it as needing more education. But for my parents it was a call, a spiritual decision. I was ordained in the first Hispanic church that had ever been created, and I was being ordained to be the pastor of this church.

> I didn't see going to seminary as a spiritual decision; I saw it as needing more education. But for my parents it was a call, a spiritual decision. I was ordained in the first Hispanic church that had ever been created, and I was being ordained to be the pastor of this church.

The first Hispanic church that had been built in the U.S.?

RR: Yes. It was a very historic moment—the first Hispanic woman being ordained in the first Hispanic church in this country. I didn't put all that together. Of course, the Hispanic community had a huge celebration. I never liked big celebrations, so I was trying not to pay attention. In the midst of it, my sister says, "Your grandmother wants to talk to you in private, in the back of the church." I go and my grandmother gives me this blessing: "God be with you, and God give you all the strength." She did this anointing ritual, and it clicked that even in my ordination that wasn't permitted. I hadn't even thought of including a blessing in the service or thought my grandmother would want to give me a blessing. For her, it was really a setting apart.

How do your faith commitments impact your work?

RR: I was taught the Gospel is about celebrating life to the fullest and to me that means every aspect. As a social worker working with high risk women, I'm trying to help people understand they're not living life at the fullest. When I have a mom who is a drug addict and she says to me, "Well I'm not using drugs anymore, but I'm drinking a lot because it's not as bad. But I go to church on Sunday," there's part of me that wants to delve into that. Why did you tell me you go to church on Sunday? I want to do more spiritual work with this woman, and I can't because I'm a social worker. I'm not there for that reason. If I did push into spirituality, it might help her clarify some issues. The challenge is how to do it in a language that doesn't come off as religious. I have to be more creative about how I dialogue with people without coming off as a chaplain. That's a big challenge.

SG: I think of Jesus not only as a savior or a teacher. You can also point to the fact that he was incredibly revolutionary in terms of going up against the powers that be and taking a stand on the side of poor and vulnerable people. Talking to the woman at the well when that was unheard of and relating with people who were shunned and frowned upon: prostitutes, tax collectors. Using that life as a model is the ultimate liberation, but it's also a constant sense of swimming upstream, against the tide, and putting your hopes in a different place. And it's hard. Through Catholic Social Ministries, I'm constantly working with people who don't have enough to eat, can't pay their light bills, and are struggling to make it financially.

And what about your individual spiritual lives?

RR: I've had to be more personal and deliberate about my faith. When I was working in the church, I was there because of my faith. I have had to remind myself that I am here [at the hospital] because of my faith and not because it's a job. I've had to be more deliberate in my prayer life. When I'm going to work, I say thank you to God for the blessings I have, prepare me for the work I'm going to do. I'm more deliberate about going to church because I'm a member of a community of faith.

SG: In my work, and also in my home, I have a sense of competence. That can be a good thing, but it can also be a slippery slope. If I begin to think that it's just me that's doing this and I lose track of that connection I have to God through praying, then things get out of balance. I start to feel overwhelmed, and I get a visceral feeling in my gut when things are off. Usually that means I need to take some space and have some quiet time where I remember about who's the creator. It's getting things back in balance.

It can only happen out of an individual longing for God. I believe that there's a space in our hearts that only God can fill. You have to get to a certain point in your life before you get to that longing, and I'm not sure some people ever do. The poet Rumi has this expression, "When I try to talk about God, the words turn to dust in my mouth." It feels bigger than words, and I certainly wouldn't offer it unless I was asked specifically about it. I think that anything about spirituality is really easily misinterpreted, seen as proselytizing or trying to save souls or judgmental. If I talk about this then somehow I see myself on a higher plane or something. But I also love a conversation like this.

stories of faith-based organizing . . . .

Scott Cooper

Scott Cooper, originally from Jackson, Tennessee, is an organizer with BUILD, Baltimoreans United in Leadership Development, and the Solidarity Sponsoring Committee. Both organizations are affiliated with the Industrial Areas Foundation. After graduating from Duke University in 1994, Scott coordinated summer programs for college students to work with grassroots organizations and worked with the Southern Rural Development Institute (SRDI).

CH: Scott tell me about your faith background.

SC: I grew up in the United Methodist church; my father is a minister. I didn't have much choice in my faith growing up. It was always explained to me by my mother that that's what put food on the table. As Methodists, we moved around from church to church every three to six years. Some were small, working class congregations in really small towns, some were large, affluent churches in the cities. As a minister's child, you learn to relate to all kinds of people. Unlike most kids who leave immediately after the service, we were always the last people to leave. You end up talking with people, ranging from 2-year-olds to 80-year-olds, all class backgrounds.

How did you get into organizing work?

Growing up in the church and in Southern communities, I had a pretty good vision of what community could be for people. As I grew older, I began to realize there was real disparity in the world. In college, it was natural to spend time volunteering at schools or doing service projects, but it didn't get at the core of what was wrong. I really struggled to find the answer to that question. It was a natural thing, to want to work like this. It wasn't a radical shift from the path I was on.

After I graduated, working with students was a way to continue to explore what I wanted to do as a vocation. I met Arnie Graff, Gerald Taylor, and Keri Miciotto from the Industrial Areas Foundation [IAF]. They were recruiting young people in North Carolina. They were talking about power and self-interest and looking at institutions like the church as being political institutions. That really struck something in me. Most training fades in your consciousness after a while; those things rattled around in my head for along time.

What was powerful for you about it?

Having grown up in church, in moderate, white Protestant denominations, there was a lot of talk, but there wasn't much real action. It seemed somewhat self-absorbed. I think mainline church denominations are in crisis right now. They've got some hard decisions to make.

Say more about the crisis.

It's a failure on the part of the church to be active in the political realm, not just electoral politics, but having a voice and being a witness in public debate. As Christians or people of faith who believe in God, we are somewhat lax in the standards that we hold one another accountable to. It shouldn't be that easy to be a Christian or person of faith. It should be something people struggle with. Look at the life of Christ, or the life of any holy figure for that matter, and look at our own lives. We're imperfect beings, but if we're seeking to imitate the life of Christ, that should be something that keeps us up at night.

> As Christians or people of faith who believe in God, we are somewhat lax in the standards that we hold one another accountable to.

Someone gave me this quote, I think it's from Ernest Hemingway: "The world breaks everyone, and out of the broken places, some grow stronger." That really resonates for me. My understanding of the story of Christ as being someone broken by this world and the story of the resurrection is being able to grow stronger and more powerful through it.

And the work you are doing with the IAF is about that?

The IAF works to build power out of institutions that share common values and that have been central to people's lives and the lives of families. In Baltimore, it wasn't until people began to talk to one another that they realized that many were only finding part-time, minimum wage jobs, jobs that used to be full-time. At the same time, there was anger on the part of the church because a great deal of public money was used to develop the Inner Harbor in Baltimore. The church agreed with the idea of redeveloping downtown, as long as good jobs were created for people. Since that promise was never fulfilled, the church began talking with the union about the idea of a living wage bill. And we passed it in 1994.

It's the first of its kind in the country. It forced the city of Baltimore to create standards. If they were going to sign contracts with private companies to provide services (cleaning, food service, transportation), they needed to be at a wage above the poverty line—$7.70 per hour. It affects the whole labor market in the city, because other companies now have to compete with those paying a decent wage. It's basic economics of supply and demand. Since we did it, 30 other cities across the country have followed our lead.

The church and workers came together, and out of that Solidarity was born, the project I work on. It is part of BUILD. The workers are all contract workers, but they work for 30-40 different companies. Many don't have a regular church or a union to belong to, so Solidarity is really important for them. You have to have an institution of people directly affected that are bringing the truth forward. Even though we forced the city to pass the law, Solidarity has been enforcing it, since companies try everything they can to get around it.

How do you get people involved?

I meet people on loading docks as they're going in to clean the schools. I have two to three minutes to engage people, and I follow it up with an individual meeting in their home. This is a chance for me to share who I am, what the organization believes, for them to share who they are and for me as an organizer to see if this person is a leader or has the potential to be a leader. Then you pull together a committee meeting or strategy meeting where there's some training going on. It's one thing to tell people things, but it's another to engage people in discussion.

What role does faith play in the work you're doing?

You can't just organize people around an issue, because politics gets boring after awhile. You have to organize people around their values. Faith adds a depth to the work. You're not just agitating someone around their need for better wages or better benefits. To have a common story—the Old and New Testament for people who grew up in the church—is really amazing. We take it another step and use it to teach.

A few weeks ago, we did a discussion of collective leadership. We used the story in the Book of Numbers when Moses has led the Israelites into the wilderness after leaving Mount Sinai. They have these new rules, the Ten Commandments, they're lugging around. Everyone comes to him saying they're hungry for meat; they're tired of manna. Moses says he can't bear this burden alone, and God instructs him to call together 70 of the elders. It's a great lesson of leadership, delegation, and not looking for one central figure. It should be a community of people that bears the burden of sustaining life for a community.

Or, look at the story of the feeding of the five thousand. People have gathered, and they want to break bread together, but all they have is five loaves and a couple of fish. At that time, people traveling carried food with them but weren't accustomed to sharing. By having them sit together and offer these loaves and fishes, people began to break out of their isolation. Whether or not Christ made food appear out of nothing is secondary to the miracle of people sharing with one another in community. You can take that to another level: people have a lot of ideas in their head but don't always have a chance to sit face to face with one another and commune.

And what about the role of faith for you?

I'm not actively involved in a church. My concept of God is a God of free will that gives us the opportunity to explore and struggle in this world and struggle with our relationship with God. It's not cut and dried. My concept is that God is love. I guess I feel the presence of God. On a certain level there is a connection that goes beyond a single issue or value. This work is scary in a lot of ways. There's something very comforting about knowing there is a higher power that reminds me not to take myself so seriously, that I can't fulfill every need for every individual. For me, having grown up in the church, being able to reconnect with that experience in my day-to-day work is really exciting.

inspiration.

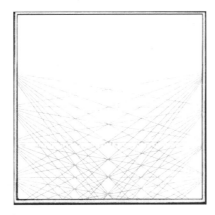

ritual

*Ritual is the way culture enacts and
affirms its values. . .[rituals] change,
grow, and develop, take root in particular
places and reflect particular moments
in a community's history.*

~ Starhawk, *Truth or Dare*

*A man without ritual cannot live;
an undertaking without ritual cannot
come to completion; and a state
without ritual cannot attain peace.*

~ Hsun Tzu (298-238 B.C.E.)

questions for reflection

What rituals were important to your family growing up?

Are they still important today?

What rituals have you created yourself?

How do you greet the morning? How do you end the day?

what is ritual? . . . .

Ritual is something—anything—that one does to draw special awareness to an event, a person, a time, or an idea. By focusing energy in a purposeful way, rituals allow us to recognize something we might not have otherwise paid as much attention to. The most important spiritual lessons are often acted out in rituals—small dramas that, in the words of anthropologist Victor Turner, "communicate our deepest values. . . and inscribe order in the hearts and minds of participants." What is truly incredible is how universal some rituals are, ignoring the boundaries of time, culture, or place:

- All over the world, birth is celebrated with namings and a blessing as a symbolic entrance into the community.
- All over the world, adolescents mark their journey from puberty to manhood and womanhood.
- All over the world, the union of two people is celebrated with feasting and dancing, elaborate costuming, and the witnessing of vows.
- All over the world, death is marked by returning the physical body to the earth and a period of mourning.

Many family traditions and holidays are rituals. Does your mother make your favorite dish when you come home? That's ritual. Returning often to the place you met your partner or spouse—that's a ritual too. Wearing a favorite shirt for an interview may sound superstitious to some, ritualistic to others. Team huddles, candles on a birthday cake, dressing up for a special event—some rituals have been around in our lives for so long, we take them for granted. Some may be repeated over many years; other rituals may last only a short while.

turning points . . . .

April, 1995. Kathleen, a young woman I know in Philadelphia, is tragically killed by a drunk driver just a few days before Easter. At her memorial service, tulips are everywhere. Many of us take the flowers home with us. A month later, I plant the bulbs in a community garden near my house in North Carolina. I gather five friends for the planting. I speak for a few minutes about Kathleen's life and her death, but mostly about her life. I ask each person to say something even though they have never met her. *I feel less alone in my grieving.*

December, 1996. A couple is leaving a house and a community they've shared for years to move across the country. On the night before their departure, I am their witness as they go from room to room; in each they take time to remember experiences in that room and what about the room is particularly sacred. At the end, they light candles to honor a house of love and caring. To celebrate the walls that heard their voices, the floors that grounded them to the earth, the ceilings that protected them. *They are able to recognize the fullness of the lives which have been lived there.*

July, 1996. I am about to turn 30. I don't want to be depressed or lonely or bored, so I plan a gathering with close friends I rarely get to see. Two friends graciously open up their home for the event. I create cards for the guests, each one with a poem picked out for the individual. The evening of the event, we gather in a circle. As I give out the cards, I speak about what each person has meant to me. In turn, they share something about our friendship. My very scattered tribe has become whole. *Suddenly, 30 feels like liberation; all things are possible.*

November, 1997. My friend Julia is getting married. The day before the wedding, 30 women—friends and family members—gather for lunch. Each woman brings with her a bead and a wish for Julia. As we go around the circle, each woman shares a wish, a prayer, or a poem, and the beads are strung, each somehow symbolic of our connection to the bride. After the luncheon, her (almost) sisters-in-law take the necklace to be restrung. Julia wears it to the party after the wedding and on many occasions afterwards. *It is a tangible reminder of a supportive circle of women.*

rituals and social change . . . .

There is something very powerful for me in the repetition of rituals
that I do on a frequent basis, like the breaking of bread, for instance.
I have found comfort in becoming one member in the "dance" of a ritual.
I am going through certain steps while others go through theirs, and together
it creates this powerful ritual. It creates space and time for me to focus,
clear my mind, and quiet the noise.

~ Heather Zorn, member of the Second Circle

Ritual creates sacred space, allowing groups greater opportunities to build trust, unity, and safety. They are a unique chance to celebrate individual and group accomplishments, the power of community, common vision and goals, beginnings and endings. Rituals can generate excitement and energy; they can also be a valuable tool when facing pain and sadness around a particular event or issue.

As illustrated by the examples above, rituals:

1. Help people mark time and/or acknowledge change.

2. Often involve the use of an object or objects which become symbolic of the ritual itself.

3. Require some thought and planning but can be done without a tremendous amount of preparation.

Rituals can be as elaborate or as simple as the situation demands. To mark the beginning of the first Training Institute stone circles ever ran, we made a talking stick together. We all walked outside to look for a stick and agreed on the most appropriate one for this group symbol. Next, each participant tied a ribbon onto the stick as they named their goals and hopes for the Institute. The stick stayed with us throughout the next two days, occupying a prominent place in discussion.

rituals for young people . . . .

In 1997, I attended two "Communal Rituals as a Means to Nonviolence" organized by mythologist-activist Michael Meade and Malidoma Somé, a medicine man and scholar from West Africa. These powerful gatherings were part of a conference called "Peacemaking: The Power of Nonviolence." The conference hotel room had been transformed for these rituals. It was lit only by what seemed like hundreds of candles. We entered under a canopy of sunflowers, held by the young people who had taken an active role in planning the ritual. Four massive altars were set up around the room, one for each element—fire, air, water, and earth.

The ritual began with quiet drumming and storytelling about the relationship between young and old in ancient cultural traditions. Participants were asked to articulate something that needed healing in their lives. From around the room, the shouts and whispers came. Young people of color whose communities had been wracked by violence. Others who had recently lost a parent, a friend, a child. Less dramatic wounds from my own mouth and others around me. The drumming grew louder; everyone was given a stone as a symbol of their particular wound, and we began moving around to the various altars to offer the stone in prayer. Time stopped as we moved in and out of each other's space, not speaking. Above the drums, I heard crying, sobbing, even a wail. In the end, it was the young people who brought us back together, and back to a place of joy, with their drumming and chanting.

everyone was given a stone as a symbol…

No one needs rituals today more than young people. Western culture provides very little for young people in the way of rites of passage, a way to mark the period of transition between childhood and adulthood, dependence, and independence. When these opportunities are not provided, young people create their own. Gangs offer much of what society has not offered—a sense of family, clear rules for success and failure, a chance to prove one's strength, and a way to earn income. Adolescents need legitimate, safe, and challenging ways to prove themselves. They need a supportive environment in which to forge their own identity independent of family and avenues to develop strong, healthy bonds with both peers and elders.

How did you mark your own transition to adulthood?
Were you the architect of this transition or did others help?
Were other peers present? What roles did they play?
Was an adult present? What role did he or she play?

rituals for facing slavery . . . .

To find our way for the next century, we must affirm and respect
the precious spiritual nature of all people,
the true source of moral power to transform our violent, materially-based civilization.
~ Organizers of the Interfaith Pilgrimage of the Middle Passage

There are events and time periods in history full of pain which, however difficult, must be remembered. For example, Jews teach their children about the Holocaust so that they will never forget it. Ritual is a way to humanize historical catastrophes, invoke the past, pay respect to those who suffered, and pass on valuable lessons to upcoming generations. How, for example, does one even begin to teach children—and adults—about the horrors of the slave trade?

For a full year, from May 1998 through May 1999, the Interfaith Pilgrimage of the Middle Passage retraced over four hundred years of the slave trade. Initiated by the Buddhist order Nipponzan Myohoji, the Pilgrimage was organized by a diverse group and endorsed by Christian, Jewish, Muslim, Baha'i, and Unitarian Universalist groups. The transatlantic voyage retraced the route of the slave trade from the east coast of North America through the Caribbean and Central America to Brazil, and finally to West and South Africa. The Pilgrimage had five purposes:

1. To offer prayers for the spirits of African ancestors and their descendants who have suffered, as well as for the spirits of White oppressors;

2. To give people of European descent an opportunity to take responsibility and repent, breaking the patterns of denial and fear that hold racism in place;

3. To reverse historical patterns by showing gratitude and respect for the African continent;

4. To educate people about the institution of slavery; and,

5. To transform the materially-based thinking that made the slave trade possible and continues to relegate millions of people to poverty.

At stops along the way, the Pilgrimage visited sites of both suffering and courage, such as slave auctions, slave quarters, and the Underground Railroad. Ceremonies were organized at many of the sites, allowing pilgrims and locals to join together for healing, learning, and community. In the words of Archbishop Desmond Tutu, Honorary Chairman for the Pilgrimage, "If we do not acknowledge our history we cannot learn from it. . . . The road they tread will be an inspiration and a means of healing for many of us who follow them by proxy in intercession and meditation."

activities to do alone

℮ simple rituals

Individual rituals can be created by thinking through your day and what aspects would be more meaningful with recognition or ceremony.

How might you give thanks for the day that stretches out before you?
How do you end the day? Do you remember or record the highlights of the day, or what you learned?
How do you begin your work day? Is there an act or set of actions that lets you know you're starting anew?
How do you leave your work behind at the end of a day?
How do you begin your meals? Do you take an opportunity to give thanks for the food and those responsible for gathering and preparing it?

activities to do with groups . . . .

ℯ exploring ritual

When talking about individual perceptions of ritual, both positive and negative, it is important to create a level of trust and safety so that each person's needs will be respected. Some people may have great memories of rituals from their childhood, while the very same things may have negative connotations for others. You can initiate a discussion of ritual by using the worksheet, "Exploring Ritual", in the Appendix. Have everyone take 10 minutes to fill it out and then pair people up to discuss their responses.

ℯ marking time: a ritual for a new year

Ask each person in the group to bring two objects to your next gathering. One object should symbolize the year just ending, and one should symbolize the person's hopes for the coming year. For this activity, you will need paper, writing implements, and a special table or cloth. Make sure you have room for everyone to sit in a circle and space in the middle to place the objects that people bring.

Start with freewriting, giving everyone five minutes to answer each of the following questions. [See the "Words and Stories" chapter for information on freewriting.]
What were the highlights of this past year for you?
What have you learned over the past year?
What are some of your hopes and dreams for the coming year?
What might hold you back from these? What will help you fulfill them?

After the writing, people can share in groups of two or three or with the whole group if there are less than 10 people. Then, as a group, have everyone talk about the two objects they brought and why. Ask everyone to lay their objects on the cloth as they speak.

ℯ focusing on each other

For a group who knows each other well, this ritual can really deepen their connections. For a group who is new to each other, this will break the ice in an innovative way. We see people differently when we are not interacting with them. Have everyone sit in a circle.

In silence, everyone will take a minute or two to focus in on every other person around the circle. This might be done by taking five deep breaths as you zero in on each individual. Think about what you appreciate about them, what you've noticed, what you are intrigued by, how they challenge you. You may look at someone while they are looking at someone else, and that's okay.

Give people a chance to say something about this afterwards if they need to. This exercise could be a prelude to something else or a way to end a difficult meeting.

activities to do with groups:
going deeper . . . .

creating a group ritual

A ritual has even more meaning when a group creates it together. Groups may decide to create a ritual for any number of reasons. You may want to deepen your connections with each other by marking a season. Perhaps you have been through a crisis, and there is still some healing that needs to happen. Or, maybe one member is moving far away, ending their work with the organization, or having a child. Below is an example of a planning outline for a ritual. It follows the worksheet, "Creating a Group Ritual," which you'll find in the Appendix.

an example of ritual planning:
The Second Circle's Autumn Equinox

1. SET GOALS: Why this ritual? What purpose do we hope this ritual will serve?
    We wanted an opportunity to mark the Autumn Equinox in a way that we had not yet done as a group.

2. DETERMINE who will be the PARTICIPANTS: Will it be group members only or open to others? How many people will attend?
    We decided this ritual would only be open to our group of 10 people. We were eager to have other folks participate but decided to save that for another time.

3. BRAINSTORM the possible elements:
    Ideas from our brainstorming session for the equinox ritual included: do something with pumpkins, string colored yarn in the trees, do a dance weaving something

At the core, grief is a form of praise. Grief carries with it the seeds of strength and hope, but if grief goes unrecognized, the seeds never grow. We are fearful of grief and reluctant to find our own ways of dealing with the pain, let alone sharing it with others. When one experiences loss, all things begin to feel unreal. There is a period of disbelief and denial, which then leads to anger and pain. Only after these stages can true healing begin.

In grief, people always have a story to tell. It is a gift to make space where people have permission to mourn. When we or someone we know loses someone (family, friend, or colleague) or even something (a job or relationship) we need ways to mark and express the loss. Ask people what they need:
Do they have memories they'd like to share?
Is there a special place they'd like to go to tell some of these stories?
Who else should be there?

together, build energy we can store for the winter, chant, drum, use leaves symbolically, see winter as a time of positive retreat, make a dream catcher, welcome the darkness, praise, harvest, focus on the heat of the earth and its warmth, bring fall foods to share.

4. Create a FINAL OUTLINE: Take a look at all of the possibilities from your brainstorming session. Which ones are people most excited about? Which seem most feasible given the size of the group, the time of year, the resources available, the space where you might gather?

Our final outline for the Autumn Equinox ritual:

As they entered the ritual space, everyone was smudged—a custom of purifying participants which begins many earth-based rituals and gatherings. One person stands at the threshold and another waves the sage smudge stick up, down, and around the outside of the body, front and back.

Each person was asked, "What do you leave behind?" This was a chance to let go of some things that would no longer serve us as we moved into a new season.

Once everyone was in the ritual space, we visited four altars, one for each of the four elements. Then, we honored the four directions, another common element of earth-based ritual. We did this by turning to all four directions and naming them and their qualities. [See the "Earth" chapter for more information on the four directions.]

Next, we gathered in a circle, and each of us spoke about what we were thankful for at this time of year. Then we spent a few minutes in individual silent prayer.

One member led the group in a guided meditation on the earth, darkness and light, and the significance of this time of year. The meditation emphasized our connection to the earth, the coming fall, and winter as a time of positive retreat. Afterwards we talked about our experience with the meditation in groups of three.

Next we created a dream catcher together. One member had already cut a piece of grapevine and created the outer, circular shape. We took

brightly colored yarn and each of us wove part of the dream catcher and then tied
our piece of ribbon onto the edges. We decided the dream catcher would be present
with us at all of our subsequent meetings.

We ended the ritual with drumming and chanting. Then we feasted on food to
accompany the time of year: squash, apples, pumpkins, cider, heavy bread, and
soup.

5. DECIDE WHO will do what:
   Four of us planned the ritual after getting ideas from the whole group. Everyone was
   asked to bring a dish for a potluck to follow the ritual. The planners got there early
   to set up, and everyone helped clean up at the end.

6. THINK about LOGISTICS:
   What are some possible spaces for the ritual? Do you want to do it outside?
   If you'll be inside, what do you need to do to transform the space?
   What materials do you need?
   What time will you start? How long will it last? Will there be food?
   We'd hoped to do our ritual outside in the woods next to one member's house, but
   it was a rainy day. The ground was too wet. So, we did the ritual inside the house.
   We set up four altars, one on each side of the room, to represent the four elements:
   fire, air, water, and earth. Each altar was a table covered in cloth holding objects
   symbolic of that element. The room was lit only by candles. We kept our ritual
   within our normal group meeting time, 7-9 P.M. We ended with a potluck supper.

7. DISCUSS how the group members might PREPARE:
   What does the group need to think about ahead of time?
   What do they need to bring?

   We asked people to think about the following:
   What do you love about winter?
   What are you thankful for?
   Does the idea of turning inward with the winter resonate with you? How?
   What impact does the darkness have on you?

   We also asked everyone to bring a piece of yarn and a dish.

resources for spiritual practice

Canada, Geoffrey. *Reaching Up for Manhood: Transforming the Lives of Boys in America.* Boston: Beacon Press, 1998. Canada draws on his own experience of working closely with young African-Americans in New York.

Cohen, David, *The Circle of Life: Rituals from the Human Family Album.* San Francisco: HarperSanFrancisco, 1991. An exquisite book of photographs and text that chronicles the rituals of birth and childhood, initiation and adolescence, marriage and adulthood, and death in cultures across the globe.

Eiker, Diane and Sapphire, eds. *Keep Simple Ceremonies.* Portland, ME: Astarte Shell Press, 1993. Hand-written guide to the home-grown rituals from the Feminist Spiritual Community of Portland, Maine. Includes rituals for life cycle events, personal milestones, and community celebration.

Estes, Clarissa Pinkola. *Women Who Dance With the Wolves: Myths and Stories of the Wild Woman Archetype.* New York: Ballantine Books, 1992. A classic collection of old tales, infused with new meaning.

Getty, Adele. *A Sense of the Sacred.* Dallas: Taylor Publishing Company, 1997. Blends personal, historical, and cultural approaches to finding spiritual life through ceremony.

Interfaith Pilgrimage for the Middle Passage. Contact: First Congregational Church, Room 11; 165 Main Street/Amherst MA 01002; 413/256-6698. Web site: www.shaysnet.com/-pagoda/

Mahdi, Louise Carus, Nancy Geyer Christopher, and Michael Meade, eds. *Crossroads: The Quest for Contemporary Rites of Passage.* Chicago: Open Court, 1996.

Mosaic Multicultural Foundation is directed by Michael Meade. They work with youth through extended retreats, mentoring programs, art projects, and public rituals. Contact: P.O. Box 364, Vashon, WA 98070; 206/463-9387. E-mail: mosaic@wolfenet.com

Somé, Malidoma. *Ritual: Power, Healing and Community.* Portland, OR: Swan Raven & Company, 1993. Somé describes the use of ritual in his native West African community which illustrates a powerful relationship between nature, people, and the spirit world.

Starhawk. *Truth or Dare.* San Francisco: Harper & Row, 1988. Starhawk offers ritual, myth, and story as tools for resisting domination ("power over") and structuring groups and leadership to maximize empowerment ("power from within").

Stein, Diane, editor. *The Goddess Celebrates: An Anthology of Women's Rituals.* Freedom, CA: The Crossing Press, 1991. Writings on ritual from women reclaiming goddess-centered spirituality. Includes essays on ritual planning and creating sacred space, as well as ideas for specific rituals.

Teish, Luisah. *Jambalaya: The Natural Woman's Book of Personal Charms and Rituals.* San Francisco: HarperSanFrancisco, 1988.

stories of ritual . . . .

Taquiena Boston

Taquiena Boston is an organizational development consultant and trainer who uses the arts and creativity techniques to help individuals, organizations, and communities empower and transform themselves. She's an African-American who descended from the Powhatan, the first native inhabitants of the Washington, D.C. region. Taquiena is a Unitarian Universalist.

CH: Taqueina, why do you think ritual is so important for communities that are struggling?

TB: Personally, what ritual does is ground me. When you enter ritual time, you're stepping out of your day-to-day concerns, and it's a way of looking at life and trying to get in touch with purpose and meaning. It's giving people a gift of time and attention, which to me is the most valuable thing we can give each other—that's what love is. So when we engage in ritual, we're saying that we're intent on making connection, whether it's with God or with spirit or with other people.

And ritual prepares us for spirit to enter, even though it may not enter every time. It's like when you're a performer. You practice so that one day you will hit the peak. You don't hit it every time, but if the muscles are primed, when it does enter, you're ready for it. Ritual constantly prepares us for our highest possibilities. Sometimes we have to transcend in order to transform, and it prepares us to do those things.

Do you remember how you first started thinking about ritual?

I was always interested in the ritual of church, which was like theater. And I've always been interested in the custom and traditions of various cultures and how they get played out in ritual. Then I began understanding that most art evolved from worship and ritual. It was just putting things together—the theater, the arts and spirituality, worship and community.

There was a theater that was written out of exposure to Western structure, and then there was a theater that evolved from myths and rituals of the African continent. Black theater artists started looking at Greek theater, which evolved from myths of ancient Greece. That took them into Africa and the Black church. They were seeking to bridge those worlds, so you had people talking back to the

> When you enter ritual time, you're stepping out of your day-to-day concerns, and it's a way of looking at life and trying to get in touch with purpose and meaning. It's giving people a gift of time and attention, which to me is the most valuable thing we can give each other—that's what love is. So when we engage in ritual, we're saying that we're intent on making connection, whether it's with God or with spirit or with other people.

stage. You had the incorporation of music and dance and storytelling and poetry, because that's what church and worship and ritual are. In all traditions, all the arts were present, until the Christian church threw them out.

What feeds you most among all of those traditions?

What feeds me most is dancing. I heard a drummer say that movement is healing, that it helps clarify whatever you have to figure out. Things can come to me, and I can see what I need to do if I can just move. I also love the sense of connection I get in doing partner and group dancing. The other day we were dancing a world dance. The instructor talked about having a connection and lining up with your partner, and I saw it as lining up hearts. That's what I'm trying to get, even with God: lined up. I may spin off, but we come back to each other.

Can you give me an example of a ritual from your own life that has been powerful for you?

When I was 39, I did a rite of passage for myself, because I had not gone through rites of passage that I thought I would have. I wasn't married; I wasn't a mother. I knew a transformation was taking place in me, and I wanted to mark it, so I invited a group of women I felt close to. I started us in a circle, with a story from *Women Who Run With the Wolves* called "Sealskin, Soulskin." I talked about someone who'd been living without their skin for so many years and that I had to go home. In the process of telling that story, other women saw themselves. They began to say things that I'd never heard them say before. The hope is that people begin to see ritual as a work of art that expresses their values.

And I know this has been particularly important for you when it comes to death and dying.

I think about it a lot because of that year, 1994. Angela, my best friend died at the beginning of the year. I feel her presence constantly. My father died six months later. The same year, a guy I admired so much was HIV-positive, and it had evolved into AIDS. We never got to see each other again; he died in 1995. So I feel now like death is a companion to me.

A friend introduced me to a book by Stephen Levine [*A Year to Live: How to Live This Year As if It Were Your Last.* New York: Crown, 1998.] One day I thought about that question: "What if you only have a year to live?" I looked at the leaves, and I thought to myself, "If I only had a year to live I would not be comparing this year's foliage to last year's foliage or hoping that next year's foliage would be more beautiful. I would appreciate the colors as they are in front of me and move out of comparisons."

Working with that idea makes me pause many times in my day and really look and experience the moment I'm in. How green things are or the pattern of birds flying or looking at a child's face and seeing what the adult is going to look like or looking at someone who's homeless and wondering, "What is this person's story?" and even why they may be where they are. And thinking about giving the gift of time and attention to people. Death is a gift that says "We don't have forever; don't put off living out what is really important. Be aware of all the gifts we are constantly being given."

Why do you think time and attention are so important for people to receive?

I see people struggling a lot to get attention. We call it status, we call it recognition, but I think that's why people do everything that they do. It's like, "Acknowledge me, I'm here." I go back to *The Color Purple* where I think it's Celie that says, "I may be Black, I may be poor, but I'm *here*." And when Shug says to her about God, "It does everything it can to please us."

Time and attention is how people say that they love us. Even though my mother worked outside of the home, I always had total access to her. If I was having a problem, I knew I could talk to her. It takes a long time to really know people, and you can't know them if you're not paying attention to all the messages they're giving you—with their body, their eyes, and the inflection in their voice. We can't know each other without time and attention.

How does this become important in the training work you do?

When I do diversity work, the youth are so thrilled that for once, somebody wants to know their opinion, what they think and why. I find that small, simple things work and give them space to express themselves. We did a "joys and concerns" where they lit candles. For this group, it was an opportunity for them to say what bugged them. They couldn't do it directly; they had to light the candle. This allowed them to step out of normal time and give each other attention.

When I go to the UUA [Unitarian Universalist Association] training, the people of color will say, "See us, we are here. We have things to offer." Alice Walker talks about how, as women, the world has tried to "disappear us." A woman in her 50s, 60s, or 70s is dealing with the fact that she doesn't matter any more; people don't care what she thinks. People put you in a box. It's an act of resistance, to refuse to let it be done to you.

> **We step out of normal time into ritual time. And by stepping out of normal time, we're focusing in a way that we don't focus if we're thinking about paying bills, washing the dishes, picking someone up, going to the store.**

We step out of normal time into ritual time. And by stepping out of normal time, we're focusing in a way that we don't focus if we're thinking about paying bills, washing the dishes, picking someone up, going to the store. I remember Joseph Campbell, and Martha Graham in a similar vein, saying that people want a feeling of being alive. Ritual is a means by which people get to the feeling of being alive, because it makes us step out of our ordinary time, consciousness, and relationships to experience them at a deeper level. Through ritual, we can give each other the gift of time and attention. It is also a gift we give to our perception of the Divine and to Life itself.

Ritual says: Pay attention to life, see it—whole.

ritual.

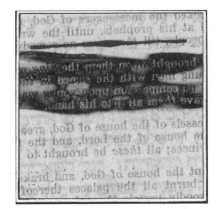

words and stories

Imagination is more important
than knowledge.
~ Albert Einstein

I refuse to become a seeker for cures.
Everything that has ever
helped me has come through
what already lay stored in me.
Old things, diffuse,
unnamed, lie strong
across my heart.
This is from where
my strength comes,
even when I miss my strength
even when it turns on me
like a violent master.
~ Adrienne Rich, *Sources, Part II*

questions for reflection

Do you keep a journal or find other ways to reflect on your life through writing?

When do you find yourself telling part of your story?

When do you hold back?

How do you learn someone else's story?

what are words and stories? . . . .

Natalie Goldberg, author of *Writing Down the Bones*, says, "Writers live twice." Writing provides a clearing process, a space to think thoughts, tell stories (real and unreal), communicate feelings, voice worries, process experiences, work through challenges, and dream big dreams. With words and stories, we can sort through all of the ideas and messages floating in our heads and get down to the truth. Writing and storytelling can be tremendous tools for spiritual exploration, vocational discernment, and community building.

There will always be the "unnameable"—that which cannot be easily spoken about—powerful experiences of love, of nature, and of spirit. Thoughts and feelings about spirituality, faith, God, and belief systems are particularly difficult to express but may flow easier when pen is put to paper. The kind of writing found in poetry or prayer may free us from having to fill in all the details or stick to a sentence structure. Regardless of the form, writing can bring about tremendous insight and healing.

turning point . . . .

In 1989, I am 22 when I become conscious of the value of journaling. I am working for the National Student Campaign Against Hunger and Homelessness, and it is my job to organize our national conference at American University in Washington, D.C. We work hard to get ready to host hundreds of students and administrators from around the country. There are meals to arrange, speakers to attract, workshops to plan, and logistics to coordinate. This means long days and little time for reflection.

The conference weekend rolls around on a clear day in October, and people pour in by the carload. The staff reconnects with friends we've made across the country and meets the faces that belong to the familiar voices on the other end of the telephone. Within hours, we go from a ten-person conference staff to a community of five hundred. The weekend is overwhelming. Intense and honest discussions about poverty in this country and abroad. New program ideas to bring back to campus. The Housing Now! rally on the mall, a gathering of over half a million low-income people, organizers, advocates. A big dance in the gym which gives everyone a chance to let off some steam. The energy is electric.

On Sunday, after a moving closing ceremony, I board a train for Philadelphia to spend Rosh Hashanah with my family. I am exhausted and drained, at a loss to explain the events of the last few days to my parents when they pick me up. Back home a few days later, I struggle to make sense of the conference. I am full—full of information, images, feelings, and questions. On a gray Sunday afternoon, I pace around my apartment, wondering what to do with all that is floating around in my head. By the grace of God, my eyes fall on a blank composition book, bought no doubt to use for conference planning and leftover, untouched.

Journaling itself is not new. I had always been a "Dear Diary" kind of kid, in love with the idea of capturing words. As a teenager, small books are filled with quotes, poems, and song lyrics. In college, journals are filled with long ramblings about the guy of the moment, the highs and lows of my social life, and a few laments about academic life. But when I pick up that composition book, I know somehow I am headed for a different journaling experience.

The story of the previous week is so complex that I cannot begin to tell it to another person. I need the sanctity of the blank page, the knowledge that this forum is completely mine to shape. The Danish philosopher Sören Kierkegaard said, "We live our lives forward but we understand them backward;" and so it is. As my words, feelings, and questions pour onto the page, I begin to process the experience, reviewing highlights, learning lessons, and bringing some closure to this rich experience.

words, stories, and social change . . . .

You can become a co-creator with God.
The act of writing is magic, one word, then another.
You create a world. You display a vision of the universe.

~ Stu Horwitz

It takes courage to tell the truth about our lives, who we are, and what has happened to us. When we begin to tell our stories out loud or on paper, we invite others to be witnesses. Somehow being seen makes us stronger. Storytelling allows us to share universal or cultural truths that we want others to know and understand. To tell the truth is revolutionary and liberating. We begin to teach people what we want them to know about us, our people, our community, our line of work, our struggles, and our joys. Throughout history, people have left written legacies, extraordinary accounts of dramatic times which open a door for others to walk through. Martin Luther King Jr.'s "Letter from a Birmingham Jail" is one example of this. So are Viktor Frankl's haunting and beautiful writings from a Nazi concentration camp in his book, *Man's Search for Meaning.*

And, our willingness to tell certain stories about the truth invites others to tell their stories. The impact of violence, the feeling of weakness, the sting of oppression, the shame of failure, the fear of mistakes—the details are intensely personal, but there is something universal about the feelings that result. Telling these stories closes the gap between us and another. It breaks the isolation of the pain, which can be as damaging as the pain itself.

Communities have vital and intricate stories to tell about injustice. Talk is a critical prelude to, and even a piece of, action. You're protesting conditions of something—a local housing development or a polluted stream or the relationship between the police and youth in the community. How do you begin to let others know what's going on? How do you start fighting for what you know is right? By telling a compelling story about what is going on. You talk to the press, to policy makers, to politicians, and to other folks who are being impacted by the same thing. Sometimes survival depends on the ability to tell a story well, to the right audience, at the right time. Enthusiasm and confidence are catching; people want to be informed and inspired. With a multitude of media outlets determining how, when, and if we hear a story, it is even more important that we master the art of storytelling.

rigoberta menchu . . . .

Because testimonies are the worlds of real individuals, they possess a flesh-and-blood authenticity lacking in the more abstract data of statistics and surveys. . . . Testimonies are life histories of women whose political engagement represents the core of their self-identity. Through their words, readers can at least partly understand the experiences of these activists absorbed in the politics of protest and resistance. . . . The evocative power of Latin American women's testimonial literature is great in that the women reveal themselves as the central actors in their own stories. They become producers of knowledge.

~ Kathleen Logan, "Personal Testimony: Latin American Women Telling Their Lives"

Rigoberta Menchú received the Nobel Peace Prize in 1992 at the age of 33 for her work to bring the abuses of the Indian people in Guatemala to light. While helping peasants resist the oppressive Guatemalan military regime, Menchú's brother, father, and mother were tortured and killed by the Guatemalan army. Menchú, a Quiche Indian, has devoted her life to overthrowing colonialism in her country, working through the Comite de Unidad Campesina (United Peasant Committee). Menchú learned to read and write in Spanish so that her story might be told more widely. Below is a brief excerpt from her autobiography, *I, Rigoberta Menchú: An Indian Woman in Guatemala.*

> *My name is Rigoberta Menchú. I am 23 years old. This is my testimony. I didn't learn it from a book and I didn't learn it alone. I'd like to stress that it's not only my life, it's also the testimony of my people. It's hard for me to*

remember everything that's happened to me in my life since there have been very bad times, but, yes, moments of joy as well. The important thing is that what has happened to me has happened to many other people too: My story is the story of all poor Guatemalans. My personal experience is the reality of a whole people.

activities to do alone . . . .

✏ write it down: start a journal

A journal is a record of experience and growth. . . .
Here I cannot afford to be remembering what I said or did. . .
but what I am and aspire to become.

~ Henry David Thoreau

Journal writing is a way to capture your story and your perspective. Journals also make room for writing that is emotional, personal, and tentative. Where else do we put these parts of ourselves? Journal keeping does not lend itself to rules. Do it whenever you want. Early in the morning and at night before bed are fruitful periods for many. Feeling like you must write every day can be death for some, discipline for others. All you need is a sturdy notebook, a writing implement, and some free time.

You can write without concern for grammar, writing style, sentence structure, or censorship. You can do it almost anywhere: alone at home, in a coffee shop, in the woods, on a bus or a plane, on your roof, beneath a tree. Sometimes 10 or 15 minutes is too long; other days an hour won't feel like enough. Carry a notebook around with you; you never know when the mood may strike you to write or you find yourself with some extra, unexpected quiet time.

Your journal might include:

quotes	lists	passages
prayers	words as art	poems
photos	colors	textures and materials
things from nature	description	dialogue
words you love	artwork	collage

℮ speaking in your own voice

Use your journal to explore: favorite ways to use your time; favorite people/ places/things; what inspires you; lessons you've learned in your life; what you believe in; seminal events and turning points; what you can do without in your life; dreams you remember; memories from your childhood; places your soul feels at ease; or a person who has been significant in your life.

Here are some questions to get you started:

What are my strengths?   *What are my limitations?*
Who/what do I love?   *What do I mock?*
Who/what do I need?   *Who/what do I fear?*
Who/what makes me sad?   *Who/what makes me happy?*
What do I have to give?   *What am I jealous of?*
Where is my path blocked?   *What would I like to see?*

You can do this journaling activity with groups. Use the worksheet, "Speaking in Your Own Voice," in the Appendix.

stories about work

Picture your work; what do you see?
What picture do you want other people to see?
Who are the main characters of your story?
Who benefits? Who does the work? If these are not the same group, what is the relationship between the two?
Can you think of a story that illustrates what you are doing?

℮ journaling for awareness

1. Awareness of self:
What is important to you in your life?
Recall a truly amazing moment you've experienced. Describe it.
What was the experience like? How did you feel at that time?
How did you feel afterwards?
What do you believe about yourself?

2. Awareness of the world:
What was your first experience working in a community?
What did you learn? How did it feel?
What would you change about the world? Who would help you?

Picture your work; what do you see?

What would it take?
Who would you most like to meet?
Where would you go and what would you talk about?
Describe a place that's meaningful for you. What is meaningful about it?

3. Awareness of spirit:
What does spirituality mean to you?
What is the difference between spirituality and religion?
What is the relationship between the two?
How do you know when spirit is present in your life?
What activities cause time to stop for you; what can you do for hours?
Who are your teachers?
Who are your students?

You can do this journaling activity with groups. Use the worksheet, "Journaling for Awareness," in the Appendix. Make sure that you have a quiet space in which to convene and ask everyone to bring a notebook with them. Have blank paper on hand also. You can do these questions in the freewriting style, with folks journaling on their own and then sharing their answers in small groups. See the section on freewriting below.

activities to do with groups: freewriting . . . .

℮ freewriting

Ed Chaney introduced freewriting to stone circles in the First Circle and during our Summer Training Institute. He had folks write for short periods of time about their passions, their relationship to spirit, and their commitment to justice. Then we took time to read them out loud. The impact was remarkable. Time and time again when I do writing or journaling exercises with groups, people respond positively:
– *I felt like I was really being listened to.*
– *Writing helps me release what is true inside.*
– *I always thought this required correct spelling and complete sentences, but I found out with free writing I can express my thoughts any way I want to.*
– *Freewriting opened me to my deeper, "unedited" thoughts.*
   I plan to use this technique for myself and in my work.

Freewriting can help people express themselves, and it can also release individuals from traditional notions of what it means to keep a journal. If a group is working together, freewriting is a way to remember how very different each person's perspective is. It's also inspiring to hear other people's writing, if people want to share.

℮ freewriting: the basics

1. In freewriting, you write for a set amount of time (usually five minutes) in stream of consciousness about a specific topic. Set aside a minimum of 30 minutes for a freewriting session. This is enough time to do two or three topics (see "Questions for Freewriting" below) and still have time for people to share at the end. Make sure everyone has a comfortable place to write, enough paper, and a pen or pencil. Provide writing boards or hard-back books if there aren't enough table surfaces to go around.

2. Each person writes for him or herself, so punctuation, grammar, and sentence structure do not matter. Encourage folks to follow their stream of consciousness, not to edit, but to keep right on going, even if it seems there is nothing else left to write. As Natalie Goldberg says, "go for the jugular," meaning go for the core of what you're thinking.

3. Each time you present a question or theme, give people five minutes to write. Have a watch or timer on hand. It helps to give a 30-second warning: "Thirty seconds left, so finish your thought or sentence."

4. After each theme, open up space for people to share what they've written if they choose. There should be no pressure, only encouragement. Or, you might ask people to pair up after writing and share that way.

Always give people the opportunity to opt out or find a different way of expressing themselves. Some people hate to write and will avoid it at all costs. Literacy levels vary widely and learning disabilities are more common than people without them know. This can cause great embarrassment for someone, and for you, if he or she is made to feel that writing is the only option. Provide suggestions for other ways to reflect on the questions at hand (perhaps through art—have some supplies on hand—or thought or movement) so people can opt out of writing without feeling self-conscious.

Also, don't worry if not everyone is getting into the exercise. Freewriting is introspective. Some people will be hungry for this opportunity and thank you profusely for it, as it will allow them to get back to something important they'd lost touch with. Others will stare around the room blankly, and you'll be sure that they are hating you. Maybe, but probably not. I did a workshop on journaling once for a statewide leadership institute in North Carolina. During the allotted time for writing, everyone seemed very intent, except for one individual who was clearly not writing. He approached me later and apologized, saying that he just wasn't into writing at that moment. A few weeks later he called to tell me that he'd been journaling ever since the workshop and to invite me to do a workshop on journaling for a new program he was starting.

warmups for freewriting

1. Powerful words
    Have everyone brainstorm a list of words that makes them feel powerful in their life and in their work.

2. Every picture tells a story
    Cut out provocative photos of a variety of topics: families, current events, travel, conflict, adventure, home life, nature, etc. Spread the photos on the floor in the middle of the room so all images are visible and ask everyone to pick one that catches their eye. Give people five minutes to write about the photograph.

TO READ TO THE GROUP:

Tell a story about this photograph. What is happening here? What happened right before the photograph was taken and/or right after? If you could add something to the story that this photograph tells, what would it be?

OR:

How does this image makes you feel? What does it remind you of? Have you seen something like this before, either in real life or in your dreams?

After this, you'll find that many people are ready to keep writing, and you can introduce one of the questions below.

questions for freewriting

What is the most important aspect of your work?
What is the hardest thing about doing what you do?
What does calm feel like to you?
What is beautiful to you?

Describe a particularly rough time you've had in the past year or two.
What place(s) on earth are the most powerful for you?
Write about one individual who has had a profound impact on your life.
Describe one time over the past couple of weeks when you were particularly frustrated at work. What was the situation? How did you handle it? What have you learned from it?

Add to the list by brainstorming questions relevant to your group or organization about what you are doing together and issues that might be of concern.

℮ back to the future: freewriting for strategic planning

When you use free writing as part of a long-term planning process, it gives everyone a chance to envision the future, generate possibilities, and set a more realistic context for the planning process. Ask people to imagine themselves and the group at a time in the future after the planning period has just ended. For example, if you're creating a two-year plan, ask folks to picture what life will be like in two years. Then, have everyone write for 10 minutes.

What is different about your life?
What is different about the organization?
What has changed in society?
What do you want to be able to say about the organization?
How has it changed?
What do you hope has been accomplished?

This is one instance when it's important that people share. Give them a couple of minutes to look over what they wrote and decide what they want everyone to hear.

activities for groups: storytelling . . . .

℮ storytelling

Gather people in your group for an evening or afternoon of storytelling. Start people in groups of three; have them answer the following questions:
What has informed your life story?
What aspects of history, culture, and tradition have been important?
Who has impacted your story? Who have you learned from?
What events in your life would help someone best understand you?

Come back together. Ask everyone to choose a story from their life to share with the group. Remind people that some of the greatest stories represent pivotal moments or turning points. Others might seem more mundane, but in fact, they reveal a great deal about our lives.

℮ name stories

One way for a group to begin telling stories is by telling a story about their name. Most names have a story attached to them. Ask each person in the group to share something significant about their name.

Where did it come from?
Do you like it?
Why or why not?
If you had the opportunity to choose your own name, what would you pick?

℮ spiritual stories

My friend David Sawyer runs a workshop on spirituality and service in which he has participants tell their "spiritual stories." It never fails to create a powerful group experience. David reminds people at the beginning that our religious traditions are full of stories, but we rarely have an opportunity to tell our own. Divide people into groups of three, four, or five; the important thing is to have the same number in each group so each group finishes at the same time.

TO READ TO THE GROUP:

All stories are holy, no matter what people have gone through or where they are now on the spiritual walk. Each of us has an inner journey. Each person will have five minutes to tell his or her spiritual story. Then there will be two minutes afterwards for the rest of the group to talk about what touched them in the story. No judgment or healing or fixing allowed. Please remember that listening itself is a sacred act. Then the next person will have five minutes to tell his or her story. This is not a group discussion. The power is in having each person speak vulnerably and deeply about his or her own journey and having others listen with an open heart.

Make sure you have a timer on hand. Announce, ideally with a bell or chime, when each person's five minutes are up, when the group reflection time is over, and when it is time to move on to the next person. When you regather as a group, ask people to share how they felt about the experience and what they learned.

Each of us has an inner journey.

℮ naming our history

1. First, have everyone do an individual timeline of their own life and what they believe is relevant about faith, spirituality, and social change. Don't give any further instructions than this; it's important that each person interpret this for him or herself. Give people 20 minutes to do this.

2. Then, begin the group timeline. On a large piece of mural paper, draw one line all the way across in the center. Ask people to begin by adding things from their personal timelines to this large timeline. Before they can do so, however, the group must establish some time landmarks to give the timeline a beginning, middle, and end. Leave time at the end to explore the lessons learned from collective knowledge. Some relevant questions:
   What seem to be the most powerful points in history?
   Why?
   What had folks never heard of?
   Are there any common denominators?

℮ analyzing the role of faith in history

For this activity, people need to come prepared. Ask everyone to think about a time when they know faith played a major role in social change work. When you come together, have people share their example in groups of four. The group should then look at the following:
What was the context/background of this example?
Who was responsible for bringing in the faith perspective?
What was the faith perspective? Was it multifaith or just one?
What role did faith play? What difference did the faith perspective bring?

Come together as a group and compare notes. What are the commonalities and differences?

℮ oral history

Oral history is the oldest history and the way we can best learn the stories of those who have gone before us. It is a great way to record details about historical events from those whose stories often go unheard. Think of someone whose story you'd like to capture. It might be an elder in your family or community. Discuss with this person the possibility of doing an interview or a series of interviews. Explain that you will be asking him or her questions and that the interviews will be taped. If you want to transcribe the interview so that it can be read on paper, let the interviewee know that as well. To do an oral history, you

Barry Hopkins, an art teacher and naturalist from upstate New York, helps his students make Earthbound Journals, a place to record their lives with personal artwork, words, and things from the great outdoors. They are collages that represent a moment in time or a walk in the woods. The multidimensional journals are more than just a scrapbook, though they might include items of significance: photographs, letters, dried flowers, leaves, and other items. Hopkins suggests the following materials for those interested in making an Earthbound Journal:

- an artists' sketchbook, unlined, at least 7 1/2" x 8 1/2"
- felt tip or rollerball pens, colored pencils
- aerosol spray to attach things; it lasts longer than glue

will need recording equipment (which you may be able to borrow or rent from a local library or university), blank tapes, a quiet space, and some questions prepared ahead of time. Think about this person's life and what you are most interested in knowing more about.

Spend the early part of the interview getting to know each other. Trust is a key ingredient of a successful oral history. You want to ask your interviewee open-ended questions; if a question doesn't seem to resonate with the person you're interviewing, move on to another question or ask it in a different way. Many colleges and universities have oral history programs; they can provide you with more information on how to conduct and transcribe a successful interview.

Minds Stayed on Freedom: The Civil Rights Struggle in the Rural South, an Oral History by Youth of the Rural Organizing and Cultural Center is an incredible collection of 15 oral histories of older folks in Holmes County, Mississippi. The histories were collected in interviews conducted by eighth and ninth graders. With so much written about the big-name leaders and organizations involved in the Civil Rights Movement, this book offers a different account. It provides the stories of men and women whose names will never end up in the history books but who worked for civil rights one voter registration drive at a time. The book also describes the impact of these interviews on both the young people and the interviewees themselves.

resources for words and stories.............

Davis, Donald. *Telling Your Own Stories: For Family and Classroom Storytelling, Public Speaking, and Personal Journaling.* Little Rock, AR: August House, 1993.

Feldman, Christina and Jack Kornfield, eds. *Stories of the Spirit, Stories of the Heart.* San Francisco: HarperSanFrancisco, 1991. Parables of the spiritual path from around the world.

Frankl, Viktor E. *Man's Search for Meaning.* New York: Simon & Schuster, 1984.

Frisch, Michael, ed. *The Oral History Review.* Buffalo: SUNY/Buffalo. This journal is published twice yearly. Contact: Oral History Association, Departments of History/ American Studies, 531 Park Hall, SUNY-Buffalo, Buffalo, NY 14260.

Goldberg, Natalie. *Writing Down the Bones: Freeing the Writer Within.* Boston: Shambhala, 1986. For people who want to explore their own talent for writing and/ or use writing as a spiritual practice. Short essays on writing and exercises to try.

_____.*Wild Minds: Living the Writer's Life.* New York: Bantam Books, 1990.

Ives, Dr. Edward D. *An Oral Historian's Work.* Bucksport, ME: Northeast Historic Film, 1998. An instructional videotape about checking equipment, researching, interviewing, and transcribing.

Keen, Same and Anne Valley-Fox. *Your Mythic Journey: Finding Meaning in Your Life Through Writing and Storytelling.* Los Angeles: J.P. Tarcher, 1989.

King Jr., Martin Luther. "Letter from a Birmingham Jail." *Why We Can't Wait.* New York: Harper & Row, 1963.

Logan, Kathleen. "Personal testimony: Latin American Women Telling Their Lives." *Latin American Research Review* 32 (1997).

Menchú, Rigoberta. *I, Rigoberta Menchú: An Indian Woman in Guatemala.* Edited by Elisabeth Burgos-Debray. Translated by Ann Wright. London: Verso, 1984.

National Storytelling Association sponsors a festival every October that attracts thousands of storytellers from all over the country. Contact: P.O. Box 309, Jonesborough TN 37659; 615/753-2171.

Nixon, Will. *"Call of the Wild."* New Age Journal, September/October 1996. A story about art teacher Barry Hopkins and his Earthbound Journals.

Progoff, Ira. *At a Journal Workshop: Writing to Access the Power of the Unconscious and Evoke Creative Ability.* New York: Jeremy P. Tarcher/Putnam Books, 1992.

Sumrall, Amber Coverdale and Patrice Vecchione, eds. *Storming Heaven's Gate: An Anthology of Spiritual Writings by Women*. New York: Plume/Penguin, 1997. A collection of poetry and prose written by a diverse and powerful group of women that addresses the search for and finding of spirit in likely and unlikely places.

Umansky, Ellen M. and Diane Ashton, eds. *Four Centuries of Jewish Women's Spirituality*. Boston: Beacon Press, 1992. An anthology of letters, prayers, speeches, rituals, poetry, and more from 1560 to today. This book brings women's voices back to the forefront of Jewish history.

Youth of the Rural Organizing and Cultural Center. *Minds Stayed on Freedom: The Civil Rights Struggle in the Rural South*. Boulder: Westview Press, 1991.

stories of history . . . .

Delia Gamble

Delia Gamble is currently pursuing a Master's degree in African-American Studies at Ohio State University. When I spoke with her, she was directing the Community Stories project at the Center for Documentary Studies in Durham, North Carolina. Community Stories is about the power to represent and define yourself. It is a community-based oral history project that uses young people to document their own stories and allows them to take ownership of the places in which they live. Originally from Washington, D.C., Delia is a graduate of North Carolina Agricultural and Technical College in Greensboro, North Carolina.

CH: Delia, tell me about your faith background.

DG: I've been a Christian for about eight years now. My faith has really grown from being something that made me feel almost better than other people, or as if I had something that they needed. I began doing Bible study with a friend. I listened and really learned Christianity, as opposed to before, when I could quote every scripture. I began to operate out of love which is different. You're coming from a completely different direction.

What impact has your faith had on some of the choices you've made about your time, your career?

Through the church, I've always been connected to groups of people. Whether it was a singing group or a singles group or visiting the sick, these were my circles, even my social circles. It's more about redemption, a circular thing. Just being a Black woman in this position is a coup for me. I really think God has placed me here, and I'm able to offer kids opportunities they wouldn't have had and I like that. I've referred to myself as a double agent. I'm aware that I'm Black and that I work with the Black community, so I'm here as a tool to gain access, but the access goes both ways.

How did this work become important to you?

I'll start with history. History was the major I settled upon, and I did not have Black history until I got to college, especially African-American history. It was eye opening. If you're a Black person and you go from a state of not knowing your history to knowing your history in six months, your whole perception of yourself has to change, and it did for me. I got excited and began to understand

> **If you're a Black person, and you go from a state of not knowing your history to knowing your history in six months, your whole perception of yourself has to change, and it did for me.**

what the possibilities are. With white culture, we know that you have your culture in front of you from day one. But to begin to know who you are is amazing.

I've always loved history, but in high school it was a means of escape. I would know everything by heart, because I was dreaming about being these people—kings, queens. Then it stopped being a means of escape and started being something that empowers me. I love it when it's visual and oral; it becomes experiential for me.

What is powerful about helping young folks tell the stories about their communities?

The goal is to work from this oral tradition where the stories are handed down, and then the stories are in them; they become the story. They know it by heart. That's the idea. Sometimes they learn it and have it for a couple of weeks, but it's the process of doing this and what they're exposed to—history lessons in the classroom.

We did an exercise. The Civil War has just ended, and your slaves are free. We put them into three groups: ex-slaves, ex-slave holders, and abolitionists. They had to make up new laws for black people, present them, and debate them. We talked about knowledge and power and what the slave codes meant in terms of control, what they could and couldn't do. They really began to get it. That's why history is exciting. I think that facts and what actually happened are important, but it matters more if they get the themes, if they begin to understand racism and how it works, what the possibilities are for them, and how to get there. I'm trying to give them a foot up in many ways. History exposes them to what is possible and gives them a better understanding of who they are in the context of the world.

stories of biblical justice . . . .

Carter Echols and Ched Myers

Carter Echols is the Canon Missioner at Washington National Cathedral in Washington, D.C. She coordinates and develops peace and justice ministries for the Cathedral, organizing churches to be more active in direct social services in Washington, D.C and around the country. Before her work at the Cathedral, Carter spent eight years as Executive Director of Samaritan Ministry of Greater Washington, a partnership of 38 congregations which helps homeless and low-income people create new lives for themselves.

Ched Myers is a fifth generation Californian living in Los Angeles. He worked for five years doing disarmament and antimilitary work, another five years with indigenous people in the Pacific Basin, and 10 years with the American Friends Service Committee. An ecumenical theologian who has published four books and numerous articles, he also consults for non-profit organizations. His itinerant teaching ministry is based on the conviction that we need to create a seminary of the street.

CH: How did each of you begin doing justice work that is faith-based?

CM: As a teenager growing up in a household that didn't have a vision of faith, I was asking: "Why bother? Why bother helping? Why bother doing?" And I didn't have a God concept so it was pretty wide open. I was impacted by the Vietnam War; my imagination was fired by the counterculture of the 60s and the peace movement. But in a few years I saw them peak and die. I was disillusioned. The vague idealism that was the 60s wasn't going to get it done. That was behind my search for a deeper vision, and there was this magnificent vision in the Bible. It made sense to struggle and work with poor people, because what is, is not the only way it can be.

But no one in secular activism was talking religion. There was a period of three or four years in the wilderness before I found people of faith who were politically active, such as Philip and Daniel Berrigan, dissident Roman Catholic priests who burned draft files, were arrested, and jailed. They became the religious symbol of the movement in the 1960s.

From 1973-1980, the anti-war movement unraveled, and the people who kept at it were disproportionately religious people. Only a few people were speaking out against militarism. The Berrigans were the people who helped me put faith and politics together for the first time. I went to Baltimore when I was 21 to sit at their feet, because here was power. I wouldn't have stayed in the church if there wasn't a political vision; I would not have sustained myself in politics had I not had a deeper vision of the work.

CE: I grew up in the church. For me, faith is about relationship, and movements are about relationships. Coming from my own personal neediness and questions as an adolescent, and knowing my own desire for inclusion, the words of the church offered such a promise. Even if the church itself wasn't inclusive. I bought into the dream of it. Somewhere there was a kingdom where everyone was okay, and we all had a place at the table.

> For me, faith is about relationship, and movements are about relationships.

For me it's been a journey through the institution, and the trick for me now is staying at peace with the fact that I'm a piece of the institution and have a ministry in the institution, because the institution is not necessarily the biblical story. If it wasn't for the faith element, I don't think I'd be in it. There are too many hard times.

CM: Why or how do you get into the struggle? How do you deepen it? I would not be doing this if not for the faith aspect. Why would anyone give up career opportunities, time, energy to do this kind of work with its relatively little gratification?

In America, we've got these root values, but our public society has betrayed the root values. I see all great civilizations or all dominant societies as made up of many layers. There's always a popular spiritual and value base that is close to the grassroots, where regular working folks are, and there's always an elite—the movers, the shakers, who usually espouse something quite different and attempt to appropriate the language of the people. The two have always been in fundamental conflict. The vision of America as religious, as peaceful, as hard-working, as thrifty, versus the vision of building a society to maximize wealth, the vision of empire.

And people read the Bible through their class filter?

CM: I do think different ways of reading texts are determined by what one has to lose and what one has to gain. That's a helpful dialectic through which to read American history. A vision of America that was fundamentally religious, was not the vision of the founding fathers. The founding fathers saw religion as auxiliary. The idea of progress has always been a vision of the elite, shaped through enlightenment, manifest destiny. Immigrants came to America with a vision of God, not necessarily a vision of progress. And our social vision is contested. Most of America would like to have safe neighborhoods, for example, but whether people actually think it's possible and that they have a role is another question. People at the top don't think it's possible.

But somehow faith makes it possible?

CM: Cornell West comments that churches may be the last institution that can engage the American public on nonmarket values. In fact, West says that "religion must be connected to public life in such a way that there is mutual respect, civility, and the protection of rights and liberties in our exchange." Religion ought to be robust and uninhibited, on the one hand, but equalizing—rendering accountable the most powerful and wealthy in society, on the other. West is interested in how we jump-start this process in a way that deals with patriarchy, class inequality, and homophobia. That is the fundamental challenge.

How might this happen? How do those of us who are committed to justice and consider ourselves faithful people begin to transform religious institutions?

CE: In my parish in Washington, D.C., we get together and talk about the scripture. Half of the people come from their own homes and half from homeless shelters. Everybody's got a spiritual journey, and it's an opportunity to be on the journey together in a way that has integrity. I really learn from those experiences.

When church says it's simple, we say, "terrific," since part of us longs for life to have simple answers. Churches are growing using market techniques and offering simple messages. How I personally get fed is different. What keeps me in the work is the visions of the kingdom that I get through my participation in events like the scripture conversation I just mentioned.

CM: To get back to Cornell West, there are very few voluntary associations left that have a language or a story that even talks about the poor, much less that the poor might have something to teach us or be important. The culture of merit is so relentless—whoever isn't upwardly mobile is invisible. But it's hard to read the Gospel and erase the poor, erase oppression. People ignore it, but to ignore it is not to erase it. As long as the Bible is still in our churches and synagogues, you still have the possibility. It's simple but subversive. There are not many places left where it's going to happen, not the YMCA, not the rotary club.

If I were an activist surveying the geography of American society today and said I wanted a grassroots movement to transform society, I'd choose churches and synagogues because they're everywhere: every neighborhood, class, race. The infrastructure is there; it's weak but it's there. The struggle to get them to be neighborhood centers is hugely important.

I have hope. An alternate vision of Sabbath economics is embedded in the tradition that we are still appealing to. It is a story that is increasingly anathema to the dominant story and dominant culture of capitalism. For a while there was an attempt to moralize capitalism using Judeo-Christian values but that project has disappeared so now capitalism is looking more like it did in the early stages—unrestrained. That's the challenge to our religious communities: continue to testify to a God that's not the patron saint of the capitalist order and may not be a perfect partner in the dance of progress.

What advice would each of you give to people who want to be a faith-based activists?

CM: First, we need you in this for the long run, and you'll only be there if you go to the roots and you find those wells to draw from. Do those wells have to be one of the great religious traditions? No. People can find spirituality through their politics. But in general, the older the tradition, the more wisdom is there.

We need people doing social change work in the long-term. To stay in it, I believe, demands that we have a vision bigger than my vision, older than my experience, and wiser than my intelligence or for that matter, the vision and intelligence of my movement, whatever that is. Because the struggle is older than we are, and we're not going to see it in our lifetime. A classic problem for activists is wanting to see the results and compromising the work to see the results. We have to think of the struggle in pan-generational terms.

CE: I would agree. Another way to say it is that it's modeling living into the faith, knowing that if we're committed to social change we always have to be open to our own change. It's the importance of the rhythm of acting and reflecting, acting and reflecting. It's easy to get one place or another. You think you've figured out the reflective piece so you just continue to act. You need to maintain both. That's also the practical thing to do since the strength comes from how they inform each other.

CM: And keep the conversation between ends and means alive. It has to do with practice and integrity. If you've got internal contradictions in your organization, you need to put time into that, not just say, "It's okay because we're working for the revolution." Even Lenin was big on the principle of self-criticism as a political principle, and Lenin was dead right. Most Leninists never practiced it. But at least religions have traditions like forgiveness and confession that invite us into self-criticism. That's wisdom.

> We need people doing social change work in the long-term. To stay in it, I believe, demands that we have a vision bigger than my vision, older than my experience, and wiser than my intelligence or for that matter, the vision and intelligence of my movement, whatever that is.

In the practice of your faith, what is most important to each of you?

CE: The first thing that popped into my mind was transcendent moments: moments in liturgy or in my prayer life or in my Christian activism in the world that I have that sense of something bigger. I don't know that I have better words for that. My faith life keeps stuff in perspective. I'm not God. There's lots bigger than I am. I sing evensong every Wednesday, and it's often just me and the boys in the choir and a few tourists, but it's always the connection with the story.

CM: This is the easiest question for me to answer. The most important thing for me in my faith life is also the most important thing in my political life: reading the Bible and always coming around to the story, trying to learn more about it. "Do I get this?" It presents such a profound alternative to the world we live in, and most of that alternative I don't grasp yet. It's like living in a paper bag and trying to imagine the world outside the paper bag, but I have this little book I read in the paper bag that talks about the world outside the paper bag. The other thing is real contact with the poor for me, both politically and spiritually— that is the bottom line. I believe the poor help us read the Bible, and the Bible teaches us to listen to the poor.

stories of writing . . . .

Ed Chaney

After graduating from the Univeresity of North Carolina at Chapel Hill, Ed Chaney worked with the Student Coalition for Action in Literacy Education (SCALE) for four years, two as Executive Director. A long-time writer of fiction and poetry, he is currently the Director of NCYT, North Carolina Youth for Tomorrow, an organization that builds the capacity of young people to serve as staff, volunteers, and board members in the non-profit sector. Ed was a member of the First Circle.

CH: Ed, why did you start writing?

EC: I really started writing with passion and vigor when I was going through a personally hard time. I came to the realization that my mother was going crazy, and I needed to process that. I needed to tell stories, and I needed the creative outlet to get through it. It was like a kind of therapy. I kept writing throughout my life, but when I started working in literacy I discovered another level of the power of writing: voice. And I mean that in two ways. One is self-discovery about who you are. When you put yourself uncensored on paper, especially if it's just for yourself, you're really surprised about what comes out. It's unbridled emotion, unbridled thought process. It's enlightening, especially on hard, big themes like faith, spirituality, social justice.

The other way is that once you put that all down, you realize the wisdom in your words, and you share it with a group. You realize the wisdom of their words. It becomes a powerful teaching and community-building tool, a way of sharing things that you wouldn't share in a normal conversation. It lends power and voice to the group, to each individual and whatever they're bringing, and it brings power to the group.

What impact has writing had on your life, your work? How has it been useful?

Social justice and non-profit work is not about institutions. It's about living intentionally and making change intentionally. In order to do that, you've got to break past the boundaries that our culture has set up and get to the heart of the spirit of the issues we're working on.

I think it all goes back to voice and stories for me. The philosophy I've developed around writing transfers into my community work, that it's important for us to connect on that level of being honest, deep, unbridled. That each person's story is powerful and needs to be heard if we're going to make any progress. And ultimately that's what the novel I'm working on is about. Unheard stories that need to be told are banging on my brain right now, telling me they want to be on paper.

> The philosophy I've developed around writing transfers into my community work, that it's important for us to connect on that level of being honest, deep, unbridled.

What advice would you give a group that was going to try a writing experience for the first time?

Make sure the space is safe enough. People feel like they're going to put risks on the paper. In order for those risks to make a difference in other people's lives, they need to hear the raw emotion. And for that to happen, people need to feel comfortable enough sharing it and not feel like they're going to get laughed at if their language is different or not as sophisticated. But you can build up to that. You can do safer topics up front to break the ice and get people used to writing and risking and sharing.

Can you tell me about a powerful time you used writing with a group, maybe within the stone circles context?

With the First Circle. We picked a free writing topic: "I knew God when. . . ," and everyone was supposed to fill in the blank. And then we made a book; everyone made a page. We gave them time to revise and decide what they wanted to put on that page and how they wanted to illustrate—collage, drawing, etc. We made a book of people's stories. It was a powerful learning experience on a number of levels, because I'm relatively sure no one had thought about that question before. It was a good reflection tool to get people to think about what that means. It was also good to capitalize on different learning styles. Hearing the stories and seeing the end product, it showed how brilliant and creative everyone was. Every page was powerful. It was all about personal reflection, journey, relationship. We could have gone a lot of places with that knowledge.

words and stories.

art

I see myself as an urban artist, using the entire environment that I work in, which includes the people in that environment. If I am talking about transforming an environment—changing, enhancing, making it more beautiful—then I am also talking about changing the people who live in that environment as well. The elements of my design are not just line, form and color but all the environmental and social factors that are inherent in the space and that cannot be separated from it. That's changing everything and not just the facade.

~ Judy Barca, *Making Face/Making Soul*

Art establishes the basic human truths which must serve as the touchstone of our judgment.

~ John F. Kennedy

questions for reflection

What are your first memories of making art?

What did you make? Did anyone help you?

Do you remember how you felt?

When did you make art recently?

How did this experience come about?

What is your favorite thing about creating something new?

what is art? . . . .

Art gives us a forum in which we can begin to explore—and trust—our intuitive side. Engaging in creation reminds us of the value of the process itself and the energy that creation brings into our lives. "Doing art" when you're not really an "artist" is a great exercise in risk-taking, in recognizing that you do not have to wait for special training, and in noticing that you have gifts yet untapped. In her article "Are You Creative?," Ann Cushman suggests that the primary purpose of creative pursuits is "to explore the act of creation as a spiritual practice, as a way of awakening to our true nature and contacting the beauty and mystery of our lives." We often build organizations and institutions without space for creativity to emerge. How do we begin to free up the kind of intuition that can usher in more of our individual spirits, revolutionize our workplaces, and increase our capacity to devise new solutions to entrenched problems? Bringing the arts into our daily lives is one way of doing this.

turning point . . . .

In 1993, I attend the National Service Learning Conference in New Mexico. I've been to so many conferences like this; I think I know what to expect. The first night I sit down for the opening program. The long flight and the time change have taken their toll. I am tired, and I haven't eaten all day. I wait for the program to begin, squirming in my seat. Happy to be there but somewhat impatient.

First I hear the drums. Then dancers emerge from all corners of the room and move down the aisles and onto the stage. A student dance troupe from the Armand Hammer World College—young people from all over the world—do a series of dances from four different continents. The performance is followed by a slide show from a Native American photographer, accompanied by live flute music. Okay, I think, I'm here. You got me. I'll pay attention now. The opening program transforms my mind set, shifts my energy, and opens my heart immediately.

The conference continues like this, filled with spirit. A roving band of troubadours from Spain make music and merriment in unlikely places. In the plaza outside the hotel conference center, people play music, look at exhibits on sustainable ecology, and paint a mural. Stories from elders are prominently featured. The conference highlight is an evening cultural festival with more performances, including an incredible improv theater troupe comprised of teenagers. I marvel at the sheer power of creation.

As human beings, we are born with creative ability, but most of us go through our lives being asked, in one way or another, to limit this potential. We're told to color inside the lines. To stay on the trail. To play the notes that are written. To spit back the right answers on the test. To follow the recipe. To follow the leader. Even with early exposure to the arts, creative muscles atrophy when not used. Suddenly, at age 25 or 32 or 50, someone asks us to participate in something arts-related, and we decline because we are not artists.

art and social change . . . .

When the artist is alive in any person, whatever his kind of work may be,
he becomes an inventive, searching, daring, self-expressing creature. . . .
He disturbs, upsets, enlightens, and he opens the way for a better understanding.

~ Robert Henri

Art gives voice to our deepest emotions—ecstasy, despair, angst, joy, and fear. There is something about the process of making art that transforms us, enabling us to come to terms with our surroundings, circumstances, frustrations, and dreams. Because creating culture is a way for people to define and represent their own identity and highlight their own strengths, art is a tool for empowerment. In cities and towns across the United States and around the world, art has always been used to chip away at old walls and open up new venues for communication. Here are examples of how art has told untold stories and built community.

the AIDS quilt . . . .

The AIDS quilt was started in 1985 in San Francisco by Cleve Jones. To memorialize the 1,000 San Franciscans who had died of AIDS at that point, he and others taped their names to the walls of the Federal Building. Stepping back from the tribute, Jones saw the resemblance to a quilt, and the idea of a memorial was born. Jones made the first panel to commemorate his best friend.

Think of the importance of quilting for women, particularly 50 or one hundred years ago. Quilts told the stories of families and family events. They were a way that women communed and connected. Today, this art form remains a tangible and collective process. Small pieces of fabric are often brought together into one integrated whole.

The AIDS Quilt brings people together and builds community in a way that begins to dissolve some of the fear, anger, and despair. When it was laid out in its entirety in the fall of 1996, just 11 years later, the Quilt stretched nearly a mile, from the foot of the Capitol building to the Washington Monument. Seventy thousand people were memorialized on thirty-eight thousand panels. The Quilt brings us face to face with the immense pain of so many deaths, disease, and the homophobia surrounding the virus.

The following is from a speech by Mary Fisher, an HIV-positive mother of two who founded the Family AIDS Network and put a new public face on AIDS when she spoke at the 1992 Republican National Convention. It is reprinted in her book, *I Will Not Go Quietly*:

> *Until the Quilt is finished, it is wise for those of us who remain to gather at the memorial from time to time, if only to remember—not so much for those who have fallen as for ourselves. . . . No matter how often we have been in its presence, we come to the Quilt tentatively, reverently, as one comes into the presence of something greater than oneself. We move from panel to panel, not only remembering but wondering. We see a name and we ask, "Why?"*

> *For those who share my virus—all those who are HIV-positive—the Quilt has a special poignancy. In remembering those who have gone before us, we see that every life has purpose and value, including our own. In hearing the names of those who have died, we remember that the meaning and legacy attached to our names will come in our living, not in our dying. As we walk amid the panels and our memories, we remember that we are human, no more and no less. And we remember this: that we are called to live with hope—not because we have all the answers, but because we have faith. And faith is the ability to live hopefully without the answers.*

making art, making change: what would you do?

Boise Peace Quilt Project started in 1981 when three people decided to make a friendship quilt for people in what was then the Soviet Union. The idea was to extend a concrete statement of their hope for world peace and their desire for friendship with "ordinary Russian people." The first quilt was presented at the Russian Embassy in Washington, D.C., and then found its way to its intended home in Alitus, Lithuania. Since then, the Boise Peace Quilt Project has continued to make peace quilts for people in other parts of the world and to give Peace Quilt Awards for peacemakers who are "blazing new trails to survival for our global family."

What are your greatest hopes for peace?
What medium might you use to express your hopes?
Who else would want to join in the creation?
To what part of the world would you send these hopes?

Culture in Action, a public art program in Chicago supported by the National Endowment for the Arts, funded many local artists. One man, Iñigo Manglano-Ovalle, founded Street Level-Video and worked with local youth, gangs, adults, and community groups to organize a video installation block party. 50 young people were taught how to use video cameras and then make videos about their neighbors and community. These were displayed on monitors set up along the street during the block party. On milk crates, in empty lots, and on the stoops of people's homes, 75 monitors offered an electronic look at the neighborhood's collective identity, linking one private experience to another in a public venue. According to one reviewer from *ArtForum* magazine, the narratives revealed, "a preoccupation with borders, generations, and isolation, but also hopes of reclamation and tolerance. . . what was visualized on the videotapes was realized on and reflected back to the block."

How do the people in your neighborhood experience each other's lives?
How could you deepen that understanding and connection?
Who would help you?
If you wanted to organize a block party with a creative component how would you begin?

Face to Face: Photographs by Don Camp and Laurence Salzmann chronicled the relationships between Jews and Blacks in Philadelphia. The two men—one Black, one Jewish—photographed individuals from both backgrounds whose lives had intersected in some way. The images run the gamut from congenial and familial to aloof and even suspicious. The exhibit portrayed Black-Jewish relationships in all their complexity, exploring issues of identity, history, belief, and community. Photographer Don Camp wrote about the process, "Myths and stereotypes, about ourselves and others, are still our primary source of information. We find ourselves unable, or unwilling, to investigate each other's presence and reality. . . I chose people to photograph who were simply unafraid to explore each other's presence."

What group(s) are you most interested in learning about?
How would you exchange this learning? In what format?
How and where would you display the results of your exploration?

From the Hip, a national photo-documentary celebrating youth activism and service, was initiated by Tony Deifell and the Campus Outreach Opportunity League. It began when 280 young photographers and writers across the country took camera and pen in hand and sought answers to two questions: *Does the public know who young people are?* and *What actions are they taking to strengthen their communities?* The result? A 13-story collection of images and words by and about young people that serves as a visual diary of their work in communities. The young artists told stories of the Berkeley Free Clinic; the Tommy Hill housing development in Newport, Rhode Island; and Fusion Cafe, a hangout for young people in Jacksonville, Florida. They chronicled the lives of a needle exchange program volunteer in New York's Lower East Side; a teen theater group in St. Paul, Minnesota; and participants in the Sex Offender Treatment Program in Giddings, Texas. Brilliant photographs and straightforward story writing created a moving and highly original portrayal of young people in the United States.

What story of community service and youth would you tell about your community?
Is there one project or organization or person you would focus on?
How would you document their activities?

YA/YA (Young Aspirations/Young Artists) works to provide educational experiences and opportunities that empower artistically talented inner-city youth to be professionally self-sufficient through creative self-expression. That means young folks learn how to paint furniture with hip, striking designs and make money selling it. Located in New Orleans, YA/YA also does custom work for individuals, hand-screens fabric, and works with school groups to design murals. There is a core group of 25 guild members and apprentices, and they reach hundreds more each year. YA/YA has their own warehouse and showroom, and their work has been exhibited around the country and throughout the world.

Who do you know who is teaching young people how to create their own artistic products?
What are they? How are they sold or distributed?
What talent would you want to share with a group of young people?

CCA Warehouse in Santa Fe, New Mexico and Appalshop in Whitesburg, Kentucky are two spaces that encourage artistic freedom and innovation in a number of media. See the "Space" chapter for more information on both.

activities to do alone ....

℮ start making art

Many of the activities in this chapter revolve around creating visual art. There are a lot of ways to begin:

1. Take a writing or drawing instrument and a piece of paper. Find an object or person that interests you. Without looking at the paper, and without lifting your drawing implement, begin to draw. Resist the temptation to look at the paper or lift up your hand. When you feel ready, look at the paper. Turn it around and look at it from all angles. What happens if you start coloring in some of the shapes?

2. Mix all your art supplies together in a bag or a box. Make sure there's nothing sharp. With your eyes closed, reach in and grab five items. Use these to create something.

3. Make a card for someone's birthday, anniversary, or wedding. You can use watercolor paper; many art supply stores now sell precut and packaged paper and envelopes for this purpose. What sentiment do you want to convey? What colors remind you of the person? Which images or shapes seem appropriate?

a word about materials

Start with the basics:

– White PAPER that's good for paint, collage, and drawing and construction paper.
– PAINTS (watercolor or water-based acrylics are best for cleanup, especially if you're working with kids).
– Colored PENCILS or CRAYONS, or even thin colored markers, the kind that come 36 or 48 to a set. You'll often find these cheaper in drug or toy stores than art supply stores, which tend to sell more high-end supplies.
– BRUSHES, old jars for water, and empty egg cartons for mixing paint colors.

Be creative when gathering additional supplies:

FOOD:	cereal, pasta, beans
NATURE:	leaves, flowers, grass, branches
HARDWARE:	old screws, nails, scrap metal, wood
MATERIAL:	fabric swatches, old curtains, bedspreads, clothes, ribbons, yarn, string
OFFICE:	rubber bands, paper clips, scrap paper, old magazines

Always be on the lookout for things that will come in handy for art projects and remember that anything goes. Once you begin to incorporate art into your life and/or your work, you are in danger of becoming an art pack rat. Find some cool containers to store everything.

In Durham there is an amazing store called the Scrap Exchange. Founded by Pat Hoffman in 1993, the Scrap Exchange gets companies to donate materials they no longer need. These are then sold to the public at very low prices. Among items always available are material, paper in all sizes and colors, wood pieces, foam in all shapes, ribbons, and funky containers. If you don't have a place like the Scrap Exchange nearby, perhaps you can get together with other people and trade materials.

activities to do with groups . . . .

the basics

1. *Think through the before, during, and after.* Give yourself plenty of time to set up and clean up and don't be afraid to ask for help. If you're using someone else's space, go the extra mile to make sure no damage is done. A big plastic tarp works well for floors. Make sure you've got extra newspaper and paper towels or rags.

2. *Extend an invitation to make art in an atmosphere of freedom.* Some people will dig right into an art project and most will eventually follow. Comfort levels will depend in part on how you set up the exercise. Remind people it's process, not product, that counts, that they are doing this for themselves and for fun. Suggest everyone work in silence or with quiet music. If some people resist, suggest a change in the directions. Be patient. Some folks just need time to sit with possibilities before jumping in.

3. *Help people to let go of judgment.* When you create an art experience for a group, you also have a responsibility to help them process it without judgmental comments. They may remember something that was squashed at an early age. There are a few ways to ensure that the process remains a safe and illuminating one for everyone:

   If you include time for verbal reflection, always let the artist speak first, about both the work itself and the process of creating it. Give some guidelines for feedback. It's important to use "I" statements here:

   I feel _____ when I look at this.
   To me, this piece looks like _____ or reminds me of _____.

   Evaluative statements, as to whether something is good or bad, are not appropriate.

Set up the reflection so that people are prepared for the impact. Natalie Rogers, who created the Person Centered Expressive Therapy Institute, suggests saying something like this:

> *Art has a lot of impact on us, so the group members will be responsive to what you have created. Be aware that the first thing to do is to discover the meaning of your art, for yourselves. Then, after exploring your personal meaning, you may ask for feedback and response from others. Know that when someone gives you an impression of your picture, they are giving you their projections. It is up to you to decide whether the feedback is useful or not. It is always interesting and fun to get such feedback, but it is crucial to understand the difference between a viewer's projection and your own understanding of yourself through artwork.*

4. *Create a silent space for looking at art.* You may want to have people just enjoy each other's work without verbal feedback. Have people stand in a circle, place their creations at their feet, and then walk in the same direction around the circle so they can look at each person's work. Or hang the pieces up and leave a blank sheet of paper or note cards next to each piece for anonymous comments about how the piece made the viewer feel and what they liked about it.

℮ collage

Collect an assortment of magazines, paper, drawing supplies, and whatever else you find that can be used for collage. Poster board makes a great base for collage. Collage is a great medium to start with when people are anxious about doing art. When a group is coming together for the first time, collage can be a great way for each person to portray themselves to others. This is particularly valuable if the group is from diverse backgrounds, regions of the country, and/or ages. Here are some possible themes to suggest to a group.

Create a collage that:
– *Conveys something about your roots.*
– *Represents God or spirituality to you.*
– *Reflects what you love most about your life.*
– *Reflects what you do and why you do it.*

At a conference for people in the non-profit sector in 1996, a colleague of mine, Jeanette Stokes, did an art workshop and encouraged participants to make collages from all of the "grab art" she had strewn around the tables. There were no guidelines other than to choose the images and materials that attracted us. Afterwards we were all asked to look at our collage, share it with the rest of the group, and notice what it was telling us. One woman, the director of a busy non-profit agency, showed us her collage, all photos of babies, children, and families. She sobbed quietly as she told us of her desire to spend more time with her three-year-old. Her experience of making art in an environment that inspired reflection was enough to bring forth her truth.

℮ group paintings

For this you will need water-based paints, brushes, jars for water, and one large piece of white paper for each person.

Have everyone sit in a circle if possible or two circles if the group is larger than 8-10 people. Give everyone a piece of paper and put the paints in the center of the circle. Ask everyone to choose or create a color they like and start painting. If they need more direction, ask them to sit quietly and think back over something powerful that happened to them during the day or the week. Without trying to paint the memory itself, encourage people to paint how it made them *feel*. Let people paint for a few minutes. Then tell everyone to pass their painting to the person on their left and resume painting. (Don't tell them ahead of time that they'll be painting on each other's pieces of paper.) Continue this pattern—everyone painting for a few minutes and then passing their paper to the left—until each paper makes it all the way around and winds up back with its original owner.

Spend a few minutes discussing what the exercise was like for people. The sheets can be cut up and made into cards or you can keep them until the next time you meet. Have people bring in prayers or quotes they want to share with others, cut the paper, and add their poem to the back or front.

℮ making music

If you can walk, you can dance. If you can talk, you can sing.
~ African proverb

1. Have people sing their name and ask everyone else to sing it back to them in the same way. This is particularly powerful when sung into some type of vessel such as a ceramic bowl. Bring the bowl up to your face and sing your name into it, in any tune that comes to mind. Then everyone else sings your name, repeating the tune you used.

2. Ask everyone to bring in a piece of music that moves them. Suggest that folks get in a comfortable position that will allow them to really take in the music. Turn the lights low or off; leave a candle burning. Sometimes the music speaks for itself and can be used as a prelude to something else—no discussion is necessary. Other times you may want to leave space for people to talk: What are the lyrics saying? How does the piece make you feel? What does it remind you of? What do you envision when you hear it?

3. Singing together as a group can be a magical experience and a powerful way to begin or end a gathering. Start with something basic, that most people know. Encourage others to bring favorite song they want to share. You are likely to have musicians among you; ask them for some assistance.

℮ making instruments

Making instruments from recycled materials can be done with kids, adults, and anyone in between. It is an inexpensive and fun way to bring out the musician in everyone. I've still never figured out whether it's more fun to make or play these instruments. The bonus here is the activity provides an opportunity to talk about recycling, where it happens in your community, what each person recycles at home, and why it's important.

- Materials for the outside: A container that has at least one open end that can be sealed easily with duct tape—plastic bottles, cardboard tubes, glass jars (don't use glass if you are doing this with younger kids)
- Materials for the inside: Anything that makes some noise when shaken such as beans, rice, birdseed, bottle caps, and nails. Consider how old your musicians are when choosing the appropriate filler. Have folks experiment with the sounds different objects make. You can get a lot of noise with just a little bit of filler.
- Materials to decorate the outside: paper, markers, crayons, stickers, paint

When instruments are complete, strike up the band. It helps to have one person volunteer to be the leader; they can set the beat for everyone else. If this activity is done outside, an impromptu parade can follow.

℮ mandalas: symbols of the spirit

When composing mandalas, you are trying to coordinate your personal circle with the universal circle. In a very elaborate Buddhist mandala, for example, you have the deity in the center as a power source, the illumination source. The peripheral images would be manifestations or aspects of the deity's radiance.

In working out a mandala for yourself, you draw a circle and then you think of the different impulse systems and value systems in your life. Then you compose them and try to find out where your center is. Making a mandala is a discipline for pulling all those scattered aspects of your life together, for finding a center and ordering yourself to it. You try to coordinate your circle with the universal circle.

~ Joseph Campbell, *The Power of Myth*

"Mandala" is the Sanskrit word for circle. Tibetan monks use them as a tool for contemplation and prayer. They can be created with a group to reflect on anything worthy of attention. We have used a very basic form: a white circle of paper the size of a dinner plate will do. Have crayons, paints, and colored pencils available. In the center, people can draw, paint, or collage a symbol of their spirit, spirit world, spirituality, or faith.

℮ fear mandalas

Fear requires deep work. Sometimes a group will come back to this topic two or three or four times before they are ready to dive in. One way to approach the topic of fear is through mandalas. The following exercise should be done in two sessions of two hours each.

FIRST SESSION:

1. Start out with an art project that is fun and light-hearted, like group paintings.

2. Ask people to sit quietly, relax into their breath, and identify a fear that is blocking them. Ask them to visualize a symbol for their fear. You may want to do this through the guided meditation. Use the full-body meditation for relaxation in the

mandalas

In the Eastern religions of Buddhism, Hinduism, and Jainism, the mandala is used as a tool for contemplation to encourage the spirit to move forward along its path of evolution. The creation of a mandala is a powerful ritual, accompanied by prayer and meditation, allowing the creator(s) to enter the state of being with the deity. The progression is one from outer to inner experience, all the way through to a point of unity and spiritual fulfillment.

The great psychologist Carl Jung discovered the mandala through dreams and artwork, not knowing of the mandala in Eastern religions. Jung used them often with patients. He believed the mandala was vital in healing psychological fragmentation because it both (1) restored a previously existing order and (2) gave expression or form to something completely new. No one mandala would ever be exactly the same as another, because each is an integration of a series of images from its creator that are projected from the psyche.

murals of a people

Diego Rivera (1886-1957) fused radical art and revolutionary politics on a grand scale. His majestic murals chronicled the history and life of the Mexican people. Rivera came of age during the Mexican Revolution of 1910, a time when artists and writers were often the conscience of their people. In the words of one biographer, "revolution turned him into a revolutionary painter—compelled to paint for the masses." And mural painting was an art form oriented for the masses. Anyone in the street could see them, and no admission could be charged. Rivera's murals adorn the walls of public buildings, so they have remained in the hands of the Mexican people. The murals detail all aspects and incidents of oppression in Mexico, from the Spanish who first conquered the land, to the landowners who ruled Mexico on a platform of corruption and great poverty. Magnificent works of art, they are also a powerful testimony to the struggles of the Mexican people.

"Meditation" chapter. Towards the end of the meditation, after everyone is relaxed, add the following: Remember to pause each time you see "..."

In this relaxed state, call to mind a fear that is present in your life... it may be a fear that is very old... that you've had for a long time... or it may be a relatively new fear... think about this fear... imagine it... do you have a picture of it in your mind... if it were going to sit next to you, what would it look like?... does it have a recognizable shape or image?... is it a certain color?... perhaps it reminds you of something or someone familiar to you... how does it make you feel, thinking about this now?... remember that you are safe here... recognize this fear as part of you... you don't have to be afraid of it right now... it cannot hurt you... you can simply notice it... it is here for you to work with....

Then, slowly bring people out of the meditation, using the end of the full-body meditation.

3. Once the meditation period is over, have people share what came up for them in pairs.

4. Using the information from the meditation and dialogues, the group is now ready to begin making their fear mandala. A symbol of their fear should go in the center of the mandala, making sure to save room around it. Request that everyone do this in silence.

5. After 20 minutes, have people wrap up. Ask them to show their mandala and talk about their fear. This will be hard for people. There may be laughter, tears, nervousness—whatever mechanisms people use to deal with tension. Go slow and honor the feelings that come up along the way.

6. People should take their mandala home with them and put it in a place where they can see it regularly. Suggest they spend time thinking about what lessons their fear. What will support them in their journey with this fear? Encourage everyone to make notes on the back of the mandala for the next session.

SECOND SESSION:

1. Starting in pairs, give each person seven minutes to answer the following questions. Have them written on paper for everyone.
    1. I'm glad/not glad to be talking with you about fear right now because. . .
    2. The fear I'm working with right now is. . .
       (*Questions 3-7 should each be answered three times. This is important. Given the sensitive nature of the subject, it is easy to give a general answer and move on. This is safer, of course, but does not get to the heart of the matter.*)
    3. This fear is most likely to creep up when. . .
    4. This fear deprives me in the following ways. . .
    5. The opposite of my fear looks like. . .
    6. My fear would hate it if. . .
    7. The cultivation of love would affect my fear in the following ways. . .

2. Bring out the art supplies again. Ask folks to start thinking of what they would want to surround their fear with, based on their answers to the questions above. The symbol in the center of the mandala should be surrounded by other symbols of those things which embrace the fear, that which might be opposite of the fear. Do this in silence.

3. Leave time at the end for people to share their finished mandalas and what it was like to create them.

@ art parties

This idea is inspired by an event that was held twice a year in Durham. The Art Parties were a chance for local artists to display their work. The parties began when a group of young artists were frustrated with the lack of gallery space interested in their work. They took matters into their own hands, organizing a party in their own house, which displayed visual art of all mediums. They made food and put out a jar for donations. Some art was for sale; some wasn't. Later, performance art was added in the basement: music, dance, poetry, video, and more. Within a couple of years, the Art Parties were attracting hundreds of people.

If you were going to throw an art party, where would you do it?
Who might help you? What artists do you know?
Whom would you invite?

℮ partnering with a local museum

stone circles has teamed up to do workshops with the Ackland Art Museum at the University of North Carolina, Chapel Hill. Ray Williams, the Ackland's director of education, and I designed one session in conjunction with the museum's "Circles of Divinity" show and a second for a show called "Identity Revealed." Be on the look-out for exhibits at local museums that are relevant to the work you are doing. Many museums make community education a priority; they might be interested in partnering with a local non-profit or individual who can bring a new perspective to a show, as well as a different constituency to the museum. The education staff will have knowledge of the exhibit and experience sharing art with people.

SAMPLE MUSEUM WORKSHOP OUTLINE:
1. As people arrive, give them time to tour the exhibit on their own. (15-20 minutes)

2. Short gallery talk by education or curatorial staff. (10 minutes)

3. Individual reflection time that allows people to go deeper with one or more of the pieces. Have thought-provoking questions available. Help people think about how a specific piece is connected to their own life. If the museum has the facilities and the inclination, do an art-related project For example, at the Circles of Divinity show, we spent time making mandalas in the museum's studio room. (20 minutes)

4. Share reflections in small groups. (15 minutes)

5. Closing and evaluation. (10 minutes)

resources for art...

American Museum of Visionary Art, 800 Key Highway, Baltimore, MD 21230-3940. 410/244-1900.

Blood, Peter, ed. *Rise Up Singing: The Group Singing Songbook*. Bethlehem, PA: Sing Out!, 1992. A wonderful, classic songbook.

Boise Peace Quilt Project, P.O. Box 6469, Boise ID 83707; 208/378-0293.

Cameron, Julie. *The Artist's Way*. Los Angeles: Jeremy P. Tarcher/Putnam Books, 1992. Cameron presents a 12-week program for reclaiming creativity based on two primary tools: the morning pages and the artist date.

Campbell, Joseph. *The Power of Myth*. With Bill Moyers. New York: Doubleday, 1988.

Chicago, Judy. *Holocaust Project: From Darkness into Light*. New York: Penguin Books, 1993. A personal account of a journey through the history of the Holocaust and creating art in memory of it.

Cornell, Judith. *Mandala: Luminous Symbols for Healing*. Wheaton, IL: Quest Books, 1994. Guide to making sacred art for healing the body, mind, and spirit. Historical information, inspiring meditations, and exercises for making mandalas and beautiful images.

Cushman, Ann. "Are You Creative?" *Yoga Journal*, September/October 1991.

Diaz, Adriana. *Freeing the Creative Spirit: Drawing on the Power of Art to Tap the Magic and Wisdom Within*. San Francisco: HarperSanFrancisco, 1983.

Fisher, Mary. *I Will Not Go Quietly*. New York: Scribner, 1995.

Goldstein, Ernest. *The Journey of Diego Rivera*. Minneapolis: Lerner, 1996. A great biography with a special focus on Rivera's murals.

Kent, Corita and Jan Steward. *Learning by Heart: Teachings to Free the Creative Spirit*. New York: Bantam Books, 1992.

Kimmelman, Michael. "Of Candy Bars and Public Art." *New York Times*, 26 September 1993. A review of the Culture in Action project, including the Street-Level Video block party.

Krishner, Judith Russi. "Street-Level Video." *ArtForum*, December 1993.

Ott, Gil. "The Village of Arts and Humanities." *High Performance*, Winter, 1994.

Rogers, Natalie. *Guidelines for Discussing Visual Art*. Santa Rosa, CA: Person Centered Expressive Therapy Institute, 1992. PCETI is a non-profit offering training in expressive arts therapy which integrates movement, art, writing, sound, and visualization. Contact: P.O. Box 6518, Santa Rosa, CA 95401.

Sark. *A Creative Companion: How to Free Your Creative Spirit*. Berkeley: Celestial Arts, 1991. Inspiring words and stories to free your creative muse.

Scrap Exchange, 1058 W. Club Boulevard, Durham NC 27701; 919/286-2559.

YA/YA, 628 Baronne Street, New Orleans, LA 70113; 504/529-3306.

stories of creativity . . . .

Jeanette Stokes

Jeanette Stokes is a Presbyterian minister and the director of the Resource Center for Women and Ministry in the South, an organization she founded in Durham, North Carolina in 1977. Through that organization and her life, she is committed to weaving together feminism, theology, social justice, creativity, and spirituality. She spends her days creating innovative programs in the areas of feminist spirituality and creativity, painting, writing, meditating, and dancing.

CH: Jeanette, when did you start making art and why?

JS: I made art as a child for entertainment. I started again in 1992 when I was 41. I had these three big disappointments: I didn't get pregnant, I didn't get a job that I wanted, and I didn't get a funded sabbatical. Someone gave me a copy of the *The Artist's Way*. First, I started writing every day. That is a practice I have continued. Then, my friend Jewel invited me to come over and play with watercolors one day. I liked it so much that I went out a week later and bought myself some brushes, paints, and paper and started painting on my kitchen table. I had been to a workshop and done real quick, rip out and slap down collages and enjoyed it. I did that with friends for a couple of years. In 1995, I quit my job and rented a studio. I spent a lot of time painting and writing and then took a bookmaking and a papermaking class and started making books.

When you quit, was making art one of the purposes?

It was one of my inklings. My first purpose was to do nothing for as long as possible, because I was completely burned out. I rented the studio immediately, which seemed like an extravagant thing to do since I wasn't generating any income, didn't have any way to pay for it, and didn't really think of myself as an artist.

And that transition really changed your life.

The Artist's Way says that if you start writing every day and listening to what it is you're saying you want, you won't be able to stand hearing yourself say the same thing over and over again without doing something about it. For me, art is about wanting and then getting what you want: wanting red here, right here in this spot, right now.

My job had devolved. I felt like I was nothing but a workshop organizer and publication producer. It had been fun and creative for a lot of years, but I was doing the same thing over and over again, and I didn't like it anymore. I knew I had to quit, because it had gotten really boring, really repetitive, and tedious. I wanted a more direct relationship with my own energy, my own inspiration, my own creativity. I get that from writing and painting and making things.

For me, art is just a way to strengthen my relationship with my own intuition. The more I practice wanting red, right here, right now and putting it there, the better I am at hearing and trusting what I want in life. I've come to believe that one of the ways the divine communicates with us is through our wanting. So I make lists of things that I want, not so much to get them but to just be able to watch the process of having things I say I want actually come to be. Making art helps that process.

How do you think this is connected to the way non-profits function?

When I'm tired at work, the image that comes to mind is trying to push dead weight. If I do that in relationship to art, what I get is really bad. The process doesn't feel any good, I have no relationship to the product, I just hate the whole thing. We do wonderful art and wonderful work when the energy comes out of the middle of us or off the top. When it's dredged up from these really tried, resentful places in us, it's not good.

In non-profits, people work way too many hours for the amount of money they might need to make or balance they need in their lives, and the work feels hard. Most of the people I know who work in non-profits are over-achievers, very responsible types who keep pushing way past the good energy. I'm not so sure that it's different from for-profit organizations, but at least people get paid a little better, so they have something left over to do something with. We value organizational efficiency really highly. I don't think there's anything efficient about making art. If I threw out as much work as I throw out art. . . and yet I expect every one of my working hours to be productive. Non-profit work has become so focused on being productive. That may be one of the enemies of creativity. I'm not sure.

Where might making art or other creative pursuits fit into shifting this?

It occurs to me that the skills that we employ in work situations are mostly the skills that I see among my friends who are trying to finish a dissertation: you keep doing it, long after you love it. You wind up with a lot of burned-out people and making art as a group can help loosen that up, but so can a lot of other things: getting people to say what they really want, what they hope for, what they like in their work. In order to get organizations to be more creative, they have to get in touch with what they really want, be willing to take risks and try new things, and be committed to the goal and ways of getting their heart's desires met in the work. The process of wanting, noticing, responding to what I want in making art, saying what's true at the moment, taking risks, trying things, being okay if they don't work out—those are all skills that are practiced in making art. They're really good skills in human relationships.

What have you noticed about groups making art together?

It's great as long as people stay focused on the process of making art and not judge the overall process. What does it feel like to rip out these magazine pages? You don't have to worry about where it's going. They stay delighted and connected to their own hearts. In an ideal situation, people in a non-profit are there because they love it. I remember when a friend went to live in East Harlem Protestant Parish. The man who ran the parish there said to him, "We don't want anybody here who thinks they ought to be here."

> I've come to believe that one of the ways the divine communicates with us is through our wanting.

What do you think the role of spirit or God is in all this?

Well to me it's all about God, it's all about spirit, it's all about mystery. I don't think any of us really know what we're doing or why we're doing it. The simplest example is that we don't know why our handwriting looks like it does. They're the doodles God gave me. When I paint, all I do is doodle with a paint brush.

I don't think it was until I started painting that I understood why people would say, "I didn't write that; God wrote that and I wrote it down." I look at what I've painted and I remember painting it, but I don't know why I made the marks I made. Why we see the world the way we do and why we want what we want—it's all very holy and very sacred to me. Which is why I get nearly hysterical if someone says, "No, no, don't paint trees like that; let me show you how to paint trees."

I lose track of that much more easily in a work situation, in the face of trying to get things accomplished. When I'm making art, partly because I'm not trying to make a living, I remember there is no place to go, there is no place we're trying to get to. It's like in a love relationship; it's like life. There's nowhere to rush to get to. All there is is living. I'm interested in the present moment, and art supports that. The present moment is the perfect teacher; it is always with us. Making art is about being in the moment. I asked a professional artist about this, and she said the only way for anyone to do work that is any good is to be present to the process. If you focus on the product, it is not possible to turn out something that is worthwhile. Making art is the way that I am the most often in contact with what I would call spirit or God.

art.

earth

Ask the beasts,
and they will teach you;
the birds of the air,
and they will tell you,
or the plants of the earth,
and they will teach you;
and the fish of the sea
will declare to you.
Who among all these
does not know
that the hand of God
has done this?
In God's hand is the life
of every living thing and the
breath of all humankind.

~ Job 12:7-10

questions for reflection

When do you feel a strong connection to the earth?

When are you most conscious of nature's rhythm?

Are you ever surprised by it?

How do you notice the passing of time?

what is earth? . . . .

The earth is our foundation. It is the very ground we walk on. It is vital to remind our feet, our hands, our eyes, and our heart that the earth holds everything upon it. We forget the earth was here long before we were. Before we built roads and skyscrapers, malls and houses, there were fields and forests and desert. The earth can be our greatest teacher about change, cycles, and sustainability. In the Book of Job, we read that the beasts, the birds, the plants, and the fish will teach you. So will the movement of the planets, the passing of the seasons, and the interconnectedness of life forms. As we observe, respect, and live in harmony with earth's natural rhythm, we learn to surrender to that which we cannot control.

turning point . . . .

September 5, 1996. Much of North Carolina is hit by Hurricane Fran. Not content to stay on the coast, the strong storm surges inward, bringing 70 mph winds and rain with her. She announces her arrival in Durham around 2:00 A.M. Venturing tentatively out of the house and into the front yard, I soon become mesmerized. This storm is beauty, drama, and power spilling out over the skies. Winds blow harder and faster than I've even seen. The trees sway, and the rain pours down in waves.

Before sunrise, trees have crushed cars and houses; natural debris litters every street. Hundreds of thousands of people are without power, and we are unable to drink our water for five days. I am one of the lucky ones; trees have fallen only across the lawn, rather than on a car or a part of the house. Folks everywhere express new levels of goodwill and camaraderie. It has taken a natural disaster to remind people how important neighbors are. Most of us are shaken out of any misconceptions we had about what authority we can exercise over the natural world around us. Before our eyes, our relationship to the earth has been redefined, and so has our relationship to one another.

earth and social change . . . .

Loving relationships are rooted in trust, truthful communication, and mutual respect. Our relationship with the Earth can also be described in these terms.

~ James A. Swan, *Sacred Places*

We can tell a lot about a society, a town, or a culture by how it treats the earth. When communities are aligned with values of cooperation and unity,

(continued top of next page)

stewardship for the planet emerges as a central tenet. As we cultivate a sense of reverence for each other and for ourselves, we nurture the same for the earth. Similarly, when we show disregard, it pervades many aspects of our being. As we assert our power for personal gain or economic growth, domination prevails—over others and over the earth.

The impact of this is evident everywhere. The Triangle area where I live in North Carolina is experiencing unparalleled growth in almost every direction. By the year 2020, our state's population will be over 8.5 million people, an increase of 31% in just 30 years. What implications does this have for our future? Every major road has been widened at least once since I moved here in 1992. Mega stores pop up where there used to be fields. Homes are built at a staggering rate. Only now, amidst this frenzy, have policy makers begun to talk about managing growth. But an inordinate amount of land has been cultivated at lightening speed; entire ecosystems which cannot be replaced have been wiped out.

All of the world's religions stress the interdependence between humanity and creation. Leviticus 25:3-5 tell us, "Six years you shall sow your field, and six years you shall prune your vineyard, and gather in its fruits; but in the seventh year there shall be a Sabbath of solemn rest for the land." On every seventh day, the Sabbath, humans must rest. Any attempts to control forces of production, namely labor and the land, are interrupted. During the sabbatical year, or the seventh year, the land must be allowed to lie fallow. After 49 years, there is a Jubilee year. In this 50th year, God commands that all land is returned and redistributed, preventing any mass accumulation of land. Through this Biblical text, we can see the relationship between how we treat each other and how we treat the earth. As one relationship deteriorates, so does the other. Just as people need rest, so does the earth.

activities to do alone . . . .

 the earth's rhythm

> *Don't push the river; it flows by itself.*
> ~ Zen saying

As mainstream society moves further away from the natural world, we lose touch with its structure, its regularity, its rhythm. In the spring, living things revive and life is renewed. Birds lay eggs, plants send out new shoots, and animals emerge from hibernation. With this rebirth, we feel hope, freedom, and a sense of possibility. In summer, nature is at her peak, creating and sustaining life. In the fall, the bounty is harvested, and we prepare for the winter ahead, a time of turning inward.

What is your favorite season? Why?

What do you associate with each of the four seasons?

What changes are you most aware of, internally and externally?

℮ learning from the earth

Think about what the most common, simplest forms in nature represent. To begin to understand what wisdom lies in these forms, we must spend time with them. This is not an intellectual exercise. Pick one, get close to it, and begin.

℮ soil

Pick up a handful of dirt.

Where do you find dirt?

How does it contribute to other life forms and the overall ecosystem?

When it's in your hand, what does it remind you of?

What is the dirt like closest to the place where you live?

How far away is it from your front door? What is it used for?

What lies in this soil?

How would you bring it inside with you? What would you do with it?

℮ river

Go to the river nearest your home and sit beside it.

Where does this river start and where does it end? Have you ever been to either place?

What lies on its banks?

What is it a boundary of?

How high is the river and how fast does it flow? What alters its course?

What is the sound of water moving?

Like many earth-based spiritual traditions, Wicca draws a connection between the four directions—East, South, West and North—with the four elements: air, fire, water, and earth. This relationship is invoked at most rituals and ceremonies. Each of the elements augment human power with their energy. Air belongs to the East, and it rules over the mind, creativity, knowledge, and communication. This direction offers inspiration and insight. Fire is the element of the South. It is faithful and energetic and rules the spirit, healing, and the sun. Water is the element of the West. Its power is intuitive, receptive and compassionate. Water rules emotions, love, and courage. Earth is in the North, and it is the seat of wisdom. Earth rules the body, nature, silence, birth, and death.

What does it remind you of?

Throw a leaf into the river. What happens? *Try a stick. Then a small stone. A bigger rock.* What impact does each of these have on the water?

℗ tree

Find a tree you like and touch it in different places.
What kind of tree is this? How old do you think it is?
What do the roots look like?
What is the relationship between the branches and the trunk?
How are they similar? How are they different?
Do the branches remind you of something? How easily do they move?
Look at the bark. Get even closer. What images do you see?
What does this tree shade?

℗ ocean

If you are lucky enough to find yourself by the ocean, make the most of it.
How quickly do the waves seem to come into the shore?
How high are they? How wide?
What patterns do you see in the waves?
Do they remind you of anything?
What does the ocean sound like? Is there a rhythm?
How does it change?
What colors do you see? What do you smell?
Pick up a handful of sand.
How many variations does the sand have?
Can you separate the grains?
What does the texture remind you of?
Where do you think it came from?
Dig deeper into the sand. What changes?

℗ sun

Choose a cool day when they sun is out. Sit outside where the trees do not block the sun. Look straight ahead.
What evidence of the sun do you see?
Where do you see shadows? Where do you see light?
Wait five minutes. Has anything changed? What is different?
Close your eyes. Where on your body do you feel the sun's warmth.
Turn you face towards the sun, leaving your eyes closed. What changes?

activities to do with groups . . . .

paying homage to the natural world

Have everyone bring in one thing that they have from the natural world that is meaningful to them. Ask each person to tell a story about it: where it came from, how and when they got it, what it means to them now. Create a living collage with all of the objects. Leave it in a place where everyone can see it for a while.

nature walk

This might be in the woods, in a nearby park, by a river, or in the mountains. Even folks living in a big city can probably get to a good walking place in less than an hour. Spend the day. Find things you've never seen before. Together, make a mental list of what is new. While you are there, try the following two activities, both of which I learned at the Haw River Festival. (See *stories of the earth: Richard Goldberg* at the end of this chapter for more information on the festival.)

find your tree

Start outside in a central place. Have everyone get a partner; one person in each pair should then be blindfolded. The seeing partner leads the blindfolded partner to a tree, being careful not to let her trip or run into anything. Once in front of the chosen tree, let the blindfolded person get to know the tree without seeing by touching it and the area around it. When the blindfolded partner thinks she has gotten a "feel" for the tree, the seeing partner leads the other person back to the central spot. It's good to do some things to throw the blindfolded person off the trail—spin them around a few times or take a longer route back. The blindfold comes off, and the person has to find the tree. Switch so the other person gets a chance.

photographs

In pairs, have one person be the blindfolded "camera" and the seeing partner be the "photographer." The photographer leads the camera to a spot he wants the camera to see and photograph. When the camera is in front of the potential picture, the photographer takes off the blindfold so the camera can take a photo in his mind. Then the blindfold is replaced. Partners should do this three times before switching. Encourage the photographers to choose pictures that are unique or beautiful in some way. For groups wanting a challenge, ask the photographer to lead the camera back to a central spot and then find the subjects of his photographs.

Find things you've never seen before.

permaculture

Permaculture is a global, grassroots movement towards sustainability, cooperation, and equality. It is based on an ethic of (1) caring for the earth in such a way that all life systems continue and multiply and (2) human access to resources necessary for existence, without accumulation of wealth or land beyond need. According to the Bay Area Permaculture Group, "Permaculture designs and nurtures agriculturally productive ecosystems which have the stability, diversity and resilience of natural ecosystems." Developed in 1970s in Australia by Bill Mollison and David Holmgren, Permaculture adopts techniques and principles from old and new traditions. These include: renewable energy sources, soil and water conservation, sustainable agriculture, and appropriate technology.

℗ start a community garden

I love people to a certain extent.
But sometimes I want to get off in the garden to talk with God.
I have the blooms and when the blooms are gone,
I love the green.
God dressed the world in green.

~ Minnie Evans, self-taught artist

Will Atwater is the garden director at SEEDS, a community gardening organization in Durham. He offers the following suggestions for groups wanting to start their own garden.

1. As a group, start by visualizing the kind of garden you want to have. Where can you see the garden? Will it have vegetables? Flowers? Both? Will you break your space into individual plots or garden as a group, which requires more cooperation? (For groups starting out, Will recommends that each person or family tend their own spot.)

2. Find a location that is accessible to everyone. Make sure it gets at least one-half day of sunlight. Consider where the closest water source is.

3. Do a soil test for quality. In many states, the local agriculture extension office will provide soil testing kits free of charge. You collect samples of the soil and send it to them, along with information about what you want to grow. They will analyze the soil and make helpful recommendations for planting. If you find a good location that doesn't necessarily have great soil, Will recommends building a raised bed and bringing in your own soil.

4. Find a planting guide at the bookstore or library. This will tell you when to plant what, how long it will take for a plant to grow to maturity, how much water it needs, and other vital information.

   To see if there is already a community gardening group in your area, contact the American Community Gardening Association, listed in "Resources for the Earth" at the end of the chapter.

℮ your piece of earth

Environmental groups speak of "carrying capacity"—the largest number of any given species that a habitat can support indefinitely *without environmental damage*. For example, when forests are clear-cut, the surrounding region's capacity to purify the air, moderate temperatures, stabilize soil, protect watersheds, preserve biodiversity, and preserve cultural, spiritual, and recreational space is greatly reduced. Start by figuring out who in your community might have answers to the questions below. Try your county or state department of environmental protection and natural resource agencies.

What is the capacity of the watershed to absorb waste and pollution while providing safe drinking water at the same time?

Are agricultural and natural ecosystems adequately protected?

How are natural, recreational, and historical areas in your community preserved?

How will the local biological diversity be protected?

How available is public transit in your area?

Where are the wild, untouched areas in your community?

What do you know about them?

medicine wheels

The Medicine Wheel dance has had a strong beginning. In the late 1970s, Spirit gave me a powerful vision. In this vision I saw a hilltop bare of trees. A soft breeze was blowing, gently moving the prairie grass. I saw a circle of rocks that came out like the spokes of a wheel. Inside this large circle was another circle of rocks, nearer to the center. As I was looking at this vision, I knew this was the Sacred Circle, the hoop of my people.

~ Sun Bear,
Dancing with the Wheel

The Native American medicine wheel is laid out on the ground with stones and other natural elements. It is a vital element in cultures where the earth is respected and protected. Each element can help human beings remember their sacred connection to nature. It begins with a circle and four spokes for the four directions: East, West, North, and South, symbolizing the universe and each person's place in it. Each of the four directions represents a different attribute. The wheel becomes a cosmic diagram.

resources for the earth . . . .

American Community Gardening Association, 100 N. 20th Street, 5th Floor, Philadelphia, PA 19103; 215/988-8785.

Anderson, Lorraine. *Sisters of the Earth*. New York: Vintage Books, 1991. Women's prose and poetry about nature from over 90 poets and writers including Annie Dillard, Alice Walker, Adrienne Rich, and Emily Dickinson.

Bernstein, Ellen and Dan Fink. *Let the Earth Teach You Torah*. Philadelphia: Shomrei Adamah, 1992. A practical guide for learning and teaching Judaism's approach to the environment, ecological crises, and the wisdom of the earth. Shomrei Adamah runs educational programs and retreats. Contact: 5500 Wissahickon Ave, #804C, Philadelphia, PA 19144; 215/844-8150.

Berry, Thomas. *The Dream of the Earth*. San Francisco: Sierra Club Books, 1988. A collection of essays on the environment and how humans might reconcile with the earth.

Bradley, Fern Marshall and Barbara W. Ellis, eds. *Rodale's All-New Encyclopedia of Organic Gardening*. Emmaus, PA: Rodale Press, 1972.

Cohen, Gary. "Toward a Spirituality Based on Justice and Ecology." *Social Policy*, Spring, 1996.

Coleman, Eliot. *The New Organic Grower*. Chelsea, VT: Chelsea Green, 1989. Manual of tools and techniques.

Findhorn Community. *The Findhorn Garden: Pioneering a New Vision of Man and Nature in Cooperation*. New York: Harper Perennial, 1975. The amazing account of the ecological community in Findhorn, Scotland, begun on just a plot of land in a trailer park.

LaChapelle, Dolores. *Sacred Land, Sacred Sex: Celebrating Deep Ecology and Celebrating Life*. Silverton, CO: Finn Hill Arts, 1988. Resource for returning to the magic within the earth and within ourselves. Includes a broad range of commentary, history, poetry, and practical suggestions.

Mollison, Bill. *Permaculture: A Practical Guide for a Sustainable Future*. Washington, DC: Island Press, 1990.

National Religious Partnership for the Environment is a coalition of religious organizations and denominations united by a biblical and religious responsibility to protect the environment. Each denomination develops the strategy and materials it needs to reach its constituency. Contact: 1047 Amsterdam Avenue, New York NY 10025; 212/ 316-7441.

Sierra Club. *Saving for the Future: A Guide to Local Carrying Capacity*. Washington, DC: Sierra Club. Contact: Sierra Club Local Carrying Capacity Campaign, 408 C Street, NE, Washington, DC 20002; 202/547-1141. E-mail: scdc1@igc.org

Starhawk, *The Spiral Dance: A Rebirth of the Ancient Religion of the Great Goddess*. New York: Harper & Row, 1989. Earth-based rituals from the practice of Wicca.

Swan, James A. *Sacred Places: How the Living Earth Seeks Our Friendship*. Santa Fe: Bear & Company, 1990.

Williams, Terry Tempest. *Refuge: An Unnatural History of Family and Place*. New York: Pantheon, 1992. In this moving personal account, Williams parallels the environmental turmoil resulting from the rising of Great Salt Lake in Utah with the turmoil of her mother's losing battle with cancer.

stories of the earth . . . .

Richard Goldberg

Richard Goldberg holds a doctorate in biomedical engineering and is currently a freelance educator and researcher. In his paid work, he has researched the eco-location used by bats and primitive human versions of the same thing, such as medical ultrasound. He has also worked on assistive technology devices for disabled kids. In his "other" life, Richard volunteers with the Haw River Festival, with Demario (a 13-year-old he met through a Big Brother program six years ago), and with Habitat for Humanity.

CH: Rich, you always strike me as someone very connected to the earth. Tell me about how this connection began for you.

RG: As a kid, our house had a lot of woods behind it and a creek, and I used to love playing out there. I had all that growing up. We lived there until I went to college. In college I got away from it. Bucknell was a beautiful place, but I didn't feel connected; I didn't take a lot of walks. When I moved here someone told me about Duke Forest early on, and I used to walk out there a lot. There were so many natural areas around here; it rekindled my connection with nature.

You've been committed to the earth on both personal and political levels. What about being outside feeds you personally?

I love walking in the woods. The other day it occurred to me that being in nature is such a spiritual place, because I'm away from all the distractions and all the human creations in the regular world. Just being around all natural objects that were created by God or some other force makes me feel closer to spirit.

It's where I go to think. It's where I go to get away from things. It's my personal retreat. Today at lunch I was processing some information. I stopped at Duke Chapel and sat there and then went to Duke Gardens and wandered around there. That's how I connect with myself. Today, I watched a duck family for 20 minutes—that's what I need to recharge myself. It was interesting watching all the little battles and their interactions and comparing them to human interactions.

> I love walking in the woods. The other day it occurred to me that being in nature is such a spiritual place, because I'm away from all the distractions and all the human creations in the regular world.

And how does this connection manifest itself on a political level?

I've always been ahead of the mainstream in basic environmental stuff, like minimizing driving and recycling. But it's really through the Haw River Festival where it really became important to me. In some ways it isn't political, because you're only working with one kid or 10 kids at a time, but I feel it is really political, because you're trying to change the way people view the earth.

How long have you been involved with the festival and how would you describe it?

Four years. It is an environmental education program for fourth graders that seeks to go beyond traditional environmental education by establishing connections with and an appreciation for nature—just by having them notice things with all their senses. And at the same time it tries to build community among the volunteers.

The first year, I helped plan, but I really didn't know what to expect when I went out there. Every year since then, I've helped plan the festival, and I'm also on the board of directors of the Haw River Assembly. The most important thing about it is that it challenges me to do things I've never done before, so I learn a lot about myself.

Such as?

How to get up in front of a 120 kids and sing. That people respect me when I try to delegate responsibility in stressful situations. Another thing about being out there is that it's a real positive, supportive atmosphere where every person, no matter what their age, is important. I brought Demario, and for someone like him, who had been kicked out of school for insubordination numerous times, to get all the positive reinforcement is really important. The atmosphere is why you can experiment and try new things that you've never done before. On a practical level, it's why the program runs as well as it does.

And it has a big impact on the fourth graders as well.

There are a number of volunteers who had come to the festival as fourth graders. You ask them what they remember, and they'll say they remember playing some games and playing with clay. But it affected them on a deeper level, which is why they return to the festival as volunteers.

The fourth graders get to use their senses. It was really apparent last week, because the river was so loud and if you put on your "deer ears" and faced the river, you heard all river, and if you turned around, you heard all birds. And the kids found, without prompting, a snake that was pretty well camouflaged. Kids got excited over every turtle, cicada, and other living things they saw and heard. I would hope they took that away with them, and I think they do.

Tell me about your faith background and what connection, if any, that has with all this earth-based work you do.

I grew up in a conservative Jewish tradition, jumped through all the hoops and hated it and made that known by getting in trouble all the time. One of the reasons I hated Hebrew School was because every Tuesday and Thursday afternoon it meant I was inside instead of outside playing. My friend Deb exposed me to how Judaism could be transformed into something that was consistent with my values. I continue to celebrate Jewish holidays with my friends. On Yom

Kippur, we fast and spend the day sitting on a riverbank. On Passover, we have a "non-traditional" seder that still incorporates all the Passover traditions. My faith ties strongly into my connections with nature, and I think a lot of the way my faith developed is because of my appreciation and fascination with life around me. I'm not sure how to be more specific than that. I just think that living things, including humans, are so amazing. That has given me faith.

How would you describe that faith?

I believe all living things are connected, and all living things are connected to non-living things, too. And that there's some force that makes that connection. There's this book I have, *The Way Life Works* written by a cell biologist, [Mahlon Hoagland and Bert Dodson; New York: Times Books, 1995] about how a cell works, and how every living thing works the same way. And that's neat because it ties it in from a scientific perspective as well, which is also a big part of me. I think the scientific and the spiritual are really related.

Maybe "related" is the wrong word, but they are a reflection of each other. They're sort of in parallel and what works on a spiritual level will also work on a scientific level. From a spiritual level, I believe all things are related, and the science agrees with that.

> Like watching the ducks today. In many ways, their interactions were very human, or maybe our interactions are very duck-like.

Like watching the ducks today. In many ways, their interactions were very human, or maybe our interactions are very duck-like. And you see so many parallels; there are so many ways that things are interrelated in nature. The fact that the physiology behind how they work is the same, then it just makes sense.

If you were speaking with someone who didn't have a connection with the earth and wanted to develop one, what would you tell them?

I would tell them to go and find a quiet place out in the woods and to just sit there. Maybe write down what you see and feel and hear and smell. I think writing down is an important step because it just reinforces everything. It makes you notice things a little bit more. It keeps you focused. Sometimes I really worry about the earth and all the things here. And I hope people can learn to respect all living things. Every thing needs a home, whether it's a person or a plant.

stories of spiritual ecology ....

Ted Purcell

Ted Purcell is the Baptist campus minister at Duke University in Durham, North Carolina. Previously, he spent 15 years in that role full-time at North Carolina State University in Raleigh. In 1989 he accepted the half-time position at Duke, which allows him to follow his calling as a retreat leader and a spiritual director. He spends much of his time addressing ecology as a spiritual issue.

CH: *Ted, tell me about your faith background.*

TP: I say I was brought up Southern Baptist, but not "South of God," in the sense of being provincial and narrow. Over the past 20 years, a lot has changed, and the Southern Baptist Convention has become more like a fundamentalist denomination. That's not where I live theologically. I belong to a church that was booted out of the Raleigh Baptist Association, the State Baptist Convention of North Carolina, and the Southern Baptist Convention, because of its stand on homosexuality. So you might say that I'm a "former Baptist" who is still a Baptist.

Traditionally Baptists have celebrated diversity of opinion. The focus was on doing our work cooperatively, doing work in hospitals, schools, and missions of various kinds around the world. The focus shifted to doctrine, and difference got politicized. One group of Baptists trying to tell another group of Baptists that they must conform or leave—that's very unBaptist. In times past, we could disagree with each other and still stay together.

When did you first realize you wanted to be a minister?

After high school, I went into the army for two years. I didn't have any other way to afford college. The army was the first real testing of my "homegrown" faith in another environment. I went to Japan and was thrown in the midst of a very diverse group of individuals. I was a chaplain's assistant, so it gave me an opportunity to see one model of ministry. The chaplain and his family were friends and very encouraging of me. I began college as a ministerial student after I served my military term.

I just really felt an overwhelming sense of gratitude and wanted to turn that gratitude into service. I had a sense that I was loved by God, and my mother assured me of this. She embodied this in her parenting. I've never had difficulty thinking of God in the feminine, because my mother was the original witness to me.

And your love for the earth started early as well?

I loved being outdoors, in close connection with the natural world. I was a natural introvert, but there was such a sense of welcoming and hospitality in the creation that I felt acceptance. I associated it with peace and comfort, as well as adventure.

And that's a part of your ministry?

I have this recurring vision that someday I might be connected with a retreat center. It's a confluence of several streams in my life—a convergence of hungers. I think that retreat vision is very much about home, being at home with myself, or at home with God. It's about finding community. It's about living a contemplative life in the beauty of creation. I found that many people resonated with that dream. At first I thought that the retreat vision was about a place that I would build or go to. Then I shifted back one gear to a portable concept of doing retreats in centers that already exist. Then I realized that I needed first to *be* a retreat, to focus more on the inner life of prayer.

That's the ferment that led me to Duke and a half-time position. I gave up half my salary and bought back half my life. It corresponds with a pull toward a more contemplative life. I really feel the need to have copious amounts of unobligated time. I had thought of ministry as being available to other people for the sake of God, and I realized that what's more basic was being available to God for the sake of other people.

Along with that, I felt this growing sense of call about being near to the earth and, in light of the environmental crisis, to make some response to that. It was a calling to "ecological spirituality," encouraged by volunteer work with the Land Stewardship Council of North Carolina. They educate people about the Jewish and Christian theology and ethic with regard to the care of creation. There are many people whose spirituality is earth-connected—people who are not connected with institutional religion but find deep meaning and a sense of the sacred in the natural world. One of the reasons we need wilderness is that there needs to be places preserved, not only for the other species but for the cultivation of the human spirit. Our culture tends to regard the earth more as a commodity to be consumed, than as a community to which we belong.

I like the way Sam Keen said it in *Fire in the Belly* [New York: Bantam Doubleday, 1992], "The new human vocation is to heal the earth." I would add myself that it's the *original* human vocation. Keen says that we can't heal what we don't love, and we can't love what we don't know, and we can't know what we don't touch. It is a call literally to reconnect with the earth, to see ourselves not just *on* but *of* the earth, to have a sense of intimate presence with the earth.

How do you make this reconnection yourself and help others do it?

We need to go back to the *other* Bible—the sacred book of nature. There was a time in Christian tradition when we spoke of the two sacred books: what has come to be written scripture and the sacred book of nature. Our scriptures are full of references to nature, so there's a tremendous symphony and unity between the written scripture and the natural world; each points to the other. Go out into the woods with a view of this being a place of sacred revelation. And, just as you would oppose any movement to burn the Bible, you need to oppose the desecration of earth that is taking place. We're poor stewards, influenced by ignorance, arrogance, and greed. We're exploiting the earth in a way that has damaged the life systems of the earth.

If you look at the primal elements—earth, fire, water, and air—and what those mean symbolically in different religious traditions, they're very powerful. No wonder Thomas Berry speaks of the earth as the primary revelation. We wouldn't have scriptures that are now in printed form without the primary revelation of the creation. It raises the great questions; it teaches the great lessons: "Who are we? What is the purpose of humankind? How can we live in relationship, in interdependent community, with the other forms of life?"

So it's a circle for you, the connections between your experience as a Baptist and someone who loves the earth?

There's no more powerful spiritual metaphor in my existence than the image of home and homecoming. To leave any of my homes, including my denominational home, fuels the hunger around the question, "What is my larger home?" When my church was expelled from the denomination, I felt loss and grief. I had a sense I was less and less at home. At the same time, I readily admit my debt to my religious background. It was a place to stand while I was sorting out my own unique spirituality.

If there's one area where I can make some contribution to other people and the earth, it seems to me it is this area. Being closer to the earth nurtures my own spirituality, my relationship to God. In retreats and seminars, I invite people to tell their earth stories about special places or special experiences they've had. These stories often reflect the human longing to feel at home in relation to the earth, to heal the sense of alienation, to love the creation.

What else would you suggest to someone who wanted to reconnect with the earth?

I can't think of a more radical act of faith than to rest. A lot of it comes from my understanding of Sabbath, which includes in the original commandment a call for earth to rest. There's a powerful connection between our restlessness and the ecological crisis. If you want to do something radically significant as an activist, just rest. Sabbath rest has many implications for the environmental crisis. Deep rest is a counter-cultural act. It involves connecting with the hospitable presence of the natural world as a place of solitude, a place of silence. Our contribution to the healing of the earth comes right back to us in a mutually enhancing way as we work and pray for the healing of the planet. Sabbath rest is about "resting in God," entrusting ourselves to something larger, and drawing nurture from that relationship with the Holy.

> I can't think of a more radical act of faith than to rest.

earth.

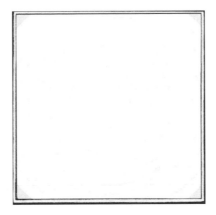

healing

*Healing occurs when you align with
the pure, positive energy that created the
planet—and that keeps your heart beating
and your blood chemistry normal. Healing
occurs when you release all your resistance
to well-being and allow yourself to be well.
Healing occurs when you're in harmony
with your life's purpose and those who are
meant to accompany you on this path.
Healing occurs when you've created a sense
of safety and security in your life. Healing is
a major leap of faith in this culture.*

~ Christiane Northrup, M.D.

questions for reflection

What activities or practices do you currently have that contribute to your own healing?

What interrupts or takes away from healing in your life?

What types of healing do you crave?

Are you healthy enough now to sustain yourself in your work over the next decade and beyond?

what is healing? . . . .

Healing is the process by which we release that which no longer serves us and cultivate that which does. Healing happens when we give up a bad habit, address an addiction, or examine old patterns. It happens when we stimulate the flow of energy in our bodies or become conscious of what we take into our bodies. Healing comes from the same word as "whole" and "holy." To be healed, therefore, is to be whole and holy.

Even the most grounded and healthy people experience stress, and most of us experience it with some regularity. We can sabotage our body's ability to move through stress (with fast food, alcohol, cigarettes, drugs, and other substances), or we can choose a different path. In the short-term, we can cultivate healthy responses: drinking enough water, getting plenty of rest and exercise, taking hot baths, getting enough fresh air, asking for support from those around us, making sure we eat well, and taking time for ourselves. In the long-term, we must realize that stress-related symptoms are a message from the body. A spiritual practice that engenders a daily commitment to healing and relaxation is one of the most effective ways to deal with ongoing stress.

turning point . . . .

In 1995, I encounter Gabrielle Roth at a conference in New York City put on by Omega Institute for Holistic Health. I have been intrigued by what I've heard about her approach to movement, her teaching style, and her percussion group, the Mirrors. Walking into the workshop, "The Mystery of Dance," I find I am one of five hundred individuals eager for a chance to study with her, if even for a couple of hours. Up until this point, most of the conference has been rather passive. But in this ballroom there are no chairs. What exactly will she have us do in here, I wonder.

The drums begin to play, and Gabrielle welcomes us to the workshop. She starts to move as she talks, inviting us all to join in. Until that moment, it had not dawned on me that we were actually going to move, such is the disconnection between my physical body and my mind. I love to dance, but suddenly I am nervous. Gabrielle immediately creates a safe and accepting environment. With the right blend of humor and intent, she coaxes out our inhibitions so we are freer to express ourselves with our bodies.

She has us start out slow, dancing with our eyes closed. At first I feel ridiculous. I am flailing around, looking crazy for sure. But it greatly reduces anxiety to know that no one else can see you. We dance, letting one body part lead us and then another. She has us open our eyes and just keep right on going.

We dance by ourselves, with a partner, in groups of four. Soon all five hundred of us are moving wildly around the room, combining our own moves with the beats of the musicians, dancing with folks we'd never met before. By the end of two hours, she has led us to the promised land. I leave the room with a new energy coursing through my body; it feels new and yet very familiar.

healing and social change . . . .

Any work can be a source of stress, but working for change presents some unique challenges to healing. The sense of urgency many of us feel about our work and the circumstances surrounding it may be a great motivator, but mismanaged, it can also be a negative force that limits our ability to act with a sound body, open mind, and loving heart.

This urgency can stem from a number of sources. Many social change organizations are plagued regularly by their quest for success and effectiveness. We wonder how we'll make payroll next month or find the money to carry us through the end of the year. Moving deeper, our health is affected greatly by the general state of things, the circumstances in which we and/or our constituents and coworkers find ourselves. The realities of poverty, violence, and oppression chip away at health, slowly and methodically, carrying pieces away from our center. One day, if we are not vigilant, there may be very little left of us at all.

Like the pursuit of justice itself, healing and self-renewal do not lend themselves to the quick fix. They require a daily commitment. Many folks who easily muster tremendous discipline and dedication for their work have a much harder time setting aside a fraction of that energy for their own healing and transformation. This can no longer be an option if we are to continue to do great work. I have witnessed too many physical, mental, and emotional breakdowns, in myself and others, made manifest in everything from repeated colds to major health crises to attempted (and even tragically successful) suicides.

We want to have a positive impact on the people and the world around us, but how can we if we don't also have a positive impact on ourselves? Healing is not just about self-preservation, though that alone is worthy of our attention. It is about preventive maintenance which in turn only strengthens the energy, intelligence, and joy that we are able to bring to our work.

activities to do alone . . . . 🖋

✏ write it down: know your energy levels

How familiar are you with your own energy level? Becoming conscious of the peaks and valleys of your day is a vital aspect of the healing process. Start by keeping track. On a scale of 1-10, write down how much energy you feel you have once each hour. One means you're ready for a nap; 10 is the best you've ever felt. Write down what you were doing that hour (working, reading, eating, driving to work, playing with your kids) and record anything else that may have contributed to that energy level (not feeling well, hungry, nervous about presentation at work). Don't change your behavior or add more movement to your daily routine. Do this for a least three days, a week if you can. Then, looking at the data you've collected, answer the following questions:

What are your most energetic times of the day, those you rated 7-10?
What were you doing during those times? List the activities. Is there a pattern?
What were your least energetic times of the day, those you rated 1-4?
What were you doing during those times? List the activities. Is there a pattern?
What can you learn from this?

Movement of any kind is a great antidote to slumps. For example, if you always hit a low after lunch, which is very common, use some of your lunch hour to take a walk. If late afternoons tend to be a black hole, figure out a way to exercise during this time. It may mean finding or asking for some flexibility in your workday.

NOTE: If you're consistently rating most of your day at 5 and under, it may be a sign that you need to take a closer look at your sleeping patterns, eating habits, stress level, or other health-related issues. This would be a good time to see a doctor or alternative health practitioner.

strengthen your relationship to your physical body

Western culture tends to teach that wisdom comes from our brain, our experiences, and our teachers. When we are disconnected from the wisdom of our bodies, we're at risk of separating ourselves from its needs and rhythms, and the messages about what it needs to function. Children intuitively are not content to stay in one place for very long. They want to move. Healing movement is any movement which deepens your connection to your physical body and unleashes energy. Here are some ideas.

Deepen your connection to your physical body. . . .

the beauty of exercise

Movement is what creates energy. Even moderate activity, 20-30 minutes, three times a week, can result in significant benefits for mind, body, and spirit. Physical activity packs a powerful punch. It strengthens the heart and the circulatory system, which increases our stamina. It improves our muscle power, our bones, our flexibility, and our joint mobility. In a 1997 report on physical activity, the U.S. Surgeon General found that physical fitness also improves one's mood, self-esteem, confidence, and cognitive functioning. Inactive people were twice as likely to have symptoms of depression as active people.

walking

I suggest a time apart or a time alone with God,
walking in receptive silence amid the beauties of God's nature.
From the beauty of nature you get your inspiration, from the silent receptiveness
you get your meditation, from the walking you get not only exercise but breathing—
all in one lovely experience.

~ Peace Pilgrim

This is by far the easiest—most of us do it every day. If you're not used to exercising a lot, have problems with your joints, or just love to walk, walking is a great way to start moving. Get out a map that includes your street and figure out one point that is a mile from your house. Use that to approximate a circle with a mile radius, the center of the circle being your home. Do the same thing for a half-mile radius. Now look at the areas contained within each of these concentric circles.
What's there?
What can you easily walk to: parks, friends' houses, school, library, work, post office, restaurants, stores?
What is your usual mode of transport to these places?

Walking is also a way to spend time quietly with someone else. Many soulful conversations happen while in motion on the sidewalk, through the woods, around the park, along the beach. Often moving side by side allows for greater intimacy than sitting across a table; perhaps folks are more likely to reveal themselves to each other. Walking is also a great way to explore new places. Like most forms of exercise, walking aids digestion, reduces anxiety, and increases your stamina, circulation, and muscle tone.

aerobic exercise

During aerobic exercise, the cardiovascular system works at a rate that demands large amounts of oxygen, much more than usual. This forces the heart to beat faster as it pumps this additional oxygen-enriched blood to the muscles. So aerobic exercise, in addition to building stronger muscles and reducing body fat, strengthens our heart and makes our lungs more efficient. More oxygen means more deep breathing. Aerobic exercise includes, but isn't limited to: running, cycling, swimming, many team sports, exercise equipment—bikes, treadmills, stair masters. Cycling is non-weight bearing, so it's particularly good for the joints, and swimming is practically stressless for the body.

yoga

The Sanskrit word yoga actually means "yoke", or "union". Yoga goes beyond the physical discipline that we normally think of when we hear the word; it includes selfless service (karma yoga), breathing exercises (pranayama), and meditation. Hatha yoga is the term used to describe the actual physical postures, or "asanas." Each posture is designed to increase body flexibility (including the health of the spine), stimulate various organs and increase circulation. Without expending enormous amounts of energy, yoga stimulates the body's energy. And, it is practiced with constant attention to the breath. It induces a state of meditation and concentration, allowing our bodies to come into a state of true physical relaxation. You can take classes at a local yoga or dance studio, rent video or audio tapes from your local library, or find books with photographs of the postures. Taking a class will give you the best sense of how to do the postures for maximum effectiveness. The benefits of yoga are immeasurable and can be felt even in as little as 10-15 minutes a day.

t'ai chi and qigong

Over four thousand years old, the Chinese arts of T'ai Chi (pronouned tie-chee) and Qigong (pronounced chee-gong) have their roots in the philosophy of Taoism. Both are based on the cultivation and direction of chi—the Chinese concept of life force or life energy. It is chi that awakens and enlivens the body. These practices can prevent illness, provide relaxation, build muscle strength, promote circulation, increase stamina and vitality, and even fight disease. Many gyms, martial arts studios, and yoga studios now offer both T'ai Chi and Qigong.

Qigong is a series of stretching exercises which lead chi to various parts of the body; breathing techniques and concentration exercises strengthen the spirit. All three of these—body, breath and spirit—work in tandem. A derivation of Qigong, T'ai Chi is a full-body movement meditation. Technically a martial art (t'ai chi ch'uan literally means "supreme ultimate boxing"), T'ai Chi is a series of

relaxation response

Dr. Herbert Benson, head of Harvard University's Mind/Body Institute, shed scientific light on the link between meditation and health with his best-selling book, *The Relaxation Response*. Published in 1975, it outlined the benefits of meditation as a powerful antidote to stress and stress-related illnesses. Meditation has the power to slow down heart rates, breathing, and brain waves. As a result of Benson's book and additional work done in the field, the relaxation response is now taught in medical schools all over the country as a way to help reduce high blood pressure, insomnia, and depression. Benson's newest book, *Timeless Healing: The Power and Biology of Belief*, examines the role that spirituality and belief play in the healing process.

A vast storehouse of wisdom of alternative healing methods, often from non-Western or indigenous cultures, are gaining more attention and credibility. Over 35 of the nation's medical schools now offer courses in alternative medicine. In 1992, the National Institute of Health initiated its Office of Alternative Medicine and appropriated limited research money to study the impact of 26 different alternative therapies. As one doctor in Philadelphia points out, "What we call *alternative medicine* is traditional medicine for 80% of the world, and what we call *traditional medicine* is only a few centuries old."

Below are only some of the primary alternative healing methods. See "Resources for Healing" for further investigation.

Acupressure: In acupressure, fingers are used to stimulate specific points along the meridians, or energy lines of the body. An ancient Chinese healing modality, acupressure is useful for preventive health care and to treat aches, pains, stress, and arthritis.
Acupuncture: Also from the Chinese medicinal tradition, acupuncture is the insertion of very thin needles into specific points. This stimulates the release of chi,

(continued top of next page)

flowing movements. Millions of Chinese, and now others around the globe, practice T'ai Chi at dawn and at dusk. During T'ai Chi, your legs and arms are in constant, fluid motion, but the movement is almost effortless.

℮ your relationship with food

How would you characterize your relationship with food?
Do you remember what you ate yesterday?
Do you know, in general, what you eat and how much?

Food means different things to us at different times. One meal might be a family or social event, another might be a cure for boredom, still another simply fuel for the day. Keep track of your relationship to food for seven days. Every time you put food in your mouth, write down:

– What you ate and how much
– When you ate, how long it took, where you were, and with whom
– Why you ate and how you felt afterwards
– Your level of hunger before eating, on a scale of 1-10

If you do this, you will be able to notice many of the patterns in your relationship with food:
When do you eat and how often? How long does it take?
Where do you eat? Are you sitting down, standing up, or in motion?
Why do you eat?
What do you eat? Which foods do you consider healthy? Unhealthy?
How do you give thanks for the food you eat?
Are you able to relax while you eat?

℮ paying attention to your emotional health

I know only a handful of women and men who have not suffered some form of mild depression or worse. Depression is more common than most of us care to admit. "What's wrong with me?" we wonder, especially when it seems like everyone else around us is fine. Of course they're not, but we may not know this or want to admit it. Healing from depression is a chance to turn our attention inward, to stop and pay attention, and to take better care of ourselves. You can begin by talking to a trusted friend or relative about how you are feeling. There are many forms of emotional ill health, ranging from the not-so-serious blues to depression and more serious illnesses.

Some forms of depression may require the attention of a medical professional. And there are some telltale signs. In his book, *Undoing Depression*, Dr. Richard O'Connor describes major depression as "a depressed mood or loss of interest or pleasure in ordinary activities for at least two weeks, accompanied by at least four of the following symptoms:

1. significant weight loss or gain (without dieting)
2. frequent insomnia
3. significant slowing of activity levels
4. fatigue or energy loss
5. feelings of worthlessness or excessive guilt
6. diminished ability to think or make decisions
7. recurring thoughts of death or suicide."

If you notice these symptoms, consult a health practitioner as soon as possible or contact your local health department or community mental health clinic. Many treatments for depression are available to you, including counseling, psychotherapy, antidepressant medication, herbal compounds, and alternative therapies.

activities to do with groups . . . .

℗ move together

Your organization has talked, planned, worked, strategized, socialized, and eaten together, but have you ever *moved* together? There are many ways to infuse movement into your daily routine at work. It may take you a little while to get comfortable with this, but you will be doing people a tremendous service by giving them a chance to get their blood moving, especially during a long day or a long meeting.

• Walk together. To work or after work, at lunch, to lunch or after lunch. 20 to 30 minutes of fresh air and movement can completely change your mood, your energy level, and your approach.

• Get a group together after work or on the weekends and dance. All you need is a big open space, music, and willing participants. Organized games of softball or ultimate frisbee after work are other options that don't require a lot of preparation.

or energy. Acupuncture is used for both acute and chronic conditions.

Ayurvedic: This healing system recognizes three main body types, each of which requires different diets. Ayurvedic medicine has been practiced in India for more than five thousand years.

Chiropractic: Chiropractors correct misalignments in the spine, which in turn impact posture, the nervous system, and overall body health.

Herbalism: Natural plants are transformed into compounds and tinctures to treat a wide array of ailments.

Homeopathy: In homeopathy, a minute amount of a natural substance is chosen to treat illness based on a series of biological and environmental factors. This substance stimulates the body's immune system.

Naturopathy: Naturopathic practitioners use nutrition, herbs, homeopathy, and other techniques to stimulate the body's ability to heal.

- Trainer for a day. If there are folks in your organization who have their own personal passion for a kind of movement or exercise, ask them to share it with everyone else. They may have to tone it down so everyone can participate.

ℚ invigorating stretches

Five or 10 minutes of light stretching before a meeting will make a difference in people's ability to stay focused. What follows is a combination of stretches and gentle yoga postures that flow together. These are easy to learn and can be done with a group of people. Attending some yoga or stretching classes will give you more background.

The instructions below are written so that they can be read aloud to a group, or you can memorize them. Just have people follow your movements. Ask people to wear loose clothing. Make sure you tell people to pay attention to their own bodies. If anything starts to hurt or feel strained in any way, they should ease up on the stretch immediately. Every time you see ". . .," pause 3-5 seconds. The questions in italics are to be asked only if you feel comfortable. Allow for people to relax into the position before you ask the question.

Head rolls. Start by standing with feet placed hip distance apart, arms at your sides. Close your eyes. . . . Let your head drop slowly forward, so your chin moves to your chest but without straining any muscles in your neck. . . . Then, again very slowly, bring your head back to center and tilt it slowly back so your neck stretches slightly but without any strain. . . . Let the head move all the way forward and then back a second time. . . Next, tilt the head to the right so the right ear moves towards the right shoulder. . . . Do this to the left side. . . . Repeat once more in each direction. . . . Do a couple of very slow full head rolls. . . . It's important to do these movements very slowly so as not to pull the neck too much in any one direction.

Shoulder rolls. Hunch your shoulders up to your ears and slowly roll them back, giving the shoulder blades a slight squeeze as you do so. . . . Repeat this five times. . . . Then roll the shoulders forward five times. . . . Next, breathe in as you hunch your shoulders up to your ears and let them drop back down as you exhale with an audible, "ha!" This is a great release of energy and tension. . . . Do this three times.
What weight do you carry in your shoulders?

Center of gravity. In this same standing position, rock forward and backwards, slowly. Find your center of gravity in the middle. . . . Stop and feel what it is to be in this place. . . . Then, rock slowly side to side and again return to the place

in the center again. . . .
How do you find your center in the world?
How do you regain a sense of balance?

The Mountain. Standing straight, raise your arms to shoulder level, turn palms so they are facing upward, and then continue raising your arms until the form a "v-shape" with your head in the middle. . . . Feel your feet planted firmly on the ground. . . . Stretch your fingers up and drop your shoulders so they're not hunched up. . . . Stand tall in this position for as long as you can. . . .
This is a posture of strength and stability. What do you need to be strong for today?
Let your arms slowly float back down to your sides.

Half-moon. When you're ready, slowly bring your arms up again as in the mountain and then together overhead so you can clasp your hands, leaving your two index fingers straight out and touching. . . . Slowly, breathing in, stretch over to the right so that your head, arms, and waist are all bending in the same direction. Stretch out as far as is comfortable and then, breathing out, return to the center position. . . . Do the same thing to the left. . . . Repeat one to two more times on each side. . . . Let arms float to the sides of your body. . . . Rest. . . .

Body twist. Begin slowly twisting your body from side to side, letting your arms wrap around your body on each twist. . . .Twist slowly for a couple minutes. . . . then hold the twist on one side so you are looking behind you over one shoulder and your hands are on your waist. . . . Do the same on the other side. . . .
What helps you gain a new perspective?

Rag doll. Drop your chin to your chest. Very slowly let your whole body begin to roll forward, as if you were going to touch your toes. . . . Instead just let your arms hang loosely, fingers a few inches above the floor. . . . If you want, you can sway gently from side to side. . . . When you've had enough, begin to roll up very slowly, taking 10 breaths to return to a standing position . . . . Leave your chin on your chest until the end. . . . Let the head be the last thing to come up. . . .

interplay

InterPlay is both a practice and a philosophy that combines dance, improvisational theater, storytelling, and singing. It grew out of the teaching and performance experiences of Phil Porter and Cynthia Winton-Henry, two self-proclaimed "body intellectuals" who were interested in finding ways to integrate dance and spirituality. In InterPlay workshops, participants are led through a progression of improvisational activities that allow them to explore the possibilities of their own power, experience the fun of playing with others, and build confidence in their bodies. It is accessible to people of all ages and abilities. InterPlay is based on the principles that we are bodies—all that we do, know, and express is physical. Through play, we can hold life both deeply and lightly.

resources for the healing . . . .

Benson, Herbert. *The Relaxation Response*. New York: Morrow, 1975.

_____. *Timeless Healing: The Power and Biology of Belief*. New York: Fireside, 1997.

Christensen, Alice. *The American Yoga Association Beginner's Manual*. New York: Fireside, 1987. Easy to follow series of three, 10-week yoga sessions. Photos of each posture and very explicit instructions.

Fluegelman, Andrew, ed. *The New Games Book*. New York: A Dolphin Book/ Doubleday, 1976. A guide with photographs to physical games for pairs, small groups, and large groups.

Huber, Cherie. *The Depression Book: Depression as an Opportunity for Spiritual Practice*. Mountain View, CA: A Center for the Practice of Zen Buddhist Meditation, 1991. An accessible look at depression as part of a spiritual journey and an opportunity to cultivate self-compassion.

InterPlay: To find out more about workshops and possible instructors in your area contact: WING IT!, 669A 24th Street, Oakland CA 94612; 510/814-9584

Jaffe, Dennis T., Ph.D., and Cynthia D. Scott, Ph.D., M.P.H. *Self Renewal: A Workbook for Achieving High Performance and Health in a High Stress Environment*. New York: Fireside/Simon & Schuster Inc., 1984.

Judith, Anodea. *Wheels of Life: A User's Guide to the Chakra System*. St. Paul, MN: Llewellyn Publications, 1997. A practical guide to working with the seven "chakras," or energy centers in the body.

Kripalu Center for Yoga and Health, P.O. Box 793, Lenox, MA 01240; 413/448-3400

Liu, Qingshan. *Chinese Fitness, A Mind/Body Approach: Qigong for Healthy and Joyful Living*. Jamaica Plain, MA: YMAA Publication Center, 1997.

Murray, Michael T., and Joseph Pizzorno. *Encyclopedia of Natural Medicine*. Rocklin, CA: Prima, 1991. Covers the use of herbs, diet, and vitamins for the treatment of various diseases.

Northrup, Christiane, M.D. *Women's Bodies, Women's Wisdom: Creating Physical and Emotional Health and Healing*. New York: Bantam, 1994. A comprehensive guide.

O'Connor, Richard, Ph.D. *Undoing Depression: What Therapy Doesn't Teach You and Medication Can't Give You*. Boston: Little, Brown and Company, 1997.

Page, Linda, N.D., Ph.D. *Healthy Healing: A Guide to Self-Healing for Everyone*, 10th ed. Healthy Healing Publications, 1997. Covers diet, herbal, and lifestyle suggestions for two hundred common ailments; provides an overview of alternative health systems with a special section on herbal healing.

Porter, Phil and Cynthia Winton-Henry. *The Wisdom of the Body: The InterPlay Philosophy and Technique*. Oakland: WING IT! Press, 1995.

Roth, Gabrielle. *Sweat Your Prayers: Movement as Spiritual Practice*. Los Angeles: J.P. Tarcher, 1998. Roth looks at movement as a medium for awakening. Through personal stories and interactive exercises, she discusses the body's five natural rhythms: flowing, staccato, chaos, lyrical, and stillness.

Sivananda Yoga Vedanta Center. *The Sivananda Yoga Training Manual*. New York: Sivananda Yoga Vedanta Center, 1991. Pocket-size book with overview of the five points of yoga (exercise, breathing, relaxation, diet, and meditation) and full explanations of the 12 basic postures, their variations, and mental and physical benefits.

_____. *101 Essential Yoga Tips*. New York: Dorling Kindersley, 1995. Photos of the basic postures and good supplementary information; good for travel.

Thorne, Julia. *You Are Not Alone: Words of Experience and Hope for the Journey Through Depression*. With Larry Rothstein. New York: HarperPerennial, 1993. The author is the director of the Depression Initiative and this book gathers the words of people who are suffering and healing from depression.

U.S. Department of Health and Human Services. *Physical Activity and Health—A Report of the Surgeon General*. Atlanta: U.S. Department of Health and Human Services, Centers for Disease Control and Prevention, National Center for Chronic Disease Prevention and Health Promotion, 1996.

Weil, Andrew, M.D. *8 Weeks to Optimum Health*. New York: Alfred A. Knopf, 1997. Weil marries Western medical training with traditional medicine. He also publishes a monthly newsletter with information on a broad scope of health issues and answers to frequently asked questions. Contact: Self-Healing, P.O. Box 2057, Marion OH 43305-2057; 800/523-3296.

stories of healing . . . .

Lori Fendell

Lori Fendell has been a traditional acupuncturist for eight years. She is also trained as a Chinese herbalist, Western herbalist, and a physician's assistant. She has a master's in International Public Health from the University of Hawaii. In the early 80s, she spent a year running an outpatient clinic and helped train midlevel health care workers in a Cambodian refugee camp. She and her partner, Walton, are committed to creating intentional community with other like-minded people.

CH: Lori, how would you describe your spiritual base?

LF: It's evolving; there's nothing stagnant. It's walking into new rooms, like "Oh, I never considered that before." The word "God" kind of turns me off. I like to call it the life force. That's how I experience it. With each step when I let go of my own will and planning and allow, there's trusting that I will be carried along with the life force. Each time I can drop deeper into that awareness, I get supported, always.

How do you remind yourself to stay in the present?

It is easy to get off track and start planning, get all your ducks in a row. It's like breathing. Sometimes you're taking a breath in, you contract and forget to really breathe. We forget, but as soon as we remember, there's the opportunity again. Life can be a breath of a reminder. Something wakes you up, and you have a choice again.

Has it always been like this for you?

For a long, long time. "The master never plans for greatness, or the one great big thing. She just pays attention. She is just with what's right in front of her." That's from *Tao Te Ching*. I never could have known that I wanted to be an herbalist and an acupuncturist because those things didn't exist. I knew I wanted to take chemistry, because I wanted to learn about the world. In high school, I was making good decisions for where I am now, but I didn't know why.

Did you want to be a healer?

I didn't want to do it because of the medical model. I wasn't attracted to working with sickness and drugs, the drama of severe illness. But a friend dragged me into what turned out to be the beginning. I worked in a hospital for four years and applied to a P.A. [physician's assistant] program.

How did you get from there to acupuncture?

I was doing research on AIDS, and we were writing a grant for alternative approaches to AIDS. We met at my house, and the one person who couldn't come was the acupuncturist. Later, he invited me to his office to observe an AIDS treatment of a patient.

When I got into his office, I felt something totally different than anything I had experienced in medicine. It was healing, and it was simple, and it was elegant. When I left his office, I had the phone number, I applied to school, and I got in, all in an instant. My friends looked at me and said, "What are you doing, career suicide?" I had a very good, professional position. I was getting all kinds of promotions, recommendations, status. It was great, but it wasn't what I loved. There's another quote from the Tao about that, "When a wise person hears the Tao, they run to it. When somebody in the middle hears the Tao, they ask questions. When a skeptic hears it, they laugh at it."

> ...when I let go of my own will and planning and allow, there's trusting that I will be carried along with the life force. Each time I can drop deeper into that awareness, I get supported always.

What is the most powerful thing about the healing process for you?

From a personal perspective, I know how much I'm growing. It demands with every encounter that I be present, beyond how I even know how to be present. And there's nothing else in life other than learning how to be present. So I'm getting the best teaching of my life.

And that's what I'm asking of my patients too—to become present to their own life. Now, to do that in a way that resonates for each person, fresh, that's the part I love. I don't always succeed. I am at a growing edge with it.

I don't know that I've ever met anyone who embodies the word "healer" more than you do.

If you're on the path that resonates for your heart, than you will be bringing about healing for the life force, in whatever modality it is for you. The Chinese say that everyone has their own heart's true note, and when you're in alignment with that, then you're living as fully as you can. The closer you are to it, the richer your life experience.

How does it feel to work with patients in this way?

I am the life force when I'm doing the work. I am the representative of it, rather than my own personal will. I'm just settling into it as I am able. The more I do it, the more it's a mystery, how profound it is. I'm just a conduit. It's phenomenal. It's just about paying attention at deeper and deeper levels.

And it is all about "chi", which I'm not sure I completely understand.

Well, guess what? Chi is the life force. It's not as mysterious as the Tao. Chi animates all of life, not just the person or the animals or the trees. It's the wind, the movement of the rivers, the tide of the ocean, the pull of gravity. We receive our chi from our breath; it comes into the lungs. And then food we eat is filled with chi, if it's good food. Another more subtle spirit level of chi is the surrounding in which you place yourself. You can elevate your chi.

If you were talking to someone who had not paid very close attention to their health, where would you tell them to start?

It's really an individual answer. I like to do gentle, steady change rather than anything to shock the body, because I think those are the lasting changes. You know people will say "Get off the coffee, get off the cigarettes." People don't change like that, really.

But I might hold a huge vision for where I know they could go over time. I've seen some people for six years here. They come in, just off chemo, drugged up, sick, entrenched in the medical model, weak through their illness, and I can't tell them to get off all their drugs. It's a slow education process of good nutrition with foods that have vitality, getting enough rest, having permission to have all the rest your body wants—going for a nap, not the coffee—and following your heart in your line of work, which includes lots of time off. Sometimes this is the only time people hear about it. Society says you're a good person if you get up early, work hard, push through. I like people to have permission to get 10 hours of sleep, plus a nap, if they need it.

And as far as self-care goes, the sooner the better?

Yes. I find that some people, when they're young they won't consider paying attention to their health, so I don't push it. I encourage them to live a joyful life and follow their heart with their work, not their pocketbook.

Some people reaching 40 or 50 are furious that they have to pay so much attention to their health. They don't want to learn about nutrition. They want their arthritis to go away. People need to realize that the body is always changing. I have compassion for them, but there's no other way around it but being with it. We're not just here to do this external work; we're here to be present to our physical bodies, too. It is the vehicle for our work, the temple for our spirituality, and we have to clean up the temple.

Ginny Going and Tom Henderson

Ginny Going spent 30 years as a non-profit administrator. She has done a lot of group facilitation and organizational development with non-profits and with churches. As a deacon in the Episcopal Church, she had a community ministry as director of the Triangle Interfaith AIDS Network for eight years. Recently her bishop approved her current ministry as an expressive art ministry for connecting mind, body, heart, and spirit.

Tom Henderson worked in the pharmaceutical industry for 25 years, the last 20 at Burroughs Wellcome as a Ph.D. organic chemist. He's trained in human interaction, group dynamics, experiential education design skills, and conflict management. He now uses these skills with non-profits and churches. A clarinet and sax player, music has always been a big part of his life.

Ginny and Tom have known each other for 20 years, been married for 8, and have 4 daughters between them. Together they founded Colleagues, a company dedicated to encouraging men and women to work, play, and be together in ways that are productive, life-giving, and joyful.

CH: I want to start by asking what got you into the world of improvisational movement.

GG: In retrospect, I was always kind of looking for opportunities to have dance and movement in my life regularly. I got introduced to modern dance by a gym teacher and then used baby-sitting money to take dance lessons in my late teens and early 20s. I always had this pull towards dance but never enough to satisfy me.

The beginnings of what we're doing now happened early in our marriage. We had been married for six months, and I had retired from my 30-year career. To celebrate, we went to Kirkridge [a retreat center in Pennsylvania] to a workshop with Walter Wink: "Sexuality and Spirituality: The Travail of Integration." That was the mountaintop experience for us. We were introduced to improvisational movement, dance, and art in a very gentle, invitational way. For six days, we did Bible study with Walter and then intense creative movement with June, his wife. And we came down from the mountain saying, "Wow."

TH: For me it starts in third grade. The class was doing *Peer Gynt*, a play, and I was a goblin and had to do a goblin dance, and I was having a great time. But the day before we were to perform for the parents, the teacher said, "Now, don't get stage fright on me," and I immediately felt something go "clench" inside me. Of course I was terrified the next day. Ever since then, I've had this angst about dancing, and I went through high school knowing I couldn't dance. I learned to play music, so I could be in the dance band and not have to dance.

That's the way things were until I was 49. We went to Kirkridge, and June said "Now, there's no wrong way to do this." It was a gradual integration. By the end of the week, we were all running and leaping and dancing with each other. I found an inner dancer. I think everybody did. That was the first time I really allowed myself to believe that my sexuality and my spirituality were intimately connected.

GG: We met in small groups every evening. People took 45 minutes to share their sexual-spiritual story. I don't think I would have dreamed of being able to do that with such honesty. In retrospect, I was learning about the power of movement and experiential arts to move individuals in a group to much more honesty and depth of sharing around whatever it is they're doing together. The movement is a metaphor for what you're doing as a group.

> It's occurred to me why movement works so quickly: we don't lie as easily with our bodies. It's harder to put on the usual masks.

TH: Movement seems to build community very quickly. Other ways of community-building take time and energy, and they're heavy. It's occurred to me why movement works so quickly: we don't lie as easily with our bodies. It's harder to put on the usual masks. What we say is more honest, and it is about a yearning for connection. Our stories come across.

Walter says, "People think that if others really knew who I am, they wouldn't love me, and just the opposite is true. If they really know who I am, they can't help but love me." That comes across in movement.

GG: Movement raises up every interpersonal issue in the world. Last night, we were introducing our class to contact, and most hadn't done this type of movement. We said the simplest thing, "When you feel your partner's touch, move into it." Then we said, "When you feel your partner's touch, move away." In that one little exercise is the tension of the coming together and the distancing that goes on between people.

TH: And questions about who's going to control that. . . .

GG: But we're doing it in a light, playful way, with a light spirit. I emphasize that it builds confidence in our bodies. I always say, "I know we're all sitting here with messages we've internalized about our bodies. They're somehow inadequate, not enough." I'll have folks make a full-page list of "My____ is too ____." We've been taught to hate our bodies. We haven't been taught anything about loving our bodies, which means we haven't been taught anything about loving ourselves.

CH: And InterPlay became a vehicle for all of this?

GG: We saw the InterPlay materials, and it seemed to circle back to where we had started at Kirkridge: movement and experiential arts as powerful tools on your spiritual journey.

I heard InterPlay described as a philosophy and a practice; that all made good sense to me. The philosophy was a way to be in my body every day, not just when we're doing movement. The fruits of it are: worrying less, going for more, deciding I can have more. Moving from a stance of judgment to a stance of affirmation. Noticing choices and exercising them. Going from a stance of scarcity to one of plenty. Wanting to see the people around me in all their fullness.

TH: One of the tenets of InterPlay is having an ethic of play. We're all familiar with the work ethic. After I recognized that I was in a midlife crisis, I realized I wanted more play in my life, but I'd forgotten how to play. So for the next few years, I worked really hard at playing. An aerobic dance class helped save my life, literally. But it wasn't until I started doing improvisational dance, that I remembered how easy and natural it is to play.

> There's something about the joy and fear and terror of being seen alive and changing in improv performance.

GG: We went to San Francisco and did the InterPlay "Wisdom of the Body" workshop. We loved InterPlay; it seemed like the natural next thing for us. And we learned about Phil and Cynthia's background of 20 years [Phil Porter and Cynthia Winton-Henry are the co-creators of InterPlay], bridging the world of dance and the world of religion.

We got introduced to improv performance by seeing WING IT!, their dance company, perform. They had the audience give them words and phrases, and they did two hours of performance with music: dance, storytelling and singing, making up lyrics and tunes on the spot. I was in disbelief. There's something about the joy and fear and terror of being seen alive and changing in improv performance. Before, if I had a presentation to do, every word had to be on paper, and perfect. Now, I get up in front of an audience, trusting that something will come that will connect me with them.

TH: We also got to perform that week in California. We didn't sign up, but at one point near the end of the performance, Cynthia said, "Tom and Ginny: following and leading," one of the forms they use. You just don't say no to Cynthia, certainly not in front of a whole room of people. We did something and that was our plunge. Cynthia has a habit of drawing people into a new place.

GG: And much to our amazement, we have our own InterPlay performance group now, *Off the Deep End*.

TH: For the next three years, I continued to say that I'm not in this to perform, it's for myself and to help men and women relate to each other better, better engage in conflict. And I still think those things are true.

CH: *What advice would you give to people who wanted to get involved?*

GG: See if you can find anyone in your area that's doing creative movement and just start with whatever you can find.

TH: And find someone who will tell you that there's no wrong way to do this, because lots of people think there's a right way.

GG: And I would say, dance at home, move at home. Put on some music and just do what feels good.

healing.

Part Three:
Turning Outward

relationships

Finally it all boils down
to human relationship. . .
whether I shall go on living in
isolation or whether there
shall be a we. . .
love alone is radical.

~ Howard Zinn

questions for reflection

What different kinds of relationships do you have?

How are these relationships significant to you?

What is hard about them? What is holy?

what are relationships? . . . .

Relationships mirror our best and worst selves. It is in relationships with other people that we get to see how present we are, how well we listen, how we judge people, how well we can see what is, as opposed to how we'd like to be. Relationships expose our own limitations and our greatest possibilities; our greatest lessons come through our relationships. These lessons are not always obvious. Sometimes it is not until years later that we see why we needed to be with or meet a certain person at a certain time. Whether a relationship seems easy or hard, enriching or draining, or all of these simultaneously, spirit is always present. With attention, we can become more aware of how we cultivate the presence of this spirit. And this is a worthy practice, for ultimately, most everything we do involves relationships.

turning point. . . . .

It is late May, 1996. In the same week, I end a significant relationship, friends suffer the loss and impending loss of family members, my car goes into the shop, my glasses break, and then, at the week's end, another disaster strikes. Stomping around the house in frustration, I miss a half step, less than three inches high. I come crashing to the floor, landing on my left foot. I hear a crack. After a day in the emergency room, my roommate's prediction comes true. My foot is broken.

With a broken heart and a broken foot, I wonder which will heal faster. If someone wrote about my life in a novel, this portion would be circled for rewrites, "too trite, they'll never buy it." Overnight my life has been transformed, and the irony does not escape me. The familiar voice at the other end of the telephone has disappeared and so has my mobility. The confluence of these events makes me suspicious of people, their motivations, and their consistency.

On crutches, I am reluctant to ask for help, because I don't want to get too dependent. But then I wonder why people aren't offering me more assistance. My daily routine shifts. Time moves more slowly; each action requires tremendous forethought, and I see humanity in a different light. Some rush to open doors, looking genuinely disturbed and sympathetic. Others are oblivious. Through it all, my expectations remain low; I cannot afford more disappointment.

Four days after my foot breaks, I head north for a previously arranged trip. I am scheduled to fly to Philadelphia, where I will rent a car, drive to Boston, and present a workshop at a conference. Somehow this all goes off without a hitch. I only need my right foot to drive, friends in Boston help out at every turn, and a woman on the plane gives up her seat for me in first class. I start making a list of small miracles.

In Boston, I accompany my friend Arrington to the convent in her neighborhood where she makes monthly overnight retreats. We each spend much of the day alone in meditation. Later I stand awkwardly during compline, the evening service. I take in the ritual, the prayers, and the beautiful sound of the nuns singing as an outsider who has been welcomed but is not so comfortable in the hospitality. After dinner, Arrington and I head to the rooftop patio which affords us a sparkling view of the city. I begin to talk about the relationship—what I'll remember, what I'll miss, what I'm glad is finished. I am crying, suddenly. This lasts a long, long time. The whole episode teaches me lessons of dependence, independence, and interdependence. Through it all, I struggle to remember one of the prime tenets of my faith—that we are all connected. And I feel blessed to have tangible reminders of it in my own life.

relationships and social change . . . .

Most, if not all, significant social change is relational. It begins when people decide that they are no longer willing to tolerate certain treatment, violence, or attitudes from others. The pursuit of justice is fundamentally about shifting the dynamics of a relationship. Efforts to right blatant wrongs depend on the strength of relationships for their success. The soundest ideas for action and organization can quickly fall by the wayside or fall apart if the relationships aren't strong enough.

Ultimately we must decide what *kind* of relationships we are going to have. Will they be based on ego or compassion, on our need to protect our own power, or on our need to love people more fully? Do we treat folks the way we want to be treated? And how do we love our neighbor in the midst of chaos? We may treat people well when things are running smoothly, but the minute our life gets hard, compassion goes out the window, and suddenly we're acting from a different place.

In the best of relationships, we stand in the truth of our experience, our own particularity, and we are better able to explore the differences and similarities between ourselves and others. It is this inspired encounter with the "other" that challenges both how we see ourselves and the rest of the world. In their multi-year study of over one hundred people who have sustained a commitment to the common good, the authors of *Common Fire: Living Lives of Commitment in a Complex World* found that "the single most important pattern we have found. . . . is what we have come to call a *constructive, enlarging engagement with the other.*" Laurent Parks Daloz, Sharon Daloz Parks, and Cheryl and Jim Keen found this goes beyond the day-to-day encounters with otherness that we all have. Rather, the transformational encounters are those that give rise to a true sense of connection and compassion, when there is "a recognition of shared capacity for the feelings that lie at the core of our essential humanity."

We need more atmospheres in which people can explore their connections to one another. In space made sacred by the presence of spirit, we begin to see each other in fuller dimensions, hear each other more completely, and sense the similarities that exist on a deeper level. Even a small amount of this kind of attention can alter our work and our lives considerably.

activities to do alone. . . . .

✎ **write it down**: looking at relationships

This activity was inspired by a set of questions that Polly Guthrie developed for the Second Circle.

1. Brainstorm a list of categories that describe the various relationships in your life. Here are some to get you started: Work, Home/Family, Community, Friends.

2. Draw two concentric circles (one inside the other) for each of these categories.

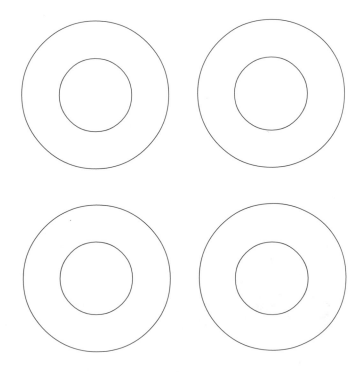

3. In the inner circle, write the names of the people with whom you have primary relationships. In the outer circle, write the names of others who are important in one way or another. Do this intuitively. There may be only one person in the inner circle, or there may be 10.
What, if anything, surprises you about these circles and the names within them?
What are your expectations of those relationships? Are these ever voiced? How?

4. Put a star next to the people who feed your spirit the most, the people you genuinely love to be with.
How do you nurture these relationships?
When do you realize you are consciously paying attention to them?

5. Next, underline the people you spend the most time with.
Are they mostly family members, coworkers, friends, others?

6. Circle the people you'd like to spend more time with.
What keeps this from happening?

7. Draw a line through the people you'd like to spend less time with.
Why? What is hard about these relationships? What do you learn from them?

This activity can also be done with groups by using the worksheet, "Looking at Relationships," in the Appendix.

activities to do with one other person . . . .

 mentoring and coaching

Who mentors you?
Whom do you mentor?
How often do you connect with him or her?
Do you wish you had more mentors in your life?
Who might some likely candidates be? Who do you know that you would love to have as a mentor? How might you ask them to participate in your life in this way?
If you could ask for coaching assistance with something, what would it be?
Whom would you ask?

℮ mentoring

(Also see "stories of mentoring: Lisa Sullivan" at the end of the chapter.)

In 12-step programs, people are asked to share their *experience, strength, and hope,* rather than give advice. I believe that this is similar to what many of the best mentors provide.

experience: We are drawn to potential mentors, because we feel they know or understand something we don't know or understand yet. A good mentor shares his or her experience when it is relevant to what you are going through, and he or she shares it in a way that is useful to you—a story, a suggestion, or a thoughtful question.

strength: The best mentors make us stronger, in our work and in our lives. Sometimes this means lending encouragement and support during rough times. Sometimes this means telling us the truth when no one else will. Sometimes it means asking a question that we might be dreading, because we fear the truth that lies in the answer.

hope: Above all, good mentors hold out hope for the best that we can be, a vision of possibility. They remind us what that is, what we're good at, and where we were headed before we got off track or sat down to rest.

Mentors can be extremely valuable. Sometimes mentors will appear, and we may not even notice them right away. Other times we may realize that we need a more consistent source of guidance in our lives, and off we go, looking for the right person. There is a saying, "When the student is ready, the teacher will appear." This is not always the case with mentors. Many of the best mentors already have full lives (You're looking for someone with a sense of purpose, right?) So persistence pays. Mentoring relationships last longer and grow deeper when there are clear expectations on both sides and these are discussed often.

℮ coaching

(Also see "stories of coaching: Julia Scatliff O'Grady" at the end of this chapter.)

Coaching is different from mentoring. It often entails more hands-on attention and assistance with a specific issue or problem. Coaching is actually a growing profession; more people are turning to coaches to help them set goals and develop the action steps necessary to achieve them. A good coach provides support and assistance along the way. Coaching may simply involve two people who are willing to listen to each other as they explore a new direction in their lives, deepen an existing commitment, or overcome a difficult situation. Like mentoring, coaching relationships work best when expectations are clearly laid out by both individuals. Pay attention to how much time you are spending together and who is benefiting.

℮ dealing with conflict

In our most important relationships, conflict is inevitable. We get angry, frustrated, or impatient, and the tension builds. The strongest relationships have conflict that gets addressed in ways that are respectful and open. The weakest relationships avoid conflict or ignore its very existence. Many of our relationships are somewhere in between: we may deal with the conflict, but we may not deal with it very well. The better we can deal with conflict, the stronger our relationships will be.

One of my mentors, George Lakey, taught me a conflict resolution technique that is still the most effective tool I know. It's simply called the X-Y-Z tool. For it to work, two (or more) people must be committed to the process. When you have an issue you'd like to address with someone, you can use the following framework, substituting your own words for X, Y, and Z:

> When you do X
> I feel Y
> Because of Z
> And what I need from you is . . .

Then the listener has a chance to respond, but *only* to the request being made. He or she can respond in one of three ways: Yes, I can honor your request; no, I can't honor your request; or maybe. In the case of no or maybe, it's helpful if the listener explains his or her response.

Here are some examples:
1. When you schedule meetings without telling me, I feel frustrated, because it often means I can't attend, and I would like to be present. What I need from you is to write me a quick note or leave me a message when you schedule something I need to be a part of.

2. When you interrupt me, especially in front of other people, I feel angry, because it makes it seem like I have nothing important to say. What I need

from you is simply to let me finish my sentence and not assume you know what I'm going to say.

3. When you monopolize the conversation in this group, I feel sad, because I feel like we are missing out on a lot of other perspectives in the room. What I need from you is a commitment to talking less and encouraging other folks to talk.

When I was first learning this tool, I was living with my brother, who was not quite as committed to kitchen cleanliness as I was. One day I came home to find many dishes in the sink. Instead of getting uptight, I calmly walked into the living room and said, "Stu, when you leave dishes in the sink, I feel sad and frustrated, because it makes me think you don't care about the state of our apartment or my feelings. What I really need from you is to make a more concentrated effort or for us to create a job chart, so you have other responsibilities instead of washing dishes."

At first, he seemed surprised. Up until this point my standard reactions to his negligence moved between scathing silence and exasperation. Now here I was, fairly calm, making a request that seemed reasonable. As a result, he was able to say that while he hated doing the dishes, he was more than willing to take on other chores around the apartment. In the end, I did more dishes (a job I've actually always enjoyed), and he took the tasks I don't like as much, like taking out the garbage and cleaning the bathroom.

The X-Y-Z formula may sound awkward the first time you use it, but stick with it because it really works. It gives people a framework to use so they can concentrate on what they need to say, without having to worry about the best way to say it. It allows for the basic information to be conveyed in a way that gives the listener specific and useful data: "This is what you do, and this is how it makes me feel." And, it allows for assertiveness, rather than passive or aggressive communication. *All of this makes it easier for people to take greater risks in their communication, which in turn leads to greater opportunities for strengthening relationships.*

activities to do with groups . . . .

@ finding out who we are
There are a million ways to do introductions when a group comes together for the first time. My friend Darryl Lester taught me these four seemingly simple questions which yield powerful answers.

Who are you?
Where have you been?
Where are you going?
Why are you here?

℮ listening with reverence

This is one of the most important building blocks in any relationship—the ability to listen well and with compassion, without responding. At first we think that our response as a listener is vital. We have been taught to nod our heads in agreement, laugh in the appropriate places, tell our own stories to demonstrate our understanding, come up with solutions, and give great advice. In all of these cases, the usual result is that the person speaking does so for our benefit and not just his own. The speaker become ultra-sensitive to our reactions and conscious of what impact their words are having. The focus subtly shifts from whatever she was speaking about to a conversation about something slightly, somewhat, or entirely different.

Listening with reverence, not reaction, gives the other person more space to tell her story without having to worry about how it will be received. The speaker actually becomes empowered to follow her own path rather than taking the direction(s) offered by the listener's questions or comments. She continues speaking in her own language, from her own frame of reference.

The time we spent together—whatever it was, twenty minutes, two hours, an evening—began to have a shape we filled better each time we met. It wasn't only that I listened to Rhoda, it was that we listened to each other. I saw after a while that each of us was concentrated on what the other had to say. It was the concentration that was so striking: I'd never before been conscious of its presence in conversation. It made me sing inside. It wasn't that I came away thinking my words brilliant; it was only that I came away feeling I had been fully heard, and because I was being fully heard I was saying everything I had to say. It seemed to me, then, that ever since I could remember I'd been fighting for someone's undivided attention in conversation. Now I had it. I could breathe easy. I didn't have to be fast on my feet. I could think before I spoke.

~ Vivian Gornick, *Approaching Eye Level*

first, organize people into pairs. you can:

1. Make two facing concentric circles, one inside the other, and have people partner with whomever they are facing.

2. Have the group count off one, two, one, two; ask all the "twos" to take off one shoe and put it in the middle of the room. Have the "ones" take one of the shoes in the middle and find the owner. That person becomes their partner. (This one takes a little bit longer.)

3. Form a circle, standing close so shoulders are touching. People should reach out one hand, and the first hand they grab is their partner.

second, decide how you want to ask questions

You can ask a question (see below for ideas) for the first partner to answer, explaining they'll have three minutes. After three minutes, ask the partners to switch, and the second partner answers the questions. After three more minutes, you ask the next question and proceed from there. With this option you have to pay very close attention to time, and you'll constantly be interrupting the group while people are talking. Give people a warning, like "Finish your thought and then switch." Each time you say a question, you may want to write it so everyone can see it. The second person to speak will then have a reminder.

TO READ TO THE GROUP:
This is an exercise in listening with reverence but without reaction. First, decide who will go first. You are going to hear questions to answer. When one person is speaking, the partner should be actively listening, not talking. You can respond non-verbally in a way that conveys support to your partner. Our natural tendency is to agree or offer advice or a similar story, but this exercise is not intended to be a conversation. There is a lot of time for that in our lives, but not a lot of time to really be heard. Notice as you do this how it feels to listen well and how it feels to be listened to.

You can also write the series of questions on a large piece of paper and give people 10 minutes each to answer them. Folks will spend less time on each question if they have all of the questions in front of them, but then they'll have more time to talk about whichever one seems the most important to them. Responses will be even more substantive and thoughtful if you begin with a few minutes of silence.

four sets of questions for listening with reverence

1. To explore your own faith tradition and find out more about each other's faith backgrounds (a particularly good idea if you are just introducing a stronger reflection component into your organization), choose the questions below that you like the best:
What faith, if any, did you grow up with?
What were your best memories of this tradition growing up?
What about that tradition is still important to you now?
Where are you now in your journey with faith or spirituality?

How is this journey connected to your work, if at all?
How has faith been a barrier or enhancement to your work?
Why do you do what you do?
What are some guiding principles or values that are important to you?

2. <u>To explore spiritual practice</u> and the presence of spirit in one's life: (You might use this in connection with activities in the "Spiritual Practice" chapter.)
What does calm feel like to you?
What do you do that heals you?
How can you tell when you feel grounded at work?
How can you tell when you're not?

3. <u>To face hard issues coming up in an organization</u>:
What do you believe is working well with the group right now?
What would you like to see improved?
What is most frustrating to you?
What do you love about this project/organization?

4. <u>To prepare for an event or initiative</u>:
What are you excited about?
What are you worried or scared about?
What do you want to make sure you're prepared for?
How will you get prepared?
What do you want to be able to say at the end of this?

℮ honoring each other

This comes from Meredith Emmett and is a great exercise for a group whose time together is ending. Write down each group member's name on a piece of paper and put them all in a hat. Pass the hat around, asking each person to draw one piece of paper out. Explain that at your last meeting each person will have the opportunity to honor the person whose name they drew out of the hat. It's optimal to give everyone 24 hours to prepare. Less time will work if necessary. You will need an evening to do this ceremony.

WRITTEN INSTRUCTIONS FOR THE GROUP:
(Hand out a copy of the instructions on the next page and explain them.)

honoring ceremony

You can honor this person in any way you see fit. Think about the following:

What have you learned from the person over the course of your time together?

What has struck you about this person?

What does he or she bring to the group, and to the world, that is unique and special?

Tangible representations have lasting impact. You can use any materials already available to you in this process, but no purchasing is allowed.

Please don't reveal whom you are honoring until the time comes.

activities for groups: going deeper . . . .

the spectrum of our beliefs

If you are working with a group or organization where people have a wide variety of feelings about faith (and this is usually the case), this activity will help folks see the spectrum of beliefs which exist. It will validate those voices that might otherwise be marginalized in the group, those who are less tied to faith, and those who are uncomfortable even talking about it.

TO READ TO THE GROUP:
This activity will allow us to see the wide range of perspectives and beliefs about faith that probably exist within this group. I am going to read you a series of statements. With each one, I am going to ask you to find your place along an imaginary diagonal line (or lay down a piece of masking tape) *from one corner of the room to the opposite corner. One end will represent those who "agree" with the statement read; the other end will represent those who "disagree."*

When each statement is read, you will name the two polar ends of the line. Repeat the directions: "Agree this corner, disagree this corner. Find your place on the spectrum." When people have found their place in the line, you can begin interviewing people. This means asking them why they are in that spot on the line. It's important to get a variety of perspectives for each question; interview people at various places along the middle and on each end.

STATEMENTS TO READ:

Faith or spirituality is an important part of my life.
Faith is an important part of my work.
Faith is important to the communities I work with.
I have a hard time understanding religious people or faith in general.

Add your own statements to the list. Let people participating present statements to the group as well. You should continue to do the interviewing.

NOTE: People may get tired of standing after a while and this will lessen their concentration. If that's happening, suggest that folks sit down right where they are while the interviewing takes place.

℮ step into the center

This is a faith-based version of a well-known diversity exercise called Cross the Line. The guidelines for Step into the Center are similar to Cross the Line, but the questions are very different.

You are going to read a series of statements to the group about faith and spiritual practice. With each one, group members will decide whether or not the statement applies to them. If it does, they will be asked to step into the center of the circle and notice who else stepped in with them and who did not. After a few seconds, they will step back into the outer circle, and the next statement will be read. For some statements, it may be that no one enters the center. Wait a few seconds anyway before asking the next question.

TO READ TO THE GROUP:

This activity is called "Step into the Center," and it will give us a chance to get to know ourselves and the group better. I am going to read you a series of statements about faith and spiritual practice. When a statement is read, those to whom it pertains will be asked to step into the center of the circle and stand there for a few seconds. Everyone will be asked to notice who is in the inner circle and who remains in the outer circle.

With each statement, it is your choice how to respond. You are under no obligation to reveal anything about yourself that you don't want to reveal. You cannot, however, ask for clarification about a statement when it is read. It will be up to you to interpret it for yourself and answer it accordingly.

This exercise should be done in silence. Resist the temptation to react verbally to the questions in any way, including laughing.

Step into the Center if you. . .

Consider yourself to be a religious person.

Consider yourself to be a spiritual person.

Worship regularly with a group.

Have ever been to the place of worship of a faith or denomination other than your own.

Grew up in an African spiritual tradition.

Grew up Buddhist.

Grew up Catholic.

Grew up Hindu.

Grew up Jewish.

Grew up Protestant.

Grew up Muslim.

Grew up in a Native American spiritual tradition.

Grew up Quaker.

Grew up Unitarian.

Grew up in a faith or spiritual tradition not mentioned.

Have ever held a position of responsibility in a religious institution or place of worship.

Believe in God.

Don't believe in God.

Believe in something else.

Were raised in an interfaith household.

Are now part of an interfaith household.

Have read the Bible all the way through.

Have read portions of the Torah in Hebrew.

Have read the Koran.

Are familiar with a sacred religious text not yet mentioned.

Perform a religious ritual regularly.

Don't believe in organized religion.

Have ever changed your religion.

Have parents who are very religious.

Find that religious people make you uncomfortable.

Find that nonreligious people make you uncomfortable.

Have ever considered being a nun or priest.

the power of relationships

There is a story about Caesar Chavez, the legendary organizer and head of the United Farm Workers. Three young organizers, eager to learn from the best, drove through the night to see Chavez at his home. When they got there, they all sat down to talk.

"Tell us, please," they said, "the secret to being a good organizer."

Chavez replied, "Well, first you talk to one person, then you talk to another person. . . ."

"No, no, no. We want to hear how it really works. What you've done here that's made farmworker organizing and the grape boycott so successful."

Chavez was silent for a moment.

"Well," he said finally, "First you talk to one person, then you talk to another person. . . ."

Have ever considered being a minister, a rabbi, or other religious figure.
Are Christian and believe in salvation only through Christ.
Are Jewish and believe Jews are the chosen people.

You can pick and choose from the list above. Add your own questions and eliminate those which seem inappropriate. Remember though that this activity is meant to be a bit risky. It will open the door to much deeper conversations about faith. After you've asked all the questions, ask the group if anyone has a question they'd like to ask.

Once all questions have been asked, move on to the small group discussion component. Do not do this exercise without time to debrief. The resulting dialogue is a vital element of the exercise.
Have people get into groups of three or four. Give the groups at least 20 minutes to talk. Set the stage for their discussion with the following questions:

> *What did you notice about yourself?*
> *What did you notice about other people?*
> *When did you feel comfortable?*
> *When did you feel uncomfortable?*

℮ clearness sessions

A clearness session is a Quaker concept, and it is a way for people to assist each other in discerning life choices. A small group of people comes together to help one person clarify a present reality or determine a future direction. They do this through compassionate listening and careful questioning.

The individual convening the clearness session might want to give information to the group ahead of time. For example, he might write a page or two about different possibilities he is considering and the questions he has been asking himself. The role of the clearness group is to hear the individual, reflect on what they have heard, and ask questions based on that. More specifically, the group should be prepared to:

- Listen carefully to the individual's story and central challenge
- Ask strategic questions
- Reflect on what is seen, heard, and felt
- Suggest possible directions, options, possibilities
- Offer wisdom, ideas, and challenges
- Point out false assumptions or other elements/aspects that are limiting

It's great to have one person facilitate the discussion and another person take notes so the person convening the session can just listen.

Strategic questions are those which. . .
- identify ideals, vision, dreams, goals:
  I hear you saying that you want to initiate a new program.
- consider obstacles:
  What gets in the way of taking six months to work overseas?
- uncover strategies for change and hidden solutions:
  Have you talked to your boss about partnering on that project?
- ask the unaskable:
  Are you wanting to leave this current job or relationship or city?
- consider consequences:
  What would happen if you cut your hours back to make space for something else?

resources for relationships . . . .

Chetanananda, Swami. *The Logic of Love*. Portland, OR: Rudra Press, 1992. Beautiful discussions of what it means to live a life of inner mastery and authentic love.

Covey, Stephen R. *Seven Habits of Highly Effective People: Powerful Lessons in Personal Change*. New York: Fireside, 1989. A principle-centered approach for solving personal and professional problems.

Daloz, Laurent A. Parks; Cheryl H. Keen, James P. Keen, and Sharon Daloz Parks. *Common Fire: Leading Lives of Commitment in a Complex World*. Boston: Beacon Press, 1996.

Drener, Henry. "Why did the People of Roseto Live So Long?" *Natural Health*, September/October 1993. Explores the miracle of a small town in Pennsylvania famous for low death rates as a result of close-knit families and communities.

Green, Tova and Peter Woodrow. *Insight in Action*. With Fran Peavy. Philadelphia: New Society Publishers, 1994. Explanation and stories of three tools for supporting a life of commitment: support groups, clearness, and strategic questioning.

Lerner, Harriet Goldhor. *The Dance of Anger*. New York: Harper & Row, 1985. Written for women, this book offers a look at how to channel anger constructively and change unhealthy patterns of relationships.

Levine, Stephen and Ondrea. *Embracing the Beloved: Relationship as a Path of Awakening*. Two Harbors, MA; Anchor Books: 1996. A look at how familial and love relationships can be an opportunity for growth and healing.

Spears, Larry C., ed. *Insights on Leadership: Service, Stewardship, Spirit and Servant-Leadership*. New York: John Wiley & Sons, 1998. Collection of essays and articles from a variety of individuals on the concept of servant-leadership and its possible applications.

Tannen, Deborah. *You Just Don't Understand: Women and Men in Conversation*. New York: Ballantine Books, 1990. Groundbreaking for many, this book explores the differences in communication between men and women.

stories of right relationship . . . .

Polly Guthrie

Polly Guthrie, a native North Carolinian, has worked in women's organizations and philanthropy for eight years, most recently with the Triangle Community Foundation. She is working on a master's degree in business administration at the University of North Carolina at Chapel Hill to pursue her interest in economic development and non-profit management.

CH: Polly, tell me first about your faith background.

PG: I was raised an Episcopalian, shopped around for different churches for a while, and ultimately came back to the Episcopal church, because I'm drawn to the liturgy and the sacramental tradition.

I know you've thought a lot about the idea of "right relationship." What does that phrase mean to you?

To me it's certainly similar to a Buddhist concept of relationship—that relationships are a way that we can make manifest between other humans the love that God chose for us. In order to move God's love from a static thing to an active presence, we can relate to other people in a just and meaningful way, through relationship.

What does that look like?

It means being intentional in relationships, which means that you sometimes choose to do the hard thing because it's the right and just thing to do. That might mean holding someone accountable or loving someone who's hard to love, or at a time when they're hard to love. It means actively seeing relationships as God's work. It means acting in such a way it's clear that you believe relationships are sacred and holy and deserve to be conducted befitting that holiness. Being in relationship is an integral way to be a person of faith.

> **Being in relationship is an integral way to be a person of faith.**

I've heard you speak often about the passage from Micah that you love, that we are called upon to "Act justly, love mercy, and walk humbly with our God."

Acting justly and loving mercy are about how you treat other people, and walking humbly with your God is certainly about how you conduct yourself. If I had to distill my faith down to a few sentences, the other one is where Jesus says: "Thou shall love thy Lord, your God, with all thy heart, soul, body, and mind. This is the first and greatest commandment, and the second is like unto it; thou shalt love they neighbor as thyself. On these two commandments hang all the law and the prophets."

Both those phrases are about relationships: your relationship with God and your relationship with other people. The way you make your relationship with God manifests in the way you treat other people.

How do you think about the idea of right relationship at work?

I think about it pretty actively. It's about nurturing people, and so it means both writing notes to people I hear won an award or remembering to commend someone at my office who's just completed some task really well. It also means challenging assumptions or statements of people when they concern me. I think about it more when particular challenges arise—someone has said something that really bothers me, and I call them on it instead of just sweeping it under the rug.

How else might people cultivate this at work?

When we're working for social change, and we treat people poorly in the process, it's not worth it. I'm a big believer that the means don't justify the ends, so how we treat each other in the process is integral to the vision for which we're working. When you call someone up to help post flyers the day before an event, you treat them with respect and compassion. If you're calling someone who didn't show up, it doesn't mean you don't share your frustration; you consider how to treat that person with respect while holding them accountable for what they should have done. It's the golden rule: treat people as you'd want to be treated. That sounds so trite, but it's a pretty darn good rule to follow.

> When we're working for social change, and we treat people poorly in the process, it's not worth it. I'm a big believer that the means don't justify the ends.

Is there a direct connection between your faith and the path you've chosen?

Certainly. As Micah says, "Act justly, love mercy, and walk humbly with your God." My work in this world has been about how I can do those things on a personal and professional level. Part of acting justly and loving mercy means looking for ways to increase social justice. And I've done that by advocating abortion rights for women, working to prevent sexual violence, targeting philanthropic dollars towards a community's most pressing needs, and I expect to be doing that next by finding ways that economic tools can help address poverty.

In both the Judeo and the Christian traditions, we will be judged by how we treat the poor among us. I have felt a calling and a drive to do what I can to work on issues affecting the poor among us, whether it be the poor in spirit or the usual interpretation regarding the lack of wealth.

Do you remember how this perspective came about for you?

It's been evolving. I had a seminal experience when I was 15 or 16, and I went to Haiti with my church. Seeing poverty of that magnitude really shifted my lens on the world. Four days after I got back from Haiti, I went to the beach with a couple I'd been baby-sitting for and their eleven-month-old infant died. Even though they had all the money in the world, they couldn't save him. And I knew if I went back to Haiti six months later, most of those babies wouldn't have been there. Those two events, so close together, set into motion a whole new way of thinking. It called into question, "What's the purpose or meaning of life? Why do people suffer?"

Faith for me is not about "Did Jesus really rise again?" or the doctrine of the Episcopal church. It's what I believe and how I try to live my life, according to that. I just sort of assumed that everyone thinks about these things. It's such a part of how I am and how I live that it's sort of like trying to describe how you breathe.

stories of mentoring . . . .

Lisa Sullivan

Lisa Sullivan recently founded LISTEN, Inc., a non-profit organization that identifies, prepares, and supports youth leadership in urban neighborhoods and communities. Lisa also serves as a consultant for the Rockefeller Foundation's Next Generation Leadership program. Prior to that she was director of the field division at the Children's Defense Fund. Her work began there in 1991, when she cofounded the Black Student Leadership Network. While pursuing a master's degree in political science at Yale University, Lisa organized youth and students in New Haven.

CH: Lisa, you've made a serious commitment to mentoring. How would you define it?

LS: I would start off by using the word "mutual," because I believe that a good mentoring relationship is mutually beneficial for both partners. The next thing is the sharing of information, and again, that's mutual. I've got several strong mentoring relationships. The one that I've been in the longest is with a young woman, Deidre, who is now 27. I've been her mentor since she was 14.

The first two years of the relationship were about me gaining her trust. I was doing community organizing in New Haven, and she was a high school student. A counselor pointed her in my direction. When you're dealing with young people of color from communities where the infrastructure has broken down—the family or the school or the neighborhood—they are used to bad things happening. They've been abandoned so many times, a mentor is just another adult who's going to let them down.

It was consistency that broke the ice. In a moment of crisis, I became the person to come to. She recognized something genuine was happening. This was a young woman who was the youngest of 12. She had raised herself and didn't know how to trust. She found herself wanting to build a relationship with me and didn't quite know how to do it. Suddenly, I had this 16-year-old ringing my buzzer every day, coming to my house, taking over my bedroom, talking on the phone, giving out my phone number. She was integrating herself into my life.

Then came the second phase: making commitments, being there through thick and thin. Together, we got her out of high school and into Spelman College in Atlanta. I had to raise Deirdre's tuition, buy her plane ticket home for Thanksgiving and Christmas. I took her shopping before college, and we actually had our first major disagreement. I had my functional "we're-going-to-college" list, and she had her "we're-going-to-Spelman-I need-fly-gear" list. It was like parenting.

When she got to Spelman, she felt out of place, because everyone was middle-class and here she was from the ghetto, the first one to go to college. I went to Family Day, and I connected her to my support system in Atlanta. As we've grown, the relationship has gone through several changes. Now we interact as peers, though I'm 10 years older. I'm providing information and perspective, but of course she doesn't have to do what I say, and I'm okay with that. All of my roommates from grad school feel like they have helped to raise her. She's in law school now at Villanova, and she gets pampered by all of the women in my life as if she's my child.

How do you balance a number of mentoring relationships and still make them meaningful?

There are different levels of involvement. There's probably a significant number of young people who claim me as a mentor. That means being accessible and responsive to them, within reason. I try to keep up with them on a quarterly basis, see what's on their radar screen. As things come across my desk, I try to make connections between them and those opportunities.

And then there's another tier—the people who have been explicit in asking me to be a mentor. Right now, that's probably 8-10 people. We've actually explored what it is they need from me, and it is clearly a mentoring relationship. It gave me an opportunity to assess what was going on in my life and whether I could show up for them. Interestingly, half of them are men.

Why is that interesting?

Because it's been my experience—and I've talked to other Black women about this—the older Black men get, the harder it is for them to relate to Black women as mentors. It's easier when they're younger, because it's a mommy or sister kind of thing. There's a bit of truth to this whole thing about Black women raising daughters and loving boys. But there are several Black men who call and e-mail me on a regular basis seeking advice and support around their life decisions.

You must have had someone who made similar commitments to you.

My father. I'm the oldest, and I was raised to be the "big sister." We were typical latch-key kids. I had the responsibility of getting my sister from the babysitter, fixing her snack, and basically taking care of her. I grew up knowing that you take care of people younger than yourself. Another piece is just who I am. I am one of those people born to support the underdog. I believe so much in young people; I feel passionately about young people who've been abandoned. And I realize I've been incredibly blessed in my life with parents who have been very supportive of me and gave me a lot. Out of five other Black women I was housed with in college, I was the only one whose father was present and who had a positive relationship with my father.

> Another piece is just who I am. I am one of those people born to support the underdog.

And there must be other shoulders that you've stood on. Who else would you consider to be a mentor for you?

Every step of the way I could say there have been people who have significantly influenced my development. Some of them have been peers; there's the traditional litany of teachers. Through age 18, it was definitely parents, godparents, and people in the neighborhood. And then from ages 18-22, being in Atlanta at Clark University, it was definitely faculty people. In New Haven, my best friend in graduate school, who is deceased, was a guy named Tony Thomas. I can honestly say that if Tony had not come into my life, I'm not sure I would have hit the level of leadership that I've hit. He saw me through Yale. He was my guardian angel, helped me demystify the place, put in it perspective. He convinced me that the world was my oyster. He was hugely significant and influential in my 20s.

The other person is Dr. Susan Lincoln. She is extraordinary. By the time she was 20, she had four children, was on welfare, and had dropped out of school. She refused to give up. She got her GED, her bachelor's degree, her master's degree, and her Ph.D. in education. Before retiring as Dean of Students, she was the bedrock of the community college in New Haven and very active in the community—politically and socially. She's amazing. Very well-known and respected by her community in New Haven, fiercely independent, and a quiet person of substance—not a lot of fanfare. When she makes up her mind she's doing something, it's done.

Dr. Lincoln tells this story: I was organizing young people in the Black community in New Haven, and I convened some of the community matriarchs for a meeting. She turned to her daughter and said, "This young woman needs our help." She came over and wrote a check for $250 for our voter registration project and said, "If you need anything, give me a call." She's been my constant from graduate school until now.

Who do I cry to? It's my father, it's Susan, a small circle of Black women peers.

What's been the role of God or faith in all of this?

Well, right now in my office I'm looking at a photograph of Ella Baker on one wall. On another wall I'm looking at Fannie Lou Hamer. Over my desk is Septima Clark, Langston Hughes, Mary McLeod Bethune, Althea Gibson, Frederick Douglas, and my friend Tony Thomas. For a while now I have known that my energy, my passion, my commitment are all things that are flowing through me. It's the spirit of these other people that lives in me. I may be tired as shit, but I go home, I get a good night's sleep, I wake up at 6:45, and I get to it. And I can't explain that. I can't explain my energy level. It's not about me.

Have you always felt that?

I've always known I was different. As a child and then a teenager, it scared me. I spent my college years trying to run away from it. My relationship with Tony and Susan was really about getting comfortable with it and naming it, that there was something very spiritual about who I was. I keep meeting older Black women who are in touch with their spiritual power, and they just lay hands on me. When I was 20, I had people telling me that I was an old soul. And sometimes there are things that I know that I don't know how I know them.

And you don't practice anything on a regular basis?

No, see, Lisa doesn't practice anything. I've got all kinds of witches and priestesses all around me. Every one of them is practicing something. I respect their spiritual beliefs, but I'm not engaged in a specific practice. I've read quite a bit about rituals and spirituality. Maybe the older I get, the more I will enter into a practice of my spiritual self, but it scares me right now because I feel very powerful and to think that I would be practicing, that's a little too much for me to handle—at least right now.

stories on coaching . . . .

Julia Scatliff O'Grady

Julia Scatliff O'Grady initiated and directed Southern Community Partners, a project of the Lyndhurst Foundation. Through Southern Community Partners, Julia provided funds, technical assistance, and coaching for 34 young people throughout the Southeast, all of whom founded community-based programs. Julia has just initiated Grace, a growing network of coaches who work with community leaders.

CH: *Julia, you've spent a lot of your time coaching young people who are doing innovative community work Why is this coaching relationship such an important part of the work you do?*

JSO: I think it's the only way people can actually reach their potential—to have someone who can challenge them, nurture them, and remember what they said they'd do. You expect to learn from a podium, but you don't embrace learning until you build a relationship with someone. I've heard a lot of lectures, and I remember the relationship learning.

It must be a new type of relationship for many with whom you work. What is the impact?

Some people are really taken aback by my desire to work with them. I met a 16-year-old at the Governor's Summit [on America's Promise] who is an amazing guy, really involved in community service. I followed up with a letter after the summit with some information he needed, and two weeks ago I sent more information, because I met someone I thought he should talk to. I got a letter from him, and I could tell by his tone that this approach was out of the blue and new, for someone to take an interest.

> One of the hardest parts of my decision to be an active coach is that I don't always know the impact I'm making in people's lives.

One of the hardest parts of my decision to be an active coach is that I don't always know the impact I'm making in people's lives. So it's lonely because I am not sure if I've been a pest or if I've been useful. At times it's hard for me to know what I've actually done when I'm not the creator; I'm the champion of the creator.

What do you think is most important in this process of coaching?

Trust is the top requirement, and I don't always have that trust with people, particularly as a funder. I am always struggling between being that caring friend and that jerk who gets people to operate around deadlines, to hold them up to their high ideals of who they are. I know I have a reputation for being a really thorough critic and asking tons of questions and just holding people to the fire until they feel comfort in that place.

What about coaching relationships that are peer-to-peer?

In being with a peer, I'm vulnerable too. That's where I grow more, because I have to put myself on the line, and I have to be open to critique as well. That's the only way the peer relationship will grow. I have really loved being more deliberate, seeking out conversations with people who have what I need. It's hard to listen well because our brains are at a much higher speed than they were a hundred years ago. Listening requires a peaceful place. I think the exercise that you pushed me to do on envisioning the future was really transformative. I didn't think I had the answer in my brain when I was asked to do it, but out comes the plan for a year and a half. That's the kind of peer-to-peer coaching outcome that's phenomenal.

I really want to see people of all different backgrounds, not flying across the country for the big answer but getting it in Durham. Peer-to-peer coaching challenges the assumption that you have to hire a consultant from five hundred miles away for your every need and pay them a lot of money. I really appreciated Evelyn Mattern's comment that it's best to surround yourself with two or three people who can help you bring your interests to life. A lot of it is getting clear about what you want in life. Peers have helped me on that front more than mentors or being a coach.

Why do you think that's true?

Peers have a similar history and day-to-day framework, so the power dynamic is not swinging in either direction, in the best of circumstances. What's key is being more honest about whether you feel competitive at that moment, or sad, or frustrated. In a typical friendship, you let most of that stay inside your body. It doesn't feel so bad when it comes out into the air.

How would you advise others to develop a coaching relationship with their peers?

First, people should know that even some of your closest friends will think you're weird when you approach them with this idea of coaching each other, because custom says wisdom comes from the elders only. But don't stay there too long. It's key to create a list of dreams, small to big, that you hope to see and then think of whom you know and how they can help you. People of all ages are so afraid to ask for help of any kind. Coaching each other helps you get over the fear.

Why do you think folks are reluctant to go beyond the normal structure of a friendship?

I think people think it's corny to be deliberate; it goes against the grain. There's our planned work time, and then there's our relaxed, free time, and this coaching relationship bridges the two. It's a kind of code-shifting that most of us haven't learn to do very well. A lot of times the traditional relationship doesn't transform into a peer-to-peer coaching one, because you're not observant. You don't see that your closest friends and colleague have certain talents. Once you pick up on that talent, you can push it. I'm really stunned by how little it takes to inspire someone to do great things.

relationships.

circles

We are all longing to go home to some place we have never been—a place, half-remembered, and half-envisioned, we can only catch glimpses of from time to time. Community. Somewhere, there are people to whom we can speak with passion without having the words catch in our throats. Somewhere a circle of hands will open to receive us, eyes will light up as we enter, voices will celebrate with us whenever we come into our own power. Community means strength that joins our strength to do the work that needs to be done. Arms to hold us when we falter. A circle of healing. A circle of friends. Someplace where we can be free.

~ Starhawk, *Dreaming the Dark*

Whether the symbol of the circle appears in primitive sun worship or modern religion, in myths or dreams, in the mandalas drawn by Tibetan monks, in the ground plans of cities, or in the spherical concepts of early astronomers, it always points to the single most vital aspect of life—its ultimate wholeness.

~ Carl Jung, *Man and His Symbols*

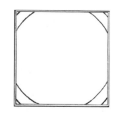

questions for reflection

How do you find like-minded people with whom you can share your joys and your struggles?

What communities or "Circles" have supported you in your life? How did they come together?

What made these groups meaningful to you?

what is a circle? . . . .

Small groups of spirited and faithful individuals coming together on a regular basis for a common purpose are nothing new, nor do they belong only to one tradition. Seekers have always needed communities to reinforce their journey and to keep themselves authentic. They have a great legacy in old and new forms that continue to thrive: in the Jewish havurah, Christian mission groups, the tribe, 12-Step programs, Bible study groups, women's spirituality groups, and many others. As we've come to define it in stone circles, a Circle is a small group of individuals who gather regularly, with intention, to support each other, renew themselves spiritually, and explore areas of common interest. Circles spark intense dialogue, ongoing challenge, new relationships, and a lot of soul-searching.

The circle is a feminine shape; a feminine sound. It is a protected and consecrated space, a space where all things and all people are equal. The circle is at the very root of equality. It is the symbol for equality. The circle is at the root of true humility where each is seen as important to the whole and none is more important than any other. God is a circle whose circumference is nowhere and whose center is everywhere. . . . We stand at the center of the Circle, always. All ceremony begins with honoring the Circle. All ceremony, all prayer, all celebration, all rituals, all moments in time. We are related to things, visible and invisible.

~ Scout Cloud Lee, *The Circle is Sacred*

turning point . . . .

It is June 1995, and I am initiating the First Circle, literally the first Circle stone circles would convene. I am not sure that I know what I am doing or why. I know now what I didn't see as clearly then—that spiritual work is always a risk with a great deal of unknowns. Unsure of how to proceed, I do what organizers do anytime they want to make something happen: I get on the phone.

I ask people what they think of the idea of a small group of activists, loosely defined, coming together for spiritual renewal. Would they come? Most people are favorable, if not a little confused, so I schedule a potluck dinner at my house. Some people can't make it on the date, so I schedule a second one as well. I send out a letter with directions, stating my intentions. I am not sure if any of it will make sense to people.

People call and say they are coming. What am I supposed to do now? The day of the first gathering I stay home and clean my house for five hours. This is about more than sweeping and mopping. I am clearing the way for new people, new energy, and new ideas. It is a chance just to be in the moment, a ritual of sorts. In the midst of this act of mindfulness, the doorbell rings. I open it to find two young men, Mormon missionaries from the Church of Latter Day Saints, standing at my door. A grin creeps across my face.

"Good afternoon, ma'am," one of them says, "We'd like to tell you about a path that you might not have considered. You might have heard about us on television or something."

"Actually, I don't watch much TV. . ."

"Good, that's good," the other one says.

"But I certainly know who you folks are. I was in Salt Lake City once. Pretty beautiful." Now I'm starting to sound ridiculous, I think.

"Yes, yes it is," they respond. "And we'd really like to share more about it with you."

"You know what?" I continue, calmly, "I'm on a path that I feel good about. I'm all about God; I just think that I think about it differently than you guys do." They stare at me blankly for a couple of seconds and then smile.

"Well, ma'am, thanks for your time. You have a great day."

"You too," I answer. "Good luck."

I closed the door and resume cleaning. Good luck? A Jewish girl wishing two nice Mormon missionary boys good luck. When I stopped to think about it, their activity wasn't all that different than mine. Wasn't I a missionary of sorts? This gathering at my house, it was a way of saying to people, "Come on, put a little more spirit in your life. Get a little more God."

circles and social change

[We need] small groups gathering and creating help for us all.
We need smaller groups now. That's all I can talk of and it's not nearly enough. . . .
Hope a new class of people who will know what's necessary. . . .
It's these small groups of people who will lead in the eventual help. . .
people who will be able to make the change to a higher place. . . .
Their small risks will become law.
~ Lewis Mumford

Small groups whose risks become law. I felt a powerful recognition with these words the first time I read them. We know that social change and social movements do not begin at mass rallies, in town meetings, or with the forming of organizations. They begin around someone's kitchen table, on the front porch, or at the local diner. They begin, and change begins, when small groups of people make commitments to each other, commitments that allow them to do something they would not do on their own. These groups or Circles provide a space in which people can heal from the past, learn to honor what is truly present, and envision a radically different future.

Church of the Savior, which runs a vast array of social service programs in Washington, D.C., believes strongly in small mission groups. These groups offer one powerful model of what is possible. These groups have at least two purposes: (1) to serve the surrounding community and (2) to support the inner and outer lives of those doing the work. In *Servant Leadership, Servant Structures*, the story of Church of the Savior, author Elizabeth O'Connor relays the importance of these groups which:

> . . . *create safe space in which the members could tell their stories—what has happened to them in the past, what is happening in their hearts in their present life situations, and their dreams, fears and hopes for the future. These groups allow for deeper and deeper levels of trust, which in turn allows people to give more and more of themselves. . . . Much more than the confession of our light or our darkness is involved. What is involved is the recovery of love, itself, the communion that is the deepest need of every life, the unlocking of that infinite capacity that each one has to be a friend and to have a friend.*

activities to do with groups

the Circle forming

What purpose might a small group like a Circle serve in your life?
What would you hope to get out of it?
Do you know of any groups in your area you might join? Ask around, check out bulletin boards and your local papers. Call people and go to a meeting or gathering if possible.
Do you have the energy and time to get a Circle off the ground?
Do you have other friends who might be interested in doing this with you?

> There is a myth that people involved in social change work take time to think and reflect,
> that their actions are grounded in all of the readings of past spiritual and political teachers.
> The reality is most of us don't.
> The union of soul and work has presented a path I did not think possible.
> ~ Julia Scatliff O'Grady, Member of the First Circle

who might come

Circles have attracted folks who:

1. Are very connected to a religious tradition but interested in discovering the spiritual elements of their religion and/or connecting with people of different faith backgrounds;

Most systems or patterns
based upon the circle or the
cycle tend to have 12 as their
end-limit. There are 12 hours
in a day and 12 months of the
year, 12 major gods of
mythologies and 12 signs of
the zodiac. There were 12
Knights of King Arthur's
Round Table, 12 apostles,
and 12 Peers of France. And,
it seems that groups of 8-12
function best to give
everyone a sense of space
while not losing momentum.

2. Have little or no connection to organized religion and are exploring avenues for bringing spirituality into their lives; and/or

3. Come expressly to make greater connections between work and spiritual practice.

My whole transformation was catalyzed by stone circles. I definitely feel more sure, more grounded, and more supported in the work that I'm doing. It's a different approach to the work I'm doing. Before I was running on two wheels: one was acting, one was reacting. It was all about motion. What the Second Circle brought in was two other pieces—groundedness and the emotional piece that helped me better understand myself. So now I'm cruising on all fours.

~ Daughtry Carstarphen, Member of the Second Circle

getting the word out

Are there one or two other people to be your partners in starting a Circle? It is infinitely easier and more fun to share the load, and the risk, of initiating something like this. Then get the word out to people. Having personal conversations with potential participants is key. I spoke with almost everyone one-on-one, either before or right after our first gathering. This personal contact made the difference. Decide on your optimal number and reach out accordingly; you don't want to invite 30 people if you're looking for a core group of 12 (and 12 is a great number for a Circle), though certainly not everyone who comes to an initial meeting will want to join.

℗ your first gathering

Start your Circle with an introductory meeting, like a potluck supper. Find a comfortable and quiet space for your first meeting. Ideally, this might be your living room (or someone else's), but if you're in a big city where folks are very spread out, you might consider using a lounge in an office building or community center that you can reserve after business hours. If you're using a space outside the home, think about how you might want to transform the space so that it creates the atmosphere you are seeking. You want your meeting space to feel intimate, safe, and sacred. And, it's good to have some consistency. At each of our Circle gatherings I set up the same simple altar with a circle of stones, candles, something from nature, and the Tibetan prayer chimes I often use to open and/or close a gathering.

The first gathering should be a time for everyone to meet each other, find out what this is all about, and begin to articulate their beliefs and needs. We did this in the following way:

1. People are always hungry. We ate first!
2. In the large group, I posed two questions. We broke into pairs to answer those questions.

What is your relationship to faith and/or spirituality?
Why are you here?

3. After 10 minutes, we came back to the large group and shared some of our thoughts.
4. I posed a third question which we discussed as a group.

What would you like to get out of this?

Then I informed people what the process would be.

5. At the end, I suggested a date for the second gathering and asked folks to think about whether or not this was something they want to participate in. I passed out a questionnaire (See the worksheet "Joining the Circle," in the Appendix), and we set a date for the second gathering.

℮ your second gathering

Ask folks to come to the second meeting having given some thought to what brought them to this point. A questionnaire like the one mentioned above is useful; the process of filling it out helps people further explore what they're looking for.

At our second gathering, I asked people go into more detail about their needs and expectations. In pairs, I had them discuss the following statements: (See the "Relationships" chapter for more information on listening with reverence.)
I hope this group might affect my life and my work in the following ways. . .
This will be a success for me if. . .
The support I need for my journey from this group is. . .
One thing I might like to share from my own experience is. . .

We came back into the large group and shared what we'd learned. Towards the end of the gathering, we began talking about when and how often we were going to meet and where. You may not find a day or a time that's perfect for everyone. You might start by just calling out times, "Okay who cannot make it on Monday evenings?" (Look for a show of hands.) "Tuesday evenings?" And so forth, until you find a time when the fewest folks will be absent. Another way to coordinate without a total headache is to pass out a blank calendar of a week (all seven days, each broken down by hour) to everyone and ask them to block off times that do not work for them.

commitments

When stone circles initiated Circles, we met every two or four weeks. People came because they wanted to slow down and feel more focused in their life and their work; to have companionship and support for their journey; to learn more about other beliefs, rituals, practices, and perspectives; to gain greater awareness of their own spirituality; to carve out quiet, reflective time to pay attention to their spirit; and to find ways to make stronger connections between their faith and their work.

Ask people to call you if they decide they don't want to participate. Don't be surprised if a couple of people are enthusiastic and then decide later against joining the Circle and try not to take it personally. There are an infinite number of reasons for deciding not to join a group, most of which will not involve you. If you are curious and feel comfortable, ask them about it.

the circle ongoing

The Circle was structured by the intentions of its members; we explored what compelled us. I miss what those gatherings added to my life, the intimate spiritual community and the time and intention to reflect, meditate, learn, move, write, share, make art, and eat in that community.

~ Heather Zorn, member of the Second Circle

stone circles provided an opportunity for me to be with people who had the same values and who even shared the same history. The jury is still out about impact. A lot is contingent on what the person does with the action, the knowledge. I've become a stronger person and more of a believer. Before it was easy to say I'm atheist or agnostic even though I wasn't. Because I had not the grounding, the language, or the support to say what I believed. But through all the work and interaction with stone circles, I now have that strength, and that's made me self-aware, more confident, ready to challenge more things.

~ Ed Chaney, member of the First Circle

format

The format of the Circle should flow directly from the desires of the group members. Combine activities from this book with those you create yourselves. I believe you need a minimum of two hours for a meaningful interaction. As the group becomes closer and more social, suggest that people arrive 15 minutes early to socialize. Another option is to have potlucks that start 30 minutes before the meeting. We met at 6:30 P.M. for a potluck dinner (which we then decided to make optional after about nine months) and started at 7:00 P.M. We rotated our gatherings between people's homes, something I recommend if it is feasible.

Here is a simple format that we used consistently; it has worked well for stone circles:

1. Opening period of silence and meditation
2. Check-in: short updates from everyone in the group on their lives and spirits
3. Discussion or activity, based on the topic chosen
4. Announcements and preparation for next meeting (location, topic, and facilitator chosen)
5. Closing ritual

roles

In the beginning, people will look to you as the leader. Every Circle needs a facilitator, but the position can be rotated. If you are interested in having the group rotate facilitation, say that at the first gathering so people know what to expect. Or, you may want to commit to planning the first three to four gatherings and then have facilitation rotate after that. People may want to pair up and facilitate together. The facilitator(s) can plan the agenda of the gathering and let people know what, if anything, they need to do to prepare.

norms or ground rules

Early on, set norms or ground rules for how the Circle will operate. This should be done as a group. We've found that folks need the following from a Circle:

> Nonjudgment and safety
> Openness
> Space to take risks
> Attention
> Challenge
> Connection and love
> Confidentiality

things to be aware of

As your Circle develops, issues of group process are bound to arise. These should be dealt with openly and honestly, as they will help you deepen your relationships with one another. Here are some of the issues that came up for us:

1. People's desire to learn individual tools for the journey (i.e., how to meditate) while experiencing community. There should be time and attention for both, in the balance that people want.

2. Creating an atmosphere of trust which allows for a truly open dialogue on issues of faith. These are not easy topics to discuss, and they are so rarely talked about. Some people feel comfortable sharing their greatest struggles and joys early on; others take more time. We reminded ourselves that trust sometimes takes a while to build, and everyone will have a different timeline.

3. Ensuring accountability so that people call if they are going to miss a meeting and follow up with someone to find out about the next one. If someone begins to miss a lot of meetings, everyone else begins to wonder why. When setting ground rules, discuss this and develop a policy. We agreed that people should call someone, preferably the host, if they weren't going to make it. At the end of the gathering, people volunteered to call whomever was missing to fill them in.

Realize that every group goes through many stages in its development. This is part of the learning and reflects our very need to be in community. For more guidance, see "Facilitating Spiritual Work with Groups" in the front of the book, which outlines other challenges that may arise and possible responses.

themes for Circles

Our Circles convened around many of the themes laid out in this book: silence, ritual, developing a practice, nature, etc. In fact, many of the activities were piloted through one of the Circles. Here are some additional ideas:

℮ in the beginning

Early on, spend time sharing information about your faith backgrounds. Have everyone tell a story about something from childhood. Use the worksheet, "Exploring Your Faith Background," in the Appendix to help people to reflect on their faith or spiritual base and provide rich information for discussion.

℮ objects that tell a story

We read the preface from James Carse, *Breakfast at the Victory: The Mysticism of Ordinary Experience*, which tells a beautiful story about a pair of boots, significant in the lives of two men. Everyone was asked to bring an object which in some way told a story about their life: a choice that was made, a transition, a turning point. It might be something associated with what Carse calls "modest events"—times and experiences whose importance may only be known much later. As we went around the room and shared our stories, we placed the objects on the altar in the center of our meeting space.

℗ photo night

This one was created by First Circle member Mitty Owens. Have everyone bring photos and/or mementos that reveal something meaningful about the past, family, childhood. We discussed the following questions in relation to our formative years:

What excited you as a child?
What "rooted" you and gave you a sense of place or belonging?
What scared or intimidated you?
What concerned you?

℗ sacred texts and social justice: what do the Hebrew and Christian bibles say?

This is a great way for people to get to know other traditions. Divide into groups of four and give each group a passage to study. Suggest that they read the passage out loud first and then consider the primary lesson or message of the passage.

How would you apply it today?
How have you heard it interpreted?
How is it ignored?

You might end by asking each person to offer a reflection in light of the passages.

Possible passages to use:
Genesis 47:13-26 —land use and economics
Exodus 4:1-31—Moses' reluctant leadership
Deuteronomy 26: 12-15—tithing
Ecclesiastes 3:1-8—for everything there is a season
Matthew 5:43-48—love your neighbor
Matthew 8:7-12—the golden rule
Mark 4:30-32—mustard seed
Luke 10: 25-37—the Good Samaritan

food

Have everyone bring a dish that is important to their cultural or faith tradition or something that was important in their family growing up. Before eating, ask each person to explain what they brought and why it is significant to them. Ask someone to prepare a blessing for the feast. You might also ask everyone to bring in copies of their recipe for the group.

Jesus

Because so many people have associations, memories, and baggage surrounding Jesus, Polly Guthrie and Charles McKinney of the Second Circle did a session on Jesus. In preparation, folks were asked to write about their associations:

What did you hear about Jesus growing up?
How did he factor into your faith?
What do you think now?
Where do these impressions come from?

They used the story of the Good Samaritan to examine what they believed to be a vital aspect of Jesus' identity as an activist.

the rhythm of the seasons

Bring a group of objects appropriate to the season and ask people to write about one of them. For example, for fall you might bring a pumpkin, squash, leaves, and some apples. This is a great way for folks to get in touch with moments from their childhood and recall what was special about the season growing up. (See the "Ritual" chapter for how to plan an Autumn Equinox ritual.)

the Circle ending

Nothing lasts forever, certainly not your Circle. Sometimes it's hard to know if you're just hitting a slump or hitting the end. The Second Circle went through a four-month low full of uncertainty before gaining steam again. If things seem to be slowing down, set aside time to talk about it as a group. Ask people to be honest about their commitment and interest level. The circumstances of our lives change constantly. People may mean well but be unable to continue. You might decide to gather less frequently, for example, quarterly instead of monthly. If it seems that the Circle has served its purpose, plan a last gathering as a final celebration. Give everyone a chance to reflect on what the group has given them, what they've learned, what's changed in their life as a result, and what they'll miss.

resources for circles . . . .

Baldwin, Christina. *Calling the Circle*. Newberg, OR: Swan Raven, 1994. Extensive information and stories on calling the circle in various contexts of work and community.

Bryant, Barry. *The Wheel of Time: Sand Mandala*. In cooperation with the Namgyal Monastery. San Francisco: HarperSanFrancisco, 1992.

Canfield, Jack, Mark Victor Hansen, Maida Rogerson, Martin Rutte, and Tim Clauss. *Chicken Soup for the Soul at Work: 101 Stories of Courage, Compassion and Creativity in the Workplace*. Deerfield Beach, FL: Health Communications, 1996. "Chicken Soup" groups have sprung up as a forum for spirit-filled storytelling at work. Contact: 64 Camerada Loop, Santa Fe, NM 87505; 505/466-1512.

Carnes, Robin Deen and Sally Craig. *Sacred Circles: A Guide to Creating Your Own Women's Spirituality Group*. San Francisco: HarperSanFrancisco, 1998. A look at how women's groups are thriving around the country; full of practical ideas and suggestions for starting your own circle.

Carse, James. *Breakfast at the Victory Cafe: The Mysticism of Ordinary Experience*. San Francisco: HarperSanFrancisco, 1994.

Jung, Carl. *Man and his Symbols*. New York: Doubleday & Company, 1964.

McLaughlin, Corinne and Gordon Davidson. *Spiritual Politics: Changing the World From the Inside Out*. New York: Ballantine, 1994. A metaphysical perspective on how spiritual politics are practiced in the workplace and in government. This book makes the connection between inner work and outer events.

O'Connor, Elizabeth. *Servant Leaders, Servant Structure*. Washington, D.C.: The Servant Leadership School, 1991. The history and struggle of The Church of the Saviour and its commitment to living and working in community.

Public Affairs Television. *Talking About Genesis: A Resource Guide*. New York: Doubleday, 1996. A companion book to the public television series, *Genesis: A Living Conversation*, this resource guide includes commentary, reflections, and activities from over 30 different contributors.

Rosen, Brant. "Community as Fellowship: The Reconstructionist Havurah." *The Reconstructionist* 60 (Spring 1995).

Wallis, Jim. *The Soul of Politics*. New York: The New Press and Orbis Books, 1994. A call for a new social vision that blends social justice with personal responsibility but rises above both the liberal and conservative movements.

Whitmyer, Claude. *In the Company of Others: Making Community in the Modern World.* New York: Jeremy P. Tarcher/Perigee Books, 1993. An anthology of writings on community: seeking it, making it , finding it, and living it. Includes essays by M. Scott Peck, Ram Dass, Starhawk, Thich Nhat Hanh, and many others.

Wink, Walter. *Transforming Bible Study: A Leader's Guide.* Nashville: Abingdon, 1980. For people interested in leading Bible study as a process of transformation; includes sections on developing questions for texts from the Christian Bible.

stories of a circle . . . .

Leigh Morgan

Leigh Morgan is an Organization Development Consultant with Glaxo Wellcome Research and Development. She has also worked with the North Carolina Commission on National and Community Service and the Carolina Justice Policy Center, where she staffed anti-death penalty and violence prevention initiatives. Leigh believes in bringing her "full self" to work to enable the people and organizations she consults with to reach their full potential.

CH: Leigh, when the Second Circle started up two years ago you came with a great deal of enthusiasm and intention. Why was it so important to you?

LM: In the year prior to the Second Circle, I had been reading more and more about Buddhism and other Eastern philosophical traditions. This peaked my interest, but I really wanted to explore, on a deeper emotional level, what spirituality meant to me. That and wanting to really embody what the Dalai Lama talks about—being compassionate to self and others, and the egolessness—led me to stone circles.

Also, I joined the Circle during a time when I was struggling with the breakup of a relationship and was in a lot of pain. When the Second Circle came along, it was a wonderful opportunity to begin to learn more about myself and what this idea of "spirituality" meant to me—especially in relation to others, the community, and my work. All arrows were pointing me to some kind of intentional spiritual community.

What do you think you've gotten out of it?

It sounds like an oxymoron, but I've developed a sense of spiritual discipline. Since joining the Circle two years ago, I have really seen a difference in the depth of spiritual experiences that I have on a daily basis. Also, I'm going to church now, and this is a very positive movement for me. I'm actually reclaiming a religious tradition as what I want to make it, whereas before I had some anger and cynicism towards Western religious traditions, especially Christianity. It feels like I've "come out" as a spiritual person.

> I find that I am kinder and more compassionate to others and myself on a more regular basis.

And, I find that I am kinder and more compassionate to others and myself on a more regular basis. I stop to look at flowers a lot more. The little things are becoming more significant in my life. I think life is about little things anyway; paying attention to those little things is important to me now.

You have a real passion, even love, for groups coming together.

Well, I get a rush when groups can capture all the good energy and passion that is out there—to me that is where human potential is unleashed. It can be unleashed individually, of course, but when a group of people finds synergy around the energy and passion, then you're just rockin' and rollin.' The potential for understanding and deep communication and changing the world is very powerful. Being a part of that process really feels good when it happens.

And you thought a lot about the group, in ways that were incredibly valuable to us.

It has to do with the notion "use of self." Whether I am in a consultant role or a member of a group, I try to trust that my own experience is important and relevant to talk about. So, if there is a difficult situation or conflict, I speak to how I'm experiencing the situation in the moment. That can be such a powerful tool for moving through conflict. Usually other people are feeling the same thing, or my comments help others express something opposite. I think it's a skill that I have that anyone can have. Part of it comes with training and experience, also.

What about a group like the Circle is most powerful to you?

Finding shared meaning. I think all people really crave to find meaning and purpose and connection in their daily life. But so often people don't talk about it, or they're not able to express it, or when they do, they get slammed. With stone circles, we created a community with a sense of shared meaning around spirituality and the role of spirituality for individuals, our group, and for the world.

> With stone circles, we created a community with a sense of shared meaning around spirituality and the role of spirituality for individuals, our group, and for the world.

What are some other signs that a group is thriving and giving people what they need?

Groups are healthy when there's a sense of interdependence—where I, as an individual, can be better because of my relationship with others in the group. A lot of groups don't get to that point. There may be a high trust level, but members don't take that extra step to say, "How can we, as a group, help each individual be all that they can be?" To me, that is the ultimate potential for an intentional group or community. The individual epiphanies come when there's a sense of "more than I." At this point, you can imagine that the group is going to take off and do great things. It takes a long time, a lot of trust, and an intentional commitment to define a group in this way. It rarely happens by accident. Also, we sat on the floor a lot, hung out in each other's kitchens, had a lot of meals together, and little things like that which helped create a good atmosphere.

What signals that a group has more work to do to get to this point?

One flag is the trust level. I think some people mistake trust for friendship. With the Second Circle, I didn't hang out with everyone to the same extent, but there still was a high level of trust so we could share and connect at a deep level.

The absence of trust can be seen when members don't use "I" statements, distance themselves from how they feel about an issue, or don't take ownership of their own thoughts and feelings. When that happens, the group tends to avoid conflict, because no one will really name what is going on. One way to develop trust is to just name what is happening.

What advice would you give to Circles that are starting up?

Talk about what type of community you want the group to be and revisit that periodically. Every time you revisit it, people can deepen their understanding of what that original vision meant and adjust as needed. It's also important to set some norms for membership and be clear about roles and expectations.

Also, I think shared leadership is important. That notion looks and feels different, to different people, but providing the opportunity for people to take different leadership roles is important. It's helpful to remember also that a group will go through different stages, and there will be times when the energy isn't going to be high. This is to be expected, and it seems like there's a real parallel here with one's own spirituality—knowing there's going to be peaks and valleys and noticing and learning from this instead of fighting it. It's doing at a group level what you hope to do with yourself.

In this society, we have religious institutions, and we have a lot of civic groups. Why do you think there's such a need for groups forming around spirituality?

Again, for me it is this idea of discovering shared meaning. Across all the many religious traditions there is a common desire to lead an ethical, moral life, to treat yourself and others well, and to find meaning in life. Yet, too often that commonality gets lost, because we focus on our own religious tradition. An intentional spiritual community with people from different backgrounds is so important in this regard—to remember and really experience the joy of different spiritual expressions.

I think too many religious traditions tend to divide people more than they bring people together. This seems to be antithetical to celebrating the different experiences that people have on the planet. Spiritual groups like stone circles can serve to build, rather than divide, and address the problem of narrow-minded religious expression.

Why has this made such an impact on you?

It's been like learning how to ride a bike—you have to practice enough in order to balance. This is a great metaphor for being spiritually centered. You have to spend time at it, fall over, get up again, etcetera. Having others remind me to keep going in my spiritual journey has made such a positive difference in my life.

circles.

interfaith celebrations

Celebration is a forgetting of ego,
of problems, of difficulties,
in order to remember the common
base that makes another's sufferings mine
and in order to imagine a relief
of that suffering. There can be no
compassion without celebration and there
will be no authentic celebration that does
not result in increased compassionate
energies.

~ Matthew Fox

questions for reflection

What do you love best about celebrating?

What form do celebrations take in your life?

Have you ever worshipped in a different faith tradition or been a part of an interfaith celebration?

What moved you about it?

what is interfaith celebration? . . . .

Communities and organizations need celebration. It is hard for people to endure, to be strong for one another, without it. When we celebrate, we celebrate each other. Birthdays, weddings, anniversaries, even funerals are a celebration of someone's life. Interfaith celebration is a particularly unique way to gather groups of people together. It does not take the place of single-faith worship or individual spiritual practice; it enhances it. Gathering with a group of people who believe in a different idea of God or read different sacred texts or pray differently opens doors of understanding. And seeing how another experiences faith or God or spirit can heighten our own experience, deepening our relationship to and pride in our own tradition or path.

turning point . . . .

I am in junior high school, and getting the house ready for Passover is an ordeal. It begins with digging the Passover dishes out of the basement. Wrapped in newspaper and packed carefully in cardboard boxes, the dishes are very old and carry the aura of most sacred family dishes. My mother is understandably protective of her bounty, and there is a limit to how many pieces my brother and I are allowed to carry up the rickety steps that lead from the basement to the kitchen.

Once all the dishes are carefully assembled on the counter, we move on to the next and more distressing phase—the elimination of all *hametz*, or leavened bread food products, from our house. For the eight days of Passover, observant Jews eat only unleavened bread, or *matzah*, in memory of what the Jews of long ago were left with as they made their hasty departure. I watch glumly as all my favorite foods—rye bread, pretzels, cereal, cookies—are deposited into a large garbage bag. What is not given to the poor is stowed away in some unsuspecting corner until the end of our eight-day breadless sentence is over. One last crust of bread is ceremoniously burned.

That evening we gather with assorted family and friends for the Seder meal. In keeping with its tradition of fostering commitment among kids, Judaism gives children two important tasks at the Seder. First, we are responsible for asking the Four Questions. This is traditionally performed by the youngest child; in an effort of fairness, my parents ask my brother and me to do these together. The second job is more fun and less stressful—the finding of the *Afikomen*—a special piece of matzah, blessed and hidden somewhere in the house during the Seder. When we find it, we ransom it back to my father for a fair price.

Years later, when I begin doing stone circles, I decide to revisit the holiday for the power and beauty of its story. I want to find a way to share it with friends and colleagues of other faiths who are curious about the Seder. Of all celebrations, those that revolve around a people's struggle for freedom are among the most compelling. And, Passover is the story of the Jew's liberation from Egypt, the much-beloved retelling of the story of freedom. Many Christians feel an affinity with the holiday; there is even some speculation that the Last Supper was really a Seder, the ritualistic meal during which the liberation story is told.

First, we organize a discussion, "Passover and Easter: Stories of Liberation," for the Third Circle. During this discussion, one member, Galia Goodman, sheds new light on the Passover story for me, reframing it as a metaphor for personal liberation as well as historical. The Jews made it through the Red Sea, the narrow place, and then wandered in the desert, moving towards their own liberation. So, too, we must come through the narrow places. Galia asks us to reflect on the narrow places in our lives, at home and at work, reminding us that the gate to salvation is narrow. A few days later, stone circles hosts a Passover Seder. Together, people of many faith backgrounds experience one of Judaism's most beautiful and sacred rituals. We discuss slavery and liberation, telling stories of freedoms won and freedoms still to be won.

celebrations and social change . . . .

Interfaith celebration—worshiping together across faith lines—reminds us of the breadth and depth of the community around us. Our spirits may have a lot in common, but our journeys on earth vary widely. We share something of ourselves, take a risk, and we gain strength in the process. The business of transforming the world is rooted in faith, and it will take more than just one faith to achieve the changes many of us are seeking. The process of worshiping together makes this possible on another level. *Webster's* defines worship as "a set of religious forms, ceremonies, or prayers, by which this love is expressed." If we can worship together, if we can begin to see on an intimate level how another person experiences spirit or praises God, then the potential for joint action becomes limitless.

Interfaith celebration requires a willingness to move from participant to observer and back again to participant. If during interfaith worship a Christian begins to praise Jesus, I become an observer, and I take that opportunity to learn more about someone else's faith tradition. If I recite a prayer in Hebrew, non-Jews in the room may not be able to participate, but they can listen and perhaps understand more about Judaism. And, in collective silence during an interfaith celebration, each of us can find our own expression of God, our own words of prayer, our own acts of praise. It provides space for diversity within an atmosphere of unity.

children's sabbath . . . .

Some interfaith celebrations follow the rhythm of the Judeo-Christian tradition. There may be prayers which look similar in format to prayers of those religious traditions, but they have been created around a specific social justice theme or issue. For the past seven years, the Children's Defense Fund (CDF) has sponsored the National Observance of Children's Sabbaths on a weekend in October. Across the country, tens of thousands of congregations—mosques, churches, and synagogues—recommit themselves to the needs of children. They may use the Children's Sabbath to design a special worship service, organize outreach activities to service agencies working with kids, or convene educational programs. The goal is to inspire people of faith to take long-term actions to protect the health and well-being of children. These might be in the form of prayer, outreach, direct service, or advocacy. The Children's Sabbath is a chance for congregations to promote education and health. The Sabbath also provides a unique opportunity for interfaith and interdenominational worship. CDF provides organizing assistance and resource materials for those interested in participating, including an outline for a sample interfaith service. (See "Resources for Interfaith Celebrations" at the end of the chapter.)

stone circles annual interfaith celebration

Since its inception, stone circles has hosted an interfaith celebration each year in mid-December. The need to convene this gathering was intuitive, and this time of year is an appropriate backdrop. As many of us prepare for our own religious holidays—Channukah, Ramadan, Kwanzaa, Christmas, and the Winter Solstice—we are also drawn into the festivity (and the madness) of the other celebrations taking place around us.

As I prepared for the first celebration in 1995, I became aware what a leap of faith it was. I'm not sure I'd ever even *been* to an interfaith service before. I began by writing a statement of my intent and passing it out to members of the First Circle, urging them to consider ways they might participate. Some were understandably perplexed by the idea or at least unsure what it was I was proposing. With some prodding, a few offered to take the leap with me. I found an appropriate space, sent out a postcard invitation with minimal explanation, and then set on the task of developing the program.

For weeks, I researched prayers from a myriad of religious and spiritual traditions. Armed with a folder three inches thick, I realized the event needed a theme to have any kind of coherence. I kept returning to the haunting beauty of the Winter Solstice. Since ancient times, the returning of the light on the shortest night of the year has been marked with great celebration. "In the darkness, there is always light," I thought, and I began to craft a program around this notion. I blended two primary components: prayers and poems from many sacred traditions and presentations from the teams of intrepid individuals who agree to design a short segment illustrating their own tradition.

Setting up the space the afternoon of the celebration, I marveled at the simplicity of the candles and the circle of stones, present at all stone circles gatherings. People began to arrive, some of whom I knew and some I didn't. We added more chairs. I gave a short welcome, explained that the prayers printed in the program would be read by whomever felt moved to speak at that moment, and we began. It was an enchanting hour and a half. One participant spontaneously led us in a dance; another offered an impromptu song. As we drank cider and munched homemade desserts afterwards, I marveled at what can transpire when people come together in a prayerful and playful way.

This celebration has grown and changed over time. One year we had a large number of young people from a local church youth group; their voices added a vibrant energy. We do more singing now, and we have started to incorporate movement as well. Some elements have stayed constant. The service always includes a candlelight prayer ceremony. As each participant lights the candle of the person next to her, she speaks her own personal prayer into the circle. And we always close with the singing of "Amazing Grace."

activities to do alone . . . .

? preparing for interfaith worship

What are your first memories of someone whose faith background was different from your own?
What were you raised to believe about people of other faiths?
What do you still believe to be true?
What has always fascinated or confused you about another faith?

@ share worship with someone of a different faith

Attend a worship service or celebration with someone of a different faith background. Enhance your visit with preparation. Think about what you expect the visit to be like.

Have you ever been to a place of worship different from your own?
How do you remember feeling the last time you went?
What was hard? What was enjoyable?
If you have never been, what are you most apprehensive about?
What are you most interested in learning?

activities to do with groups . . . . 🎎

℗ faith and culture-sharing

One simple way to initiate interfaith celebration with a group is
through faith and culture-sharing. Ask everyone to bring something
from their faith or cultural background to share with the group. It
might be an object that tells a story, a prayer or song, a ritual
everyone can participate in, or something else entirely. Set up the
room so everyone can sit in a circle and light candles. Facilitate the
sharing Quaker-style: individuals should take their turn sharing
whenever they feel moved.

℗ organizing an interfaith celebration: 8 steps

See the worksheet, "Designing an Interfaith Celebration," in the
Appendix to use in the planning process.

1. GOALS:
What are your primary reasons for convening this type of gathering?
Do you want to:
Create common ground between various faiths?
Involve a wide spectrum of people?
Educate folks about various religious and spiritual traditions?

2. PLANNING GROUP:
Find people from a range of faith and spiritual backgrounds. Having
a clergy member present can be great, as long as he or she is clear
about the intent of the service. Clergy who have had experience with
interfaith dialogue or worship will be particularly helpful additions.
You will always need more volunteers than you think for setting up,
greeting people, handing out programs, assisting with refreshments,
and cleaning up.

come sunday. . . come saturday

Interfaith celebrations can be
held as part of related
events. stone circles has held
many interfaith gatherings
at youth service conferences,
for example. We also
collaborated with the Bridges
Project at the Center for
Documentary Studies to
convene an interfaith
celebration in conjunction
with a photography exhibit.
"Come Sunday" was a
photographic pilgrimage to
the Black churches of
Brooklyn. Held on a
Saturday after the exhibit
opened, we called the
celebration, "Come
Sunday. . . Come Saturday."
We gathered on the grass
outside of the center. The
celebration consisited of
readings, prayers, songs, and
movement from Baha'i,
Buddhism, Christianity,
Hinduism, Islam, and
Judaism, as well as original
poetry.

Who else do you know who might want to be involved?
What other interfaith gatherings have been held in your town or city?
Who has organized and led them?

3. CONTENT:

Do some meditating and brainstorming on content with your planning group. Ask folks what is most special to them about worship. You may even want to lead a short guided meditation, asking everyone to sit quietly and think back to a meaningful worship experience they've had. [See guided meditations in the "Meditation" chapter.]

What are you most interested in seeing included in the service?
Do you have a favorite prayer or know of an easy movement that a large group of people can do?
Have you been to interfaith gatherings in the past? What made them special?
What are you most interested in learning or seeing from other faith traditions?

The more interactive the service, the better. People in the planning group can collect readings, poetry, prayers, and songs. Encourage people to write something themselves and to look in likely and unlikely places for inspirational passages. Readings may come from places as conventional as the Bible or as unconventional as the inside of a Celestial Seasonings tea box. Maybe you will invite people to bring a percussion instrument.

4. LOGISTICS:

place: The right location is vital; it will set the tone for the event. Possible locations include schools, dance studios, art galleries, a university commons room, libraries, and community centers. Any space can be transformed with flowers, candles, material, sacred objects, and other decorations. And, always consider seating possibilities. An hour and a half is the ideal length for an interfaith gathering. If you're planning to invite a lot of kids, keep it to an hour.

Serving food afterwards gives people a chance to meet others with whom they've just shared this experience. Ask people on the planning group to make or bring desserts and very light snacks. Hot apple cider has become a tradition at our interfaith celebrations.

Are there enough chairs or do you have to rent/borrow some?
Can people sit comfortably on the floor?
If you're planning an outdoor location, is there a rain site nearby?

5. PARTICIPANTS:

In addition to those in the planning group, you may know people who are committed to their religion or spiritual practice and who may be willing to share something from their tradition. Brainstorm with them. People might want to share a poem, read a passage from a sacred text, lead everyone in singing a song, or do some movement. Here are examples of how people can get involved:

- Christians from different denominations might read a scripture about the birth of Jesus, light Advent candles, and lead the rest of the group in singing a Christmas carol.

- Jews can team up to tell the story of Channukah, light the Channukah Menorah, and sing a traditional Channukah song.

- African-Americans might share their celebration of Kwanzaa with drumming, lighting the Kinara, and teaching the seven principles of the holiday.

6. INVITATIONS:

Invitations to your service can be as simple as a postcard. Make sure to include all the vital information: time, date, location, directions if the place is difficult to find, a note if refreshments will be provided, and a phone number to call for more information. If you want folks to bring anything, like a candle or an instrument, make sure to note that on the invitation. (We always ask people to bring a candle for the final candle-lighting prayer ceremony but have extras on hand just in case.)

7. PROGRAM:

A program is a great addition to the event itself and serves as a reminder for people long after the celebration is over. Include the text of the readings and songs so people will have these as part of their own collection. The program does not have to be anything fancy, unless you have a design/graphic arts person in the planning group who wants to work on it. A sample program from a recent stone circles interfaith celebration appears in the Appendix.

8. THE DAY OF:

Take some time in the afternoon to quietly collect your thoughts, maybe with a walk or a meditation. Give yourself plenty of time to set up and get ready. If you are serving food, make sure you have what you need. Ask everyone in the planning group to get there at least a half hour early, more if they need to set up anything. Provide a table or space in the center of the room where people can put any ceremonial objects they are going to use. If your location is hard to find, post signs in the appropriate places. Run through the program with everyone a few times.

interfaith celebrations.

resources for interfaith celebrations

Alternatives. *To Celebrate: Reshaping Holidays and Rites of Passage*. Ellenwood, GA: Alternatives, 1987. Alternatives is a non-profit organization providing resources for responsible living and celebrating. Contact: Alternatives for Simple Living, P.O. Box 2857, Sioux City IA 51106; 800/821-6153. Web site: www.simpleliving.org

Budapest, Zsuzsanna E. *The Grandmother of Time*. San Francisco: Harper & Row, 1979. A book of celebrations, spells, and sacred objects for every month of the year that draws on goddess spirituality.

Children's Defense Fund. *Seeking Shalom: Healthy Children, Healthy Nation*. Washington, D.C.: Children's Defense Fund, 1997. This guide to organizing a Children's Sabbath is published yearly and available for Catholic, Jewish, and Protestant congregations. Contact: Religious Affairs Division at CDF: 25 E Street, N.W., Washington, D.C. 20001; 202/662-3693. Web site: www.childrensdefense.org

Eck, Diana. *Encountering God: A Spiritual Journey from Bozeman to Banaras*. Boston: Beacon Press, 1993. One woman's journey across continents and faith traditions and the universal implications for religious pluralism.

Magida, Arthur J., ed. *How to Be a Perfect Stranger: A Guide to Etiquette in other People's Religious Ceremonies, Vol. 1 and 2*. Woodstock, VT: Jewish Lights Publishing, 1996. All basic questions are answered here: custom, attire, behavior. The first volume covers the ceremonies of all the major religious traditions; the second volume, edited by Magida and Stuart M. Matlins, covers those religions and denominations with smaller memberships.

National Conference for Community and Justice, originally founded as the National Conference for Christians and Jews, promotes understanding and respect among all races, religions, and cultures. They sponsor interfaith dialogues and publish a yearly listing of major holidays from different faith traditions. Contact: 71 Fifth Avenue, Suite 1000; New York, NY 10003; 212/206-0006; Web site: www.nccj.org.

Teish, Luisah. *Carnival of the Spirit*. New York: Harper Collins. Folks tales, wisdom, and stories of celebrations and festivals from all over the world, with a special focus on Africa and the Carribean.

Tobias, Michael, Jane Morrison, and Bettina Gray, eds. *A Parliament of Souls: Conversations with 28 Spiritual Leaders from Around the World*. San Francisco: KQED Books, 1995. A companion to the 26-part television series of the same name, the interviews in this book offer insight into a range of personal faith journeys and the dilemmas and truths which unite these spiritual leaders.

space

*We create sacred space to bring our
spirit into harmony with life in
our daily environment.
When our mind is clear and
we are fully present to life and
the world around us, we are in
sacred space. And creating
sacred space, by ritually
changing and rearranging our
outer environment, is a means
both of focusing our mind—becoming
present to the sacred, which is always
within us—and of anchoring and
aligning the flow of Spirit
in our physical environment.*

~ Margo Anand, *The Art of Everyday Ecstasy*

questions for reflection

What are the central spaces in your life?

How would you describe your relationship to these spaces? To space in general?

What makes you feel connected to where you live?

what is space? . . . .

The relationship between human beings and our environments is reciprocal; one reflects the other. Turning inward, the spaces where we live and work and play impact how happy, productive, distressed, overwhelmed, or calm we might be at any one time. Turning outward, public space impacts our notions of community, of connectedness, of what is possible. When cities and towns fall into physical decay and disrepair, so do our spirits. In many areas, public space is rapidly disappearing or being developed for exclusive use. Space is what allows us to come together for a common purpose. We cannot continue to build strong organizations for change without places where people can gather, talk, exchange, scheme, learn, plan, and celebrate.

turning point . . . .

When I visit the Highlander Center in 1993, I go with much anticipation; I have heard some of the legends and the stories. But nothing could have prepared me for the experience of walking into the main house, whose giant windows overlook grassy fields and the Smoky Mountains. The inspiration of the view provides a fitting backdrop for the famous circle of rocking chairs that I'd heard so much about. As I walk the outer circumference of the room, not wanting to even touch these sacred seats at first, my mind drifts into the past. I begin imagining the conversations that might have taken place, who might have been sitting with whom. As the sun slowly sinks outside, the room seems filled with a thousand spirits.

The Highlander Research and Education Center was started in 1932 by Myles Horton and Frank Adams with a mission to train leaders in the South and preserve local culture. It has been training grassroots activists in a variety of arenas ever since. In the heart of Appalachia, one of this country's poorest regions, workshops and discussions at Highlander give people a sense of their own power and their connection to one another. In the 1930s and 40s, Highlander worked to develop the skills, strategies, and networks of labor organizers and displaced factory, mill, and mine workers. In the 1950s and 60s, Black and white activists congregated at Highlander to build bridges that would build a movement. It was, in fact, one of the only places in the South where Blacks and whites could meet openly and safely. Martin Luther King, Jr. spent time at Highlander, so did Rosa Parks.

Carrying this spirit and commitment onward, Highlander continues to provide training and act as a true gathering spot for activists. Since the 1980s, Highlander has organized schools, workshops, and training institutes around the issues of environmental degradation, global economic restructuring, and youth leadership.

? space and social change . . . .

Gathering places have played a major role in building the relationships that have given birth to movement organizing. From coast to coast there are examples of thriving spaces that facilitate new levels of relationship-building and community dialogue, places where voices are heard, spirit felt, and powerful new directions forged. Some spaces are a twist on the familiar; others are the result of a radical revisioning of what walls and a roof can provide for folks. Here are five examples of spaces that pay homage to what is while laying groundwork for *what will be.*

> *Free spaces are settings between private lives and large-scale institutions*
> *where ordinary citizens can act with dignity, independence and vision. . .*
> *environments in which people are able to learn a new self-respect,*
> *a deeper and more assertive group identity, public skills,*
> *and values of cooperation and civic virtue.*
>
> ~ Sara M. Evans and Harry C. Boyte, *Free Spaces*

Appalshop Located in Whitesburg, Kentucky, Appalshop acts on the belief that the people of Appalachia and other cultures can tell their own stories and control their own images. Appalshop is an amalgam. They produce films on issues of critical importance to Appalachia; run WMMT-FM, a non-commercial radio station that broadcasts mountain music, storytelling, and reporting on the region; and operate Roadside Theater, a traveling ensemble that has developed plays from the rich culture and history of Appalachia. They also run June Appal Recordings, featuring both traditional and contemporary mountain music, and the Appalachian Media Institute, which trains students in media production and leadership. Their building in Whitesburg houses all of the above projects, as well as a gallery and theater, and hosts numerous concerts, plays, art exhibits, and forums.

Consider each of the elements that comprise Appalshop. Do any of these exist where you live?
Where are they located? Have you ever seen or visited them?
Is there a place in your hometown that tells the stories of your community? How are these stories told?

CCA Warehouse/Teen Project The Center for Contemporary Arts helped birth the Teen Project, a multifaceted, youth-driven initiative in a four thousand square foot warehouse on the edge of downtown Santa Fe, New Mexico. The warehouse includes a recording studio, small meeting rooms, and a large open space for concerts and workshops. The Teen Project was created in response to a lack of arts institutions with a commitment to young people. They offer a number of opportunities, run mostly for and by young people. Activities include free, weekly arts workshops; "Free Food/Comida Gratis," an independent and alternative newspaper; weekly dance parties and band nights; video forums; and "Ground Zero," a weekly radio show.

Where do young people in your community hang out?
What empty or abandoned buildings do you pass by on a regular basis?
What were they once used for? What else can you see happening in that space?
Who in your community needs a place to gather?

St. Joseph's AME Church Founded in the late 1800s, St. Joseph's was the heart of Hayti, Durham's Black community, for generations. During the Civil Rights Movement, St. Joseph's was often the congregating spot for organizers, marchers, and citizens. When much of the neighborhood was destroyed through various "urban renewal" projects, the church was saved through a communityled effort to place it on the National Register of Historic Places. Hayti Heritage Center, built next to the church, is a gathering space for art-related events, exhibitions, and non-profit organizations. St. Joseph's is undergoing $2.5 million worth of renovations, which will create a 350-seat performance space to host traveling and local entertainment, meetings, and lectures.

What religious institutions or congregations in your neighborhood act as gathering
*   places?*
What do they offer? Who meets there?
Are you affiliated with a place of worship? Who uses the space when services aren't
*   being held?*

Village of Arts and Humanities was initiated by artist Lily Yeh in 1986. What began as a mural project and sculpture garden in North Philadelphia is now a series of parks, community gardens, a community center, performances, and events (dance, theater, and ritual), and exhibitions. There are arts education and after-school programs, GED and vocational training programs, and resident-led construction projects to renovate nearby buildings and homes. The Village also seeks resources to provide jobs, housing, food, and counseling for people in the

pilgrimages: the journey to holy space

Pilgrimages have been around for thousands of years. In making our way to holy or sacred space, we are transformed, both by the journey and the destination. Followers of Buddhism visit the Buddha's birthplace, the place of enlightenment, and where he died. Catholics travel faithfully to the Shrine of Our Lady of Guadalupe in Mexico City where it is said the Virgin Mary appeared in 1531. Hindus take a sacred plunge into India's Ganges River. Every year on Easter, Christians follow the Stations of Cross, reenacting the last days of Jesus. And Jews find renewal in a trip to pray at the Wailing Wall in Jerusalem.

Perhaps the holiest of all pilgrimages is that of the Hajj, the trip to Mecca that all Muslims who are able must complete at least once in their lifetime. Mecca, a city in Saudi Arabia, attracts millions of people every year from all over the world. First, Muslims must enter *ihram*, a state of purity and cleanliness. Then they go to the *Ka'bah*, the first temple, which is circled counter-clockwise seven times. People then travel through the desert of the Mina Valley to the hill where the Prophet Muhammed gave his last sermon. They perform *sa'i*, or "hastening," traveling seven times between two hills near the Ka'bah to replicate Hagar's frantic search for water for her son, Ishmael. Muslims also throw stones at pillars symbolizing Satan and the rejection of evil. Pilgrims feast together and trim a lock of hair to symbolize the end of the Hajj.

neighborhood. Working with residents, Yeh and the Village have developed a crafts industry which markets images associated with the Village and sells baked goods and vegetables. They are acquiring more vacant lots for community gardens and parks. Yeh's ongoing collaboration with artists and residents in the neighborhood of North Philadelphia is an example of the best that community-based art has to offer.

What changes have occurred in your neighborhood over the past year? Who was responsible for them?
Are there public parks? Who takes care of them?
Is there a space for public art close to your home? Whose art is there? How did it get there?

The White Dog Cafe is the brainchild of Judy Wicks, a one-time VISTA volunteer who came of age during the 60s. What began as a muffin shop in West Philadelphia is now one of the most vibrant and committed restaurant enterprises around, serving up an incredible menu of speakers, cultural events, volunteer opportunities, and great food. The White Dog sponsors an ever-evolving series of community events. "Table Talk" invites speakers of all backgrounds and areas of expertise to share their knowledge and engage in discussions over an early morning breakfast. There are trips to sister restaurants in Vietnam, Cuba, Iraq, and other countries with whom the United States has tenuous relations, as well as in other neighborhoods throughout Philadelphia.

What restaurants, cafes, or diners near your home or work bring different people together?
Do they host any events like music, poetry, speakers, etcetera?
What are your favorite places to go? Why?
What could you imagine happening in the space?

activities to do alone . . . .

✎ write it down: memories of space

Reflect on the spaces that were important in your childhood.
What influence did they have on you? What control did you have in shaping them?
Were there any spaces that were particularly special to you as a child?
What happened there?
Who else was a part of it? Was the space a secret?
*What were the characteristics of spaces that you knew as a child were sacred
   or religious?*
(These questions, and many others in the activities that follow were inspired by
Annice Kenan, a member of the First Circle.)

℮ everyday space: home and work

Our homes and workplaces are obvious places to start when thinking about the
transformation of space.

1. Draw a diagram or map of the living space in which you spend the most time.
It might be your bedroom, a living room, an entire apartment or house, or
somewhere else. Do this from memory, when you are not in the space.
What are the most important things about this space to you?
What do you like the most about it?
What do you like the least?

2. Take the diagram and stand in the middle of the space.
What did you remember to include in your diagram? What did you forget?
Look around. What is the space set up for?
What are the activities that this room/space invites?

3. Think about how you and your family or housemates use your time at home.
Write down the three activities that are most important to you and/or consume
the most of your time at home.
How does the room arrangement match up with how you spend your time?
Are there gaps between how you use this space and what it feels most conducive to?
Do you need to change anything to greater align this space with its primary purposes?

Repeat this exercise for your workspace.

How do you create sacred space?

ancestor altars

Billie Burney, program director with North Carolina Public Allies, offers the following story about her ancestor altar:

When I first decided to create my altar, the first thing I did was look at my house and figure out a space that was safe, a space where someone couldn't accidentally knock something over or trample on it, but a space that was central to the room. An ancestor altar is something that anyone can establish. A lot of people have them, and they don't realize it. They may have a section of their house with a lot of photographs of relatives, maybe a candle. They don't realize they've already begun an altar, a way to honor those people.

With my altars, I'm more aware of my living space and the energy that I invite into my house. With my mom passing, my ancestor altar will eventually provide a place where she and I can talk. It makes you more aware that even if people aren't around in a physical sense, they're there in a spiritual sense, which gives me hope. The ancestor altar is designed to embody the "asé" of family members and friends who had transitioned. Asé is a word of African origin that means essence or power.

If you have a parent who's deceased, or a grandparent or friend, create an altar for them. Get a white cloth, a white candle, some incense, and a glass of water. Spend at least 15 minutes a day having a conversation with that person. Share some food with them. Keep the water fresh. Give them fresh flowers. It's a powerful thing to know your ancestors can still help you if you open yourself up to it.

creating sacred space

What if anything has to be present for space to feel special to you? How do you create sacred space where you live and work?

There are many ways to transform "ordinary" space at home, at work, or anywhere else you might find yourself. When I first began meditating, a corner of a room set aside for that purpose enhanced my practice; this is still true today. A small altar in my bedroom, consisting only of a candle, a plant, and a group of stones, is my space for daily meditation and prayer. When I travel, I usually carry a stone, a candle, some incense, and my favorite prayers with me. Here are some ways to transform space that do not take a lot of time or cost a lot of money:

- Find a tapestry, beautiful piece of cloth, or a scarf to lay over the floor or on top of a table. Use this as a surface or altar for objects of significance.
- Change the lighting by adding candles, different colored light bulbs, or small tree lights.
- Scour thrift shops for large pillows.
- Burn incense or sage.
- Take away whatever furniture is unnecessary and easy to move.
- Add plants, stones, leaves, flowers, sand, water, and/or wood.

What else comes to mind?

finding sacred space

Where do you go when you need to be quiet?
What spaces make you feel calm?
What spaces remind you of God or spirit?
What are your places of inspiration?
How accessible are these spaces for you? Are they inside or outside or both?
How often do you go to them?

Make a list as you answer these questions. Find a map of your hometown and enlarge it, if possible, on a photocopier. Post it on the wall. Mark the spaces on the map; notice and add those spaces that are far away. Exchange ideas with other people you know. Read a travel book written about where you live. Are there other spaces or places you want to explore?

activities to do with groups . . . . 👥

℮ community spaces

(For this activity, you can also use the worksheet "Looking at Space," in the Appendix.)

First, ask each person to answer the following questions. You might set this up as a freewriting activity; see the "Words and Stories" chapter for more information on freewriting.
What is your favorite place in your city or town? Describe it. How did you find it?
Why do you love it? What goes on there?
When you want to gather with colleagues or friends, where do you go?
How do you choose this location? What do you use the space for?

Then, divide into groups of three and share your answers. Come back together as a group. Notice where the answers overlap and where they are different. What can people learn about each other and about your community? If people are interested, suggest meeting for an afternoon to visit these spaces together. You might also think about:

What are the most popular gathering spaces/places in the town where you live?
Who spends time there? Why? What activities take place there?
Are these places similar or different to those your group listed?
What do you notice?
What space is missing in your town?

℮ histories of space

Ask everyone in your group to choose a different space or place in your city or town that interests them and research its history using the following questions:
How old is this place? How did it come into being and why?
Who was instrumental in its creation or development?
For what was the space initially intended?
Who uses the space now and for what? How is it maintained?

Come together to share what you've learned. If time allows, visit these spaces and do your "reports" on-site.

---

stonehenge and other stone circles

In the first written mention of Stonehenge in 1130 A.D., Henry of Huntingdon remarked that "stones of wondrous sizes are raised in the manner of doorways, in such a manner that door seems superposed upon door, yet nobody knows how or why." Stonehenge is a ring of open doors which invite entry. Stone circle formations like Stonehenge are found around the world amd remain a mystery. We don't really know exactly how they were built or why. One thing most anthropologists and archaeologists agree on is that Stonehenge was created as sacred space for worship and ritual. Rituals depend on a laying out of sacred time and space. Built in alignment with the solstices and the paths of the moon, Stonehenge enabled people to see the changing relationship of sky and earth.

resources for space . . . .

Appalshop, 306 Madison Street, Whitesburg, KY 41858. 606/633-0108.

Bledsoe, Thomas. *Or We'll All Hang Separately: The Highlander Idea*. Boston: Beacon Press, 1969. This book tells the story of Highlander's first three decades, following it from labor struggles to the freedom movement. The emphasis is on the people who made it happen and the real challenges they faced.

CCA Warehouse/The Teen Project 1614 Paseo de Peralta, Santa Fe NM 87501; 505/989-4423

Cochran, Kelly Thompson. "Bedrock of African-American Tradition Now a Durham Showcase." *Raleigh News and Observer*, 28 March 1997. About St. Joseph's AME Church.

Evans, Sara M. and Harry C. Boyte. *Free Spaces: The Source of Democratic Changes in America*. New York: Harper & Row, 1986.

Horton, Myles and Paolo Freire. *We Make the Road by Walking: Conversations on Education and Social Change*. Philadelphia: Temple University Press, 1990. Engaging dialogue between these two veterans of popular education and social change. Horton was the founder of the Highlander Research and Education Center.

Philadelphia Inquirer. "Pilgrimage." *Philadephia Inquirer*, Sunday 12 April 1998. sec. T.

"Building Movements, Educating Citizens: Myles Horton and the Highlander Folk School" *Social Policy*, Winter 1991. An entire issue of social policy devoted to Highlander.

Streep, Peg. *Altars Made Easy*. New York: HarperCollins, 1997.

White Dog Cafe, 3420 Sansom Street, Philadelphia PA 19104. 215/386-9224.

Our Black Church, by Charles McKinney

Charles McKinney is a partnership manager at North Carolina Public Allies and in the midst of finishing a Ph.D. in history at Duke University. Raised Pentecostal in Southern California, Charles now attends Mount Level Baptist Church in Durham, North Carolina. He originally wrote this piece for the Afroam List Serve, April 7 1995.

I went to church last Sunday. Hardly a noteworthy action. It's a straight-up little "country" church: off the paved road, in a sanctuary that's too small, replete with mothers with loud children, and predominated by men and women who remember the Great Depression. Yet, as I took in the service, a number of things occurred to me about church, religion and black people.

I've always enjoyed going to this particular church. It's always had the right combination of singing, preaching, and good ol' worship (grandma would say "wu-ship") but on this day, something about the whole thing moved me. As the men's chorus stood to sing "Can't nobody do me like Jesus," heads nodded and shouts of "Amen!" arose to greet the senior men as they struggled out of their chairs. They were affirmed and it showed in their singing. The slow, methodical singing, and the heartfelt foot-tapping was contagious. The chorus and the audience fed off of one another; the men singing their hearts out, and the audience responding with shouts of "Amen!" and "Preach!" after a number of extended choruses, the men sat down to shouts of joy and appreciation.

> It is a community of old and young, male and female, brought together by cultural, social and religious bonds. It is a place we come to when we want to charge our batteries for the week.

So, I'm sitting there, in this little church, tryin' to figure out why I enjoy it so much. As a budding historian, perhaps I get a kick out of the old people. When you think about it, the practice of worship for black people hasn't changed very much in a couple of centuries. Perhaps the rhythms and sounds that I hear evoke images of old slave men and women—heads bowed and eyes closed as they perform the West African ring shout. Maybe they make me think of the religious processionals of the motherland, as the elders pour libations under a starry sky. Maybe the old people remind me of my own family—a grandmother and father (on both sides of the family) who claim that they got through only by the grace of God. Maybe that's why I love this place so much.

Then it hits me. I love this place so much because it is a community. It is a community of old and young, male and female, brought together by cultural, social and religious bonds. It is a place we come to when we want to charge our batteries for the week. The young come together with their elders—to both inject new blood into the church and to glean some of the elders' wisdom and insight into life. The old people come to be affirmed and recognized as individuals who have made it through. They have stories they want to tell us, little tidbits of life they want to give us, and this is the place where it happens. Can you think of any better place to affirm the elders and teach the young?

It's a place that we've carved out where it's all right to tell someone that you're thinking about them or praying for them throughout the week. And, for the spiritually-minded among us, it's a place we can come in order to get another set of helpful hints (and admonitions at times) on how to get through to the end of the day.

Yeah, that's what I like about this place.

space.

appendix

list of activities

worksheets

sample program: interfaith celebration

retreat centers

list of activities

All of the activities in the book are listed below by chapter. <u>Time</u> is the minimum time needed for the activity; many can take longer. When a range is listed, this indicates how minimum time increases when the group size increases from approximately 12 to 24 people. The <u>risk</u> factor for each activity is rated L for low, M for medium, or H for high.

*Activities with corresponding worksheets have an <u>asterisk</u>.

Name	Time	Alone/ Group	Risk	Preparation	Page #
how to use this book					
faith stories	20 min	G	L	No	8
words of power	30 min	G	L	No	9
faith maps	45 min	G	M	Materials	9
silence					
silence in daily life	1 hour	A	L	No	26
silent retreats	1 day	A	M	Yes	26
experiencing silence	1 hour	G	M	Some	27
silence with others	2 days	G	H	Some	29
meditation					
basic meditation	10 min	A/G	L	No	41
full-body meditation	20 min	A/G	L	Some	42
walking meditation	15 min	A/G	L	No	44
guided meditations	30 min	A	L	Some	45
leading meditation	30 min	G	M	Yes	45
meditating on challenge	30 min	G	M	Some	46
meditation in pairs	30 min	G	H	Some	47
prayer					
beginning to pray	15 min	A	L	No	63
prayer as daily practice	20 min	A	L	No	64
centering prayer	20 min	A	L	No	64
prayer journal	10 min	A	L	No	64
write your own prayer	45 min	A	M	No	64
prayer bundles	30 min	G	M	Materials	65
communal prayer	1 hour	G	H	Yes	66

Name	Time	Alone/ Group	Risk	Preparation	Page #
spiritual practice					
*developing a practice	1 hour	A/G	L/M	Yes	79
retreats	2 days	A	M	Some	81
organizational practice	20 min	G	M	Some	82
stations of reflection	60 min	G	M	Setup/ materials	83
inspiration					
*seeking inspiration	20 min	A/G	L	Materials/ worksheet	102
models of faith	20 min	A/G	M	Some	102
outings	30 min	A	L	No	103
sharing inspiration	60 min	G	M	Yes	103
personal models of faith	30 min	G	M	No	103
spiritual biographies	3 hours	G	M	Research	104
ritual					
simple rituals	20 min	A	L	No	125
*exploring ritual	20-30 min	A/G	L	Worksheet	126
marking time	45-60 min	G	M	Some	126
focusing on each other	15-30 min	G	M	No	126
*creating a group ritual	3 hours	G	H	Yes	127
words and stories					
start a journal	15 min	A	L	No	140
*speaking in your voice	20 min	A/G	L	No/worksheet	141
*journaling for awareness	30 min	A/G	M	No/worksheet	141
freewriting	30 min	G	M	Some	142
storytelling	2 hours	G	M	No	145
name stories	15 min	G	L	No	146
spiritual stories	60 min	G	M	No	146
naming our history	60 min	G	M	Materials	147
role of faith	1 hour	G	L	Yes	147
oral history	3 hours	A/G	H	Yes	147

Name	Time	Alone/Group	Risk	Preparation	Page #
art					
start making art	30 min	A/G	L	Materials	166
collage	30 min	A/G	L	Materials	168
group paintings	20-40 min	G	M	Materials	169
making music	30 min	G	M	Materials	170
making instruments	60 min	G	M	Materials	170
mandalas	4 hours	G	H	Materials	171
art parties	4 hours	G	H	Yes	173
partnering w/ museum	2 hours	G	H	Yes	174
earth					
learning from the earth	20 min	A/G	L	No	185
paying homage	60 min	G	L	Some	187
nature walk	60 min	G	L	No	187
find your tree	20 min	G	M	No	187
photographs	20 min	G	M	No	187
gardening	Days	A/G	L	Yes	188
your piece of earth	60 min	G	M	Yes	189
healing					
know your energy	30 min	A/G	M	Yes	203
walking	30 min	A/G	L	No	204
aerobic exercise	30 min	A/G	M	No	204
yoga	20 min	A/G	M	Some	205
t'ai chi/quigong	30 min	A/G	M	Some	205
relationship to food	30 min	A	L	No	206
move together	20 min	G	M	Yes	207
invigorating stretches	20 min	G	M	Yes	208
relationships					
*looking at relationships	30 min	A/G	L	No/worksheet	225
dealing with conflict	30 min	G	M	No	228
finding out who we are	10-30 min	G	L	No	229
listening with reverence	30 min	G	M	Some	230
honoring each other	60 min	G	M	Yes	232
spectrum of our beliefs	30 min	G	M	Some	233
step into the center	60-90 min	G	H	Yes	234
clearness session	2 hours	G	H	Yes	236

Name	Time	Alone/Group	Risk	Preparation	Page #
circles					
first gathering	2 hours	G	M	Yes	252
second gathering	2 hours	G	M	Yes	253
in the beginning	1-2 hours	G	L	No	256
objects	2 hours	G	L	Some	256
photo night	1-2 hours	G	M	Some	257
sacred texts	1-2 hours	G	M	No	257
food	2 hours	G	L	Yes	258
Jesus	1-2 hours	G	M	Some	258
rhythm of seasons	1 hour	G	L	Some	258
interfaith celebrations					
share worship	2 hours	G	L	Some	270
faith & culture sharing	1-2 hours	G	M	Some	271
*interfaith celebration	2 hours	G	H	Yes	271
space					
memories of space	20 min	A	L	No	283
everyday space	30 min	A/G	L	Some	283
creating sacred space	15 min	A/G	M	Yes	284
finding sacred space	30 min	A/G	M	Yes	284
community spaces	60 min	G	M	Some	285
histories of space	60 min	G	M	Yes	285

worksheets

Worksheets have been designed for the activities listed below. They can and should be copied; please make sure to include the copyright information at the bottom of each sheet. Read over the description of the activity in the chapter when using the worksheet with a group. Please note that some of the worksheets first appear in the "activities to do alone" section of the chapter.

creating a group ritual . . . .

1. GOALS:
Why this ritual?
What purpose do we hope this ritual will serve?
What are some common themes among individual answers?

2. PARTICIPANTS:
Who will participate in this ritual? Group members only or open to others?
How many people will attend altogether?

3. BRAINSTORM the possible elements:
Will there be singing, dancing, meditation, prayer, talking, art, writing, drumming, etc.?

4. Create a FINAL OUTLINE:
Based on your brainstorming and the needs of the group, come up with a plan for your ritual. Look back over your list.
Which ideas is the group most excited about?
What will be most accessible to your group?

5. WHO will do what?

6. LOGISTICS:
What are some possible spaces for this ritual?
Do you want to do it outside?
What do you need to do to transform the space?
What materials do you need?
What time will you start? How long will it last?
Will there be food?

7. PREPARATION for the Group:
What does the group need to think about ahead of time?
What do they need to bring?

designing an interfaith celebration . . . .

GOALS:

Possible PLANNING GROUP MEMBERS:

BRAINSTORMING CONTENT:

Possible LOCATION:

DATE?   TIME?

What kind of INVITATIONS will you send out?

Will there be a PROGRAM?

Will there be FOOD?   Where will it come from?

WHO will do what ahead of time?   WHO will do what on the day of
                                               the celebration?

developing a spiritual practice . . . .

1. What do you currently do in your life that you consider spiritual? Fill in this grid to help you determine what you do, how often, and with whom. Don't worry about how many boxes you leave blank and how many you fill in.

	alone	with others	at work
daily			
weekly			
monthly			
yearly			

2. What do you notice from the grid?

3. What don't you want as part of your practice? What turns you off?

4. What do you want more of in your life? What helps you during difficult times? What have you experienced that has brought you calm or peace?

(over)

developing a spiritual practice worksheet, page 2

Here are some possibilities; note your reactions to them:

reading	art	keeping a Sabbath
meditation	music	silence
prayer	dance	planting/gardening
yoga	exercise	sports
writing	fasting	other?

Now, fill out the second grid with practices or activities you might like to start doing. Don't worry if you find yourself writing down things you don't know much about.

	alone	with others	at work
daily			
weekly			
monthly			
yearly			

For daily practice: What is the best time?   Best place(s)?

What do you need to develop your practice and stay faithful to it?

What might stand in your way?

Who can support you?

exploring ritual . . . .

1. What rituals do you remember from your childhood?

2. What did these rituals mark and how?

3. Who was involved?

4. Did these rituals change over time?

5. What rituals exist in your life right now?

6. Do you have any rituals connected to work?

7. How did these rituals come about?

8. What purpose do they serve?

exploring your faith background . . . .

Think back to your experiences with faith growing up. For the words listed below, what memories, images, and associations come to mind? For each word or phrase, jot down a few words that are relevant to your experience.

Holidays

Worship

Religious education

Service, volunteer, or missionary experiences

Music and ritual

Food

God

What are some of your earliest experiences with religion?

Your most vivid memories from childhood? Which of these were positive?

Which were negative?

(over)

exploring your faith background, page 2

Rate the truth of these statements on a scale of 1-5; 1=not at all true; 5=very true

I grew up in a family with a strong religious affiliation.

     1   2   3   4   5

I grew up with strong religious teachings.

     1   2   3   4   5

I grew up with a strong belief in God.

     1   2   3   4   5

I grew up in a family with different religious affiliations.

     1   2   3   4   5

My religion brought me joy.

     1   2   3   4   5

My role in my religion was limited.

     1   2   3   4   5

I am currently very connected to the religious tradition that I practiced as a child.

     1   2   3   4   5

List two ways that religion was in some way enlightening or uplifting while you were growing up.

List two ways that religion was alienating or disturbing to you.

Thoughts this activity may have sparked:

joining the circle . . . .

In preparation for joining the circle, please answer these questions thoughtfully.
Please write as legibly as possible.

Name: _____

Address: _____

_____

Phone: _____ Fax: _____ E-mail: _____

Why have you made the decision to participate in this circle?

What do you want people to know about any spiritual questions you have right now?

What do you want people to know about the work you do in the world?

What are you most interested in doing with this group?

journaling for awareness . . . .

AWARENESS. . . of self

1. What is important to you in your life?

2. Recall a truly amazing moment you've experienced. Describe it. What was the experience like? How did you feel at that time? How did you feel afterwards?

3. What do you believe about yourself?

AWARENESS. . . of the world

4. What was your first experience working in a community? What did you learn? How did it feel?

5. What would you change about the world? Who would help you? What would it take?

6. Whom would you most like to meet? Where would you go and what would you talk about? (If you've answered a question like this before, pick a different person.)

7. Describe a place that's meaningful for you. What is meaningful about it?

AWARENESS. . . of spirit

8. What does spirituality mean to you?

9. What is the difference between spirituality and religion?

10. What is the relationship between the two?

11. How do you know when spirit is present in your life?

12. What activities cause time to stop for you; what can you do for hours?

13. Who are your teachers? Who are your students?

looking at relationship . . . .

1. Brainstorm a list of categories that describe the various relationships in your life.
   Here are some to get you started:

   Work   Home/Family   Community   Friends

2. Draw two concentric circles (one inside the other) for each of these categories; label
   each one.

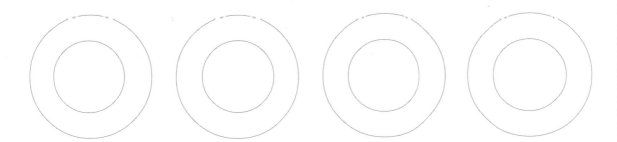

3. In the inner circle, write the names of the people with whom you have primary
   relationships. In the outer circle, write the names of others who are important in one
   way or another. Do this intuitively. There may be only one person in the inner circle, or
   there may be 10.

   What, if anything, surprises you about these circles and the names within them?
   What are your expectations of those relationships? Are these ever voiced? How?

4. Put a star next to the people who feed your spirit the most, the people you genuinely
   love to be with.

   How do you nurture these relationships? When do you realize you are paying attention to them?

5. Next, underline the people you spend the most time with. *Who are they?*

6. Circle the people you'd like to spend more time with. *What keeps this from happening?*

7. Draw a line through the people you'd like to spend less time with.
   Why? What is hard about these relationships? What do you learn from them?

looking at space . . . .

everyday space

Reflect on the spaces where you grew up. What influence did they have on you? What control did you have in shaping them?

Describe a space in or around your childhood home that you shaped as your own. What happened there that was special? Who else was a part of it? Was it a secret?

What is the impact of space on your everyday life? Reflect on your daily pattern of moving through your day, from home to work to play to rest? What role does space play?

sacred spaces

What were the characteristics of spaces that you knew as a child were sacred or religious? Did people behave differently within them? Did you?

What do you consider sacred space today? How do you find or create this for yourself?

What or where are your resting places or spaces of inspiration? How often do you go to them?

(over)

looking at space, page 2

Below, draw and/or describe your ideal environment, real or imagined.

What is the closest you have ever come to experiencing this?

community spaces

What are the most popular spaces/places in the town where you live? Who spends time there? Why? What activities take place there?

What is your favorite place in your city/town? How did you find it? Why do you love it?

When you want to gather with colleagues or friends, where do you go? How do you choose this location?

What space is missing in your town?

seeking inspiration . . . .

Gather different colored pens, magic markers, paints, or colored pencils and one sheet of 8 x 11 paper.

1. Draw your favorite shape so that it fills the entire space.

2. Figure out a way to divide it into six parts, any way that you want. Be creative.

3. In each of the parts put one of the following words:

> Written sources (books, poetry, magazines, etc.)
> Music
> Visual sources (art, movies, video, etc.)
> Colors
> Places
> People

4. Fill in each section, slowly, with the relevant sources of inspiration. Brainstorm possibilities. Create other categories and add to the shape to make room for them.

5. Notice any patterns or themes. What images came to mind while you were making your lists?

speaking in your own voice . . . .

Use a notebook or journal to begin exploring the center of who you are.
Write about:

Favorite ways to use your time

Favorite people/places/things

What inspires you

Lessons you've learned in your life

What you believe in

Seminal events and turning points

What you can do without in your life

Dreams you remember

Memories from your childhood

Places your soul feels at ease

A person who has been significant in your life

What are my strengths?

What are my limitations?

Who/what do I love?

Who/what do I need?

Who/what do I fear?

Who/what makes me sad?

Who/what makes me happy?

Who/what makes me angry?

What do I have to give or share?

What do I mock?

What am I jealous of?

Where is my path blocked?

What would I like to see?

Whatever . . .

stone circles 4th Annual

Interfaith Celebration of Community, Spirit, and Change

December 20, 1998

7:00 pm

WELCOME: Claudia Horwitz

MOJUBA: To Give Thanks to the Ancestors
Jessica "Torkwase" Alarcon and Amoke Tolukun (Nakia Ocean)
The libation ritual will be done in Yoruba and English.

"WE GATHER": written by John Parker
We gather to remember
We gather to remember all our beloved ones, to remember how each came, lived and passed to the spirit
world.
We gather because they love us, they speak to us and tell our hearts how to survive.
We gather and we remember the ones before us - the children, the elders, the struggle, the lives - all our
relations.
Spirits, Ancestors!
You are with us.
You whisper to us.
You breathe on us.
You are more powerful than memory.
And so - we gather.

ZOROASTRIAN SUN DANCE: led by Lucy Oliver
from the Dances of Universal Peace
Shining, Undying, Swift-Horsed Sun
Ahura Mazda
Shine, Shine, Shine

REFLECTIONS ON CHANNUKAH: Richard Goldberg and Edie Kahn
The dreidel game is traditionally played during Channukah. The four Hebrew letters on the dreidel
are *nun, gimmel, shin, heh,* which is an acronym for the Hebrew phrase translated as "a great miracle
happened there." Each player puts an ante (piece of candy) into the pot and one player spins the

dreidel. If it lands on *nun*, then do nothing, *gimmel* means take the whole pot, *heh* means take half the pot, and *shin* means add to the pot. This is repeated as they take turns spinning the dreidel.

SONG: I HAVE A LITTLE DREIDEL

REFLECTIONS ON KWANZAA: Darryl Lester
7 Principles of Kwanzaa:
1st Day: UMOJA/*Unity*
We are one people, one impulse, one drumbeat.

2nd Day: KUJICHAGULIA/*Self-Determination*
Each of us must be able to name our own self, speak for our own self, lead our own self and our own people.

3rd Day: UJIMA/*Collective Work & Responsibility*
We strive to produce a good harvest, build homes and develop our communities.

4th Day: UJAMAA/*Cooperative Economics*
We must put our money together for the collective good.

5th Day: NIA/*Purpose*
Our purpose in life must always be clear, for a people without a purpose, without a destination is like a ship without a navigator.

6th Day: KUUMBA/*Creativity*
We must use our natural creative ability to beautify our total surroundings.

7th Day: IMANI/*Faith*
For all of the other principles to succeed, we must have faith in our parents, our leaders and most importantly, in ourselves.

SONG: BEAUTY AM I
Beauty am I
Spirit am I
I am the infinite
Within my soul
I can find no beginning
I can find no end
All this I am

REFLECTIONS ON THE WINTER SOLSTICE: offered by Susanya Schuett
Tomorrow, December 21st, marks the Winter Solstice, the longest night of the year. It is a time to recognize the darkness, and celebrate the returning of the light.

"BEATITUDES" AND REFLECTIONS ON CHRISTMAS: led by Scott Pryor

"THE INVITATION": written by Oriah Mountain Dreamer (an Indian elder)
read by Molly Milroy and Vanessa Davis

"I BOW TO THE LIGHT IN YOU": led by Terry McCarthy, music by Blaise Keilar
I bow to the light in you; I bow to the mystery
We sing and we dance our prayer; Glory to you.

PERIOD OF MEDITATION AND SILENCE

"NAMASTE": played by Scott Pryor

PRAYER CIRCLE
This candle lights. . . a prayer for. . .
As your candle is lit, you are invited to share a prayer with the community.

SONG: AMAZING GRACE

retreat centers

Avila Retreat Center, 711 Mason Road, Durham, NC 27712; 919/477-1285
Catholic retreat center that runs a great range of day-long and weekend workshops. Also provides space for directed and private retreats.

Center for Life Enrichment/Nonprofit Holistic Resource Centers, 1509 S. Hawthorne Rd, Winston-Salem NC 27103; 910/768-0558; in Greensboro - 910/299-7999
Offers courses in yoga, astrology, ayurveda, reflexology, reiki, homeopathy, meditation, etc.

Elat Chayyim: A Center for Healing and Renewal, 99 Mill Hook Road, Accord, NY 12404; 914/626-0157; 800/398-2630
Inspired by the Jewish renewal movement. Runs weekend and week-long workshops in a variety of areas—dance, drama, writing, spirituality, Jewish texts, holidays.

Gampo Abbey, Pleasant Bay, Cape Breton, Nova Scotia, BOE 2PO, CANADA; 902/224-2752; Fax 902/224-1521 E-mail: gampo@shambhala.org
Monastery of the Kagyu lineage of Tibetan Buddhism. Pema Chödrön is the resident teacher.

Greenfire, HCR 35, Box 436. Tenants Harbor, ME 04860; 207/372-6442; Fax 207/372-0561
Small community of women that enables the creative work of the deepest self through retreats, structured and spontaneous events, and individual consultations.

Green Gulch Farm, 1601 Shoreline Highway, Sausalito, CA 94965; 415/383-3134
Classes in Zen Buddhism, meditation retreats, workshops, and family events. The famed Green Gulch Garden has a volunteer program and numerous workshops.

Insight Meditation Society, 1230 Pleasant Street, Barre, MA 01005; 508/355-4378
Wonderful place for the intensive practice of insight meditation; retreats from a weekend to three months.

Kirkridge Retreat and Study Center, 2495 Fox Gap Road, Bangor, PA 18013; 601/588-1793

With their motto, "Picket and Pray," Kirkridge is committed to the integration of personal growth and social change. They run retreats, workshops, seminars, and conferences.

Kripalu Center for Yoga and Health, Box 793, Lenox, MA 01240; 413/448-3400

Runs weekend and weeklong workshops. It is also possible to be in residence doing *seva*, or selfless service, for longer periods of time.

Southern Dharma Retreat Center, 1661 West Road, Hot Springs, NC 28743, 704/622-7112; E-mail: sdharma@juno.com

Located in the western North Carolina mountains. Sponsors teachers from a variety of traditions for meditation retreats.

Vallecitos Mountain Refuge, P.O. Box 1507, Taos, NM 87571; 505/751-0351; Fax 505/751-1775

Wilderness mountain ranch in Carson National Forest, Vallecitos is a refuge for contemplative practice and spiritual renewal for environmental and social activists.

stone circles

stone circles are universally holy.
They symbolize sacred doorways,
the center of the universe,
the dwelling place of the life force.

stone circles finds unique ways to integrate faith, spiritual practice, and social justice. Our work is based on values and beliefs supported by lessons from historical movements, political realities, and personal journeys. We do this in three ways:

1. by providing training & organizational development that reconnect people and organizations to their core values and passions, to each other, and to their work. Many media are used, including discussion, reflection, writing, ritual, art, silence, brainstorming, readings, and music;
2. by helping people convene Circles, collectives of activists who meet regularly for reflection, renewal, and peer education; and
3. by organizing interfaith gatherings and events that encourage exchange, discovery, learning, celebration, reflection, and understanding.

Join us!

We want to keep you informed about stone circles and our programs, and we are interested in your experiences using this book. Please send us feedback, comments, and questions.

Contact us at:
stone circles, 301 West Main Street, Suite 280, Durham NC 27701
919/682-8323; Fax 919/956-5349, astonesthr@aol.com
And coming soon to the Web at www.stonecircles.org

✂ —

Please send me information about upcoming stone circles events and trainings:

Name: _____

Address: _____

_____

Organization/School, if applicable: _____

Phone: _____ Fax: _____ E-mail: _____

a stone's throw:

living the act of faith

published by stone circles
301 West Main Street, Suite 280, Durham NC 27701
919/682-8323; Fax 919/956-5349, astonesthr@aol.com

Please send me _____ additional copies of *A Stone's Throw* at $17.00 per copy, plus $3.00 for shipping and handling for the first book and $1.00 shipping and handling for each additional book. A reduced price is available to those ordering 10 copies or more; please contact stone circles for more information.

Name: _____

Organization/School, if applicable: _____

Address: _____

City: _____ State: _____ Zip Code: _____

Phone: _____ Fax: _____ E-mail: _____

Quantity:

_____ copies of A Stone's Throw X	$17.00 each	$ _____
Shipping and handling:	$3.00/first book	$ _____
	$1.00/ each additional book	$ _____
	TOTAL ENCLOSED	$ _____

Please make check or money order payable to "stone circles."

If you would like copies mailed to an address different from the one above, please note that here:

stone circles is sustained by those who believe in
and benefit from its work.

We give thanks and praise to the following individuals, organizations, and
institutions who made this book possible:

Maya Ajmera
Cal Allen
Natalie Ammarell
Betsy Alden & Mark Rutledge
Will Atwater
Scott Barber
John & Wanda Beilenson
John Bell & Judy Whisnant
Shawn Bohen & Richard Morehouse
Debra Brazzel
Brenda Brodie
Kristin Bull
Hunter & J.B. Buxton
Sarah Carroll
Daughtry Carstarphen
Elizabeth Catlin
Chris Chafe
Jenny Chafe
Arrington Chambliss
Ed Chaney & Rekha Chandrabose
Ginny & Richard Chorley
Ed Cohen
Scott Cooper
Tony Deitell
David DeVito
Meredith Emmett
Chris Estes
Jess & Frank Fischer
Fran Fogelman
Robert & Sharon Freedman
Katherine Fulton & Kathy Kunst
Richard Goldberg
Thomas Goldstein
Galia Goodman
Polly Guthrie
Diane & Bobby Hackett
Kelly & Seth Collings Hawkins
Manny Horwitz
Margot & Ellis Horwitz
Dawn Hutchinson
Diane Johnson
Kippy Joseph & Jason Scott
Cheryl & Jim Keen
Amy Kellum
Anne Kenan

Annice Kenan & Jesse Smith
Joan Kofodimos & Kyle Dover
Louise Kowalsky
Bob Korstad
Colleen McCauley
Charles & Natalie McKinney
Anita McLeod
Stephe McMahon
Wayne Meisel & K.P. Weseloh
Evelyn Mattern
Atiba Mbiwan
Leigh Morgan
Thérèse Murdza
Christy Nordstrom
Hez Norton
Julia & Brian Scatliff O'Grady
Tema Okun & Tom Stern
Lucy Oliver
John Ott
Mitty Owens
John & Kathryn Parker
Lori Pistor
Julie & Ted Purcell
Charlotte Richardson
Sandra Robinson
Allan Rosen
David Sawyer
Susan Schroeer & Susan Powell
Bob Sigmon
Nancy Stark
Jeanette Stokes
Zemo Trevathan
Gina Upchurch
Don & Darlene Wells
Melinda Wiggins
Ray Williams
Maura Wolf
Ginger Young & Jonathan Wiener
Heather Zorn

The Blessing Way Foundation
echoing green Foundation
Institute for Public Media Arts
Judea Reform Congregation
North Carolina Public Allies
The Rockefeller Foundation

index